CALGARY PUBLIC LIBRARY

FEB   2013

THE BLOOD
of
FREE MEN

Also by Michael Neiberg

Dance of the Furies: Europe and the Outbreak of World War I
The Second Battle of the Marne
Fighting the Great War
Foch
Making Citizen-Soldiers
Warfare in World History
The Western Front: 1914–1916
The Eastern Front: 1914–1920 (with David Jordan)
Warfare and Society in Europe: 1898 to the Present
Soldiers' Lives Through History: The Nineteenth Century

THE BLOOD

of

FREE MEN

❧

The Liberation of Paris, 1944

MICHAEL NEIBERG

BASIC BOOKS
A Member of the Perseus Books Group
NEW YORK

Copyright © 2012 by Michael Neiberg

Published by Basic Books, A Member of the Perseus Books Group

All rights reserved. Printed in the United States of America.
No part of this book may be reproduced in any manner whatsoever
without written permission except in the case of brief quotations embodied
in critical articles and reviews. For information, address Basic Books,
250 West 57th Street, 15th Floor, New York, NY 10107.

Books published by Basic Books are available at special
discounts for bulk purchases in the United States by corporations,
institutions, and other organizations. For more information, please contact
the Special Markets Department at the Perseus Books Group, 2300 Chestnut
Street, Suite 200, Philadelphia, PA 19103, or call (800) 810-4145,
ext. 5000, or e-mail special.markets@perseusbooks.com.

Designed by Linda Mark

Library of Congress Cataloging-in-Publication Data
Neiberg, Michael S.
 The blood of free men : the liberation of Paris, 1944 /
Michael Neiberg.
  pages cm
 Includes bibliographical references and index.
 ISBN 978-0-465-02399-8 (hardcover : alk. paper)—
 ISBN 978-0-465-03303-4 (e-book) 1. World War,
 1939–1945—Campaigns—France—Paris. I. Title.
 D762.P3N45 2012
 940.54'214361—dc23
                                    2012016282
        10 9 8 7 6 5 4 3 2 1

*I dedicate this book to my daughters,
Claire and Maya, and my Parisian goddaughter,
Chiara Noël, in the hopes that for them Paris
will always be a place of peace and happiness.*

CONTENTS

*Map of Key Sites to the
Liberation of Paris, 1944*   ix

Introduction   xi

CHAPTER ONE
The End of This Nightmare   1

CHAPTER TWO
Resistance   27

CHAPTER THREE
Berlin, Washington, London, and Paris   55

CHAPTER FOUR
The Smasher of Cities   83

CHAPTER FIVE
The Guns Go Off, August 15–18   111

CHAPTER SIX
**"The Most Beautiful Days of Our Lives,"
August 19–20**   135

CHAPTER SEVEN
The Days of the Barricades, August 21–22   165

CHAPTER EIGHT
Deliverance, August 23–24   195

CHAPTER NINE
Apotheosis, August 25–27   221

CONCLUSION
247

Acknowledgments   *261*

Notes   *263*

Index   *299*

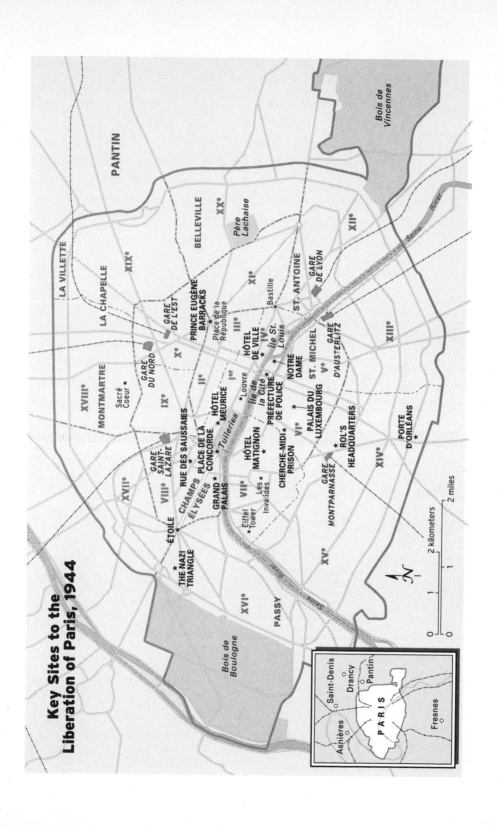

Key Sites to the Liberation of Paris, 1944

PANTIN

Bois de Vincennes

Seine River

BELLEVILLE

XXe

Père Lachaise

XIIe

LA VILLETTE

XIXe

LA CHAPELLE

XIe

GARE DE LYON

ST. ANTOINE

GARE DE L'EST

PRINCE EUGÈNE BARRACKS

X^e

Place de la République

Bastille

IIIe

IVe

HÔTEL DE VILLE

Île St. Louis

GARE D'AUSTERLITZ

XIIIe

MONTMARTRE

Sacré Coeur ■

GARE DU NORD

IXe

IIe

Ier

Louvre ■

Île de la Cité

NOTRE DAME

PREFECTURE DE POLICE

ST. MICHEL

V^e

HÔTEL MEURICE

Tuileries

XVIIIe

XVIIe

GARE SAINT-LAZARE

VIIIe

RUE DES SAUSSAIES

PLACE DE LA CONCORDE

HÔTEL MATIGNON

CHERCHE-MIDI PRISON

PALAIS DU LUXEMBOURG

VIe

ROL'S HEADQUARTERS

XIVe

PORTE D'ORLÉANS

CHAMPS ÉLYSÉES

ÉTOILE

GRAND PALAIS

VIIe

Les Invalides ■

Eiffel Tower ■

GARE MONTPARNASSE

THE NAZI TRIANGLE

XVIe

PASSY

XVe

Seine River

Bois de Boulogne

N

2 kilometers

2 miles

1

1

0

0

PARIS

Saint-Denis

Asnières

Drancy

Pantin

Fresnes

INTRODUCTION

Fʀᴏᴍ ᴛʜᴇ ᴍᴏᴍᴇɴᴛ ɪᴛ ʙᴇɢᴀɴ, ᴛʜᴇ ʟɪʙᴇʀᴀᴛɪᴏɴ ᴏғ Pᴀʀɪs ᴡᴀs an almost mythical affair. Even while some of the city's German occupiers still remained in the city, a visiting American journalist described Paris as "a magic sword in a fairy tale, a shining power in the hands to which it rightly belongs." Even American general Omar N. Bradley, who had never been to the city and had some deeply ambivalent feelings about liberating it, came to understand that Paris meant much more than any other city in Europe, not just to the French but to the Americans as well. Recalling the fever that "seized the US Army" as it approached Paris, he wrote in his memoirs that, "to a generation raised on fanciful tales of their fathers in the AEF [American Expeditionary Forces from World War I], Paris beckoned with a greater allure than any other objective in Europe." In the heated days of August, when the fate of the city still hung in the balance, Albert Camus, writing in the clandestine newspaper *Combat*, spoke of Paris returning to its historic role of purging tyranny with the "blood of free men." The liberty that the city was buying with its own blood, Camus argued, was the liberty not just of Paris and not just of France, but of mankind itself. Parisians and visitors alike could not help but see in the events of 1944 clear reverberations of the history-making Paris of 1789, 1830, and 1848—revolutionary years when the people of the city had taken a stand against tyranny in the name of democracy and freedom everywhere.[1]

No other city in the world captured peoples' imaginations like Paris. No other city could have motivated such intense feelings of love from people around the world. And no other city during World War II so symbolized freedom and liberty suffering under the boot of naked aggression and bloodthirsty hatred. When, after more than four years under Nazi rule, Paris returned to French control, church bells across the globe rang out in celebration. As far away as Santiago, where members of the Chilean Parliament joined together to sing *La Marseillaise*, the liberation of Paris represented the end of one era and the start of another, more hopeful one. A free Paris meant that, even if the war was not yet over, the outcome could no longer be in doubt. A free Paris meant that the end of the Nazis was near.

War correspondents were so awed by witnessing the liberation that men who relied on words to make their living were rendered speechless. One Australian correspondent wrote a dispatch that simply read, "The whole thing is beyond words," signed his name, and sent it to his editor. *Time* magazine's chief war correspondent walked around Paris with photographer Robert Capa. Their eyes were too filled with tears of joy to report anything for hours. The city also attracted the rich and the famous, many of whom sped to Paris as quickly as they could. Ernest Hemingway assembled his own private platoon and drove through the night to see Paris at the greatest moment of its illustrious history—and to liberate the wine cellar of one of his former haunts, the elegant Ritz Hotel on the Place Vendôme.[2]

But if Paris in 1944 appeared as a magic sword to foreign journalists and others attached to the liberating armies, it did not seem so magical to those living there. Before the liberation Paris bore only the faintest of resemblances to the majestic city that had once captivated people from all over the world. Four years of Nazi occupation had reduced the City of Light from the world's once-proud capital of art, diplomacy, and fashion to a place that a Swiss diplomat called "black misery" for its inhabitants. Hungry, desperate, and terrified, Paris in 1944 sat on the abyss of yet another period of the violence and bloodshed that had so often marked its history.[3]

Nor would the liberation of Paris come without a price. Cut off from the outside world for four years, the members of the city's various Resistance cells had developed their own view of what the future of France should hold, including the proper punishment for those who had collaborated with the Germans. Having suffered directly under the Nazi regime, moreover, they believed that they were due a disproportionate voice in deciding France's future. Ecstatic though they were to see Allied, especially French, troops liberate their city, they remained anxious about ceding power that they felt they had earned through their blood. Paris, they wanted the world to know, had liberated itself. Not all of their fellow countrymen agreed with either their interpretation of the liberation or their plans for the future, leading to widespread fears of a civil war once the Germans left. Expatriate English journalist Sisley Huddleston was among those who saw in liberated Paris not just sheer joy but a dangerous political brew that had the potential to be no less savage than the French Revolution's Reign of Terror.[4]

As Huddleston and others knew, Paris's long and tortured history of revolution and political turmoil hung over the ecstasy of the liberation like a dark cloud. The real and ever-present specter of widespread famine made many Parisians think of the terrible days of the Paris Commune in 1871, when the city was starving and surrounded by Prussian troops. The Commune was part of a bloody civil war that followed the Franco-Prussian War. It left thousands of Parisians dead and bitterly divided the Left and the Right. The 1930s reawakened those divisions and made them even more intense. What would happen if Paris were again cut off from the outside world and on the verge of starvation? Could the liberation lead not to joy and freedom but to a new round of civil war, bloodshed, and revolution? The specter of 1871 hung over the city as surely as the presence of the Germans did, and the lack of food underscored the desperate plight and uncertain future that the city faced.

Those who had seen Paris before the war knew firsthand the depths to which it could sink. In the 1930s Paris had been the scene of constant political chaos and, at times, violence. The rise of fascism on France's borders and the civil war in neighboring Spain both highlighted the complexity of Parisian politics and brought into sharp focus the essential divisions that characterized them. The formation of the antifascist Popular Front in 1936 temporarily united the Left and center of French politics against the growing fascist tide that had already swept Italy and Germany and threatened to sweep Spain as well. Although France avoided the fate of those three nations until 1940, it nevertheless had a powerful and violent fascist movement of its own that shared the anticommunist and antidemocratic beliefs of its fellow travelers across Europe.

In France, as elsewhere, fascist ideologies were popular not just with avowed racists, although avowed racists there surely were. Extreme right-wing and fascist ideas also had their supporters among conservative Catholics and members of the urban middle class who feared communism's atheism and opposition to private property more than they feared the unknowns of fascism. Paris, with its history of class struggle and its tradition of political agitation, always stood at the center of these disagreements. The outbreak of war with Germany in 1939 did surprisingly little to quell these intense debates, so deep were the hatreds that had built up inside France. Although few people realized all of its implications, the decade of internal fighting had left France unable to meet a challenge from the outside.

The humiliating and disorienting collapse of the French Army in May and June 1940 led to the decision of the French Parliament to ask the aging World War I hero Marshal Henri-Philippe Pétain to assume control of the government. In impossible circumstances, he did so, surrendering the northern and western parts of the country, including Paris, to outright German occupation. A rump state, with its capital at the spa town of Vichy and maintaining formal, if limited,

control of the overseas French empire, remained as a legally independent political entity with the authoritarian and antirepublican Pétain
as its head of state. Pétain placed the blame for France's failures on
Freemasons, Jews, and communists, as well as the weaknesses of the
French Third Republic, with its divisive and corrosive party system.
He promised a National Revolution to return France to its traditional values—which were, in the Vichy formulation, largely agricultural and Catholic. Revolutionary and democratic symbols like
Bastille Day, *La Marseillaise*, and the French tricolor flag vanished in
favor of more traditional, rural symbols. Even France's legendary
motto "Liberty, Equality, Fraternity" disappeared in favor of Vichy's
"Family, Work, and Fatherland."

In order to achieve their domestic goals, Vichy officials needed to
come to terms with the Germans. In October 1940, Pétain coined the
term *collaboration*, which, in his eyes, meant that France and Germany would work together under French recognition of German
dominance in Europe. Pétain and Hitler met at Montoire, in the occupied zone, for a meeting and a photo opportunity that cemented
the new relationship between the triumphant Germans and the defeated French. Pétain and the collaborationists hoped in exchange for
their cooperation to get a guarantee from the Germans of Vichy
French sovereignty in the unoccupied zone and in the French overseas empire, a return of the 1.6 million French prisoners of war in
German camps, and a reduction of the enormous indemnity the
armistice of 1940 required the French to pay to cover the costs of
Germany's war in the west.

Defenders of collaboration argued that it promised the best future
that France could expect given the collapse of French arms and the
inability of Great Britain to defeat Germany on its own. Collaboration also put an end to the fighting, the dying, and the killing; recalling the murderous 1916 battle that claimed 163,000 French lives
(and 143,000 German lives), some Frenchmen concluded "better
Vichy than Verdun." That Pétain, the great French hero of Verdun,
was the man in charge of the Vichy state only made it seem all the

more legitimate in the eyes of many of his countrymen. So great was Pétain's reputation that even many of those who vilified his Vichy state refrained from attacking him personally and held out hope that he alone could forge a better future for France.[5]

The United States and other nations recognized Vichy France as an independent nation, giving it diplomatic legitimacy to match the veneer of legality it had inside France. Vichy's retention of control over the powerful French fleet (based in Toulon and Algeria), and the support given to it by most senior French officials, bestowed upon it the aura of a long-term solution to the new power structure in Europe. To be sure, not all French officials supported Vichy, but the armistice had been a legally binding agreement approved by both the French Parliament and the cabinet that brought with it the force of law; thus did many officers feel honor and duty bound to respect Vichy even if they disliked the circumstances of its birth. For this reason, many of Free France's future heroes, such as Generals Alphonse Juin and Jean de Lattre de Tassigny, offered Vichy their support in 1940.[6]

Most French citizens, stunned by the pace of events in 1940, saw little choice but to accept the new regime. Indeed, until 1943, Pétain had the support of the French people, who grudgingly accepted his Vichy government because he had kept France out of the fighting then raging across Europe. The Vichy regime could plausibly claim to be the legitimate government of France, and it had the recognition of many foreign governments as well. Until 1944, moreover, neither the Soviet Union, nor the western Allies, nor the Free French movement of Charles de Gaulle in London were urging the Resistance to start an uprising. As a result, most Frenchmen saw little choice but to become *attentiste*, a word that came to signify those who were waiting for something better. An early Resistance pamphlet, "33 Hints to the Occupied," advised, "On the outside, pretend you do not care; on the inside stoke up your anger. It will serve you well."[7]

For those on the French Right, however, collaboration opened up opportunities to rid France of traditional domestic enemies—the same Jews, communists, and Freemasons whom Pétain blamed for

France's troubles. As a result, the war years in France resembled a civil war, fought not so much between Germans and French as between collaborationists and their real and perceived enemies. Vichy officials and collaborationists imprisoned 135,000 people (many for little more than their political beliefs), sent 650,000 more to Germany as "guest workers" under an obligatory labor scheme, and, most notoriously, sent 76,000 Jews to Nazi death camps. Less than 3 percent of those Jews survived.

The reconstruction of France after this civil war bequeathed a series of myths to an already wounded French nation. Perhaps the most persistent posited that the Germans had forced unwilling French officials to commit atrocities against other French people. Another suggests that the vast majority of French people supported the Resistance from an early date. Neither one is correct, but both proved useful in reuniting France after 1945 and preventing a repetition of the discord of the 1930s. It was easy for postwar French politicians, some of whom had worked for Vichy, to blame Nazi Germany for all of the crimes and horrors of the war years, but such allegations were historically nonsensical. For decades afterward, the skeletons in the closets of France continued to haunt the nation, reigniting debates and reheating leftover passions. The skeletons also underscored how much more complicated the truth was than the myths.[8]

The story of the liberation of Paris is the story of much more than the Germans and the French. It is a story of the Germans who physically held the city, the willing collaborationists who made that hold possible in order to serve their own agendas, the various and diverse people inside Paris who hoped to break that hold, and the advancing Allied armies, who had given surprisingly little thought to Paris. Each of these groups brings to the story its own plans for the city and its own agendas. In some ways, the Germans are the least important of the actors in this story. Most members of what became the French Resistance, made up of more than a dozen different groups, had considerably more hatred for the collaborationists among their own countrymen than they did for the Germans. They knew that the Germans were headed at the end of the war for defeat, punishment, and occupation. The *collabos*, however, would have to answer for the crimes they committed against their fellow citizens inside France. Most members of the French Resistance and others with scores to settle looked forward to a postwar *épuration*, a purging of those who had worked with the occupiers. The potential of the épuration to turn violent and get quickly out of hand frightened Parisians who worried that the liberation might mean not the end of the bloodshed, but just the start of a new phase of violence.

For their part, the Germans saw Paris quite differently than they saw most other conquered capital cities. In German eyes, especially the eyes of the Nazi leadership, France was an obstacle that the German Army needed to overcome before it could turn the full power of its military might east to fight the Slavs, whom the Nazis despised. Haunted by the two-front nightmare that Germany had faced in the last war, German diplomats had even cut a deal with the Soviet Union in 1939 to ensure that the Wehrmacht could focus on just one front at a time. German generals had deep respect for the French Army before 1940; only after they had defeated it could the Nazis truly think about shaping a world order.

Most German generals were as surprised as most French and British generals at their ability to do in six weeks what the German Army a generation earlier had not been able to do in four years. Still, success in France did not make the Germans eager to reach for too much. Knowing that Great Britain's continued belligerence meant that the two-front dilemma remained, and knowing that a war with the Soviet Union was becoming ever more likely, German leaders wanted a calm, easily manageable France. Thus to the Germans, Pétain's offer of collaboration came as a welcome gift. The Germans could remain in direct control over much of France, including its clear center of gravity in Paris, but the French themselves would do most of Germany's work. Paris figured so lightly in Hitler's own plans that he visited the city only once, getting his picture taken like any other tourist at the Trocadéro opposite the Eiffel Tower, but not even staying long enough to eat a meal. In an ideal world, the Germans hoped to occupy Paris as lightly as possible. The gentler the occupation, and the more reliable the French collaborationists, the less need the Germans would have to devote resources to its security. German officials courted the French Right accordingly; during his visit, Hitler agreed to transfer the body of Napoleon's son, the Duc de Reichstadt, from Vienna to Les Invalides as a gesture of affection for Paris and a symbol of his admiration for another man who had dreamed of continental conquest.[9]

As the war dragged on, and as the Russian Front demanded more and more of Germany's best combat units, Paris increasingly became a rest center for worn-out units and a destination for second-line soldiers. An artificially inflated currency exchange rate between the franc and the mark (to the latter's great favor) meant that German soldiers could live unusually well in Paris and buy luxury items— often from Parisians who were impoverished as a result of the German takeover—that they could never have owned in Germany. They could also take possession of apartments once owned by the city's deported Jewish community or those imprisoned for running afoul of the new regime.

German soldiers in Paris could enjoy pleasures unlike any they could have known in their native Germany. First-class tickets to the city's artistic and cultural wonders were theirs for the asking. For the most part, only Germans could drive cars or ride in taxis in Paris because of the lack of gasoline. Parisians had to content themselves with walking, taking the Métro, or riding the bicycles that soon filled the city's streets. Even then, Parisians had to cede their place on public transportation and yield on the sidewalks to German officers. Many extended the same courtesy to German enlisted men out of reflex or out of fear. The allure of Parisian women may have trumped all of the city's other legendary charms; German soldiers could now approach these women with money in their pockets and an aura of power surrounding them. Few of these women could have envisioned the bitter reprisals they would face once their German lovers left.

Like most occupiers, the Germans took the best of the best whenever they wanted to do so. The Luftwaffe took over the city's most beautiful palace, the Palais du Luxembourg, formerly the home of the French Senate; its magnificent gardens became parking lots for the Luftwaffe's vehicles and, eventually, for German tanks. The city's best hotels served as residences and headquarters for German officers; the dining room of the elegant George V hotel (named for the British king who had allied with France in World War I) became a fancy mess hall for senior German officials. Theaters began to put on shows in German, often with distinctly anti-Semitic themes, although French theater continued with little direct censorship. The German commander of the military district of Paris took possession of the French president's box at the famous Longchamp racetrack, and his officers took the first-class seats alongside well-connected collaborationists. Street signs, too, began to appear in German, and even the clocks were adjusted one hour to conform with German time. The Germans also banned the flying of the French flag, the playing of the French national anthem, and the celebration of French republican holidays.

Still, in the early months the Germans did what they could to conduct the occupation as lightly as possible. Rather than brutally oppressing the conquered French, as many Parisians had feared, the Germans came to Paris in 1940 trying to seem agreeable, appearing as lambs rather than wolves. Few German soldiers wanted to ruin the cushy and privileged assignment they had doing occupation duty in Europe's most beautiful city. At least in the early months of the occupation, one Parisian recalled, German soldiers were "sweet and affable. . . . They smiled at children, gave them candy (which they had taken from us), paid properly in the stores (with money they had assessed from us), gave their seats to ladies, and picked up the gloves [that women] had dropped." They also applied surprisingly few restrictions on French literature, art, and drama. Nor did Parisians have a curfew until April 1942. All in all, Paris had, at least in the early stages, avoided some of the worst aspects of occupation.

It had certainly avoided the miserable fate of conquered and contested cities in Eastern Europe like Warsaw, Leningrad, and so many others. In Leningrad alone more than 1 million Soviets died, most of them civilians. Collaborationists took much of the credit, often blaming the British for continuing the prosecution of an unnecessary war and a blockade that shut off much of France's commerce (and food supply) from the outside world.[10]

Over time, of course, German avarice and collaborationist vengeance began to take their toll. As one Briton living in France during the war noted, the occupation began "'correctly,' but degenerated into an orgy of assassination. We were plunged back into the horrors of the Middle Ages." Three events in particular changed the character of the German occupation and concurrently undermined the legitimacy of the Vichy system. The first was the new regime's targeting of its traditional enemies and scapegoats. As early as September 1940, the Germans began taking a census of the Jewish population in France and dissolved the French Communist Party. By the following summer, Germany and the Soviet Union were at war, meaning that the Communist Party became an even more intensive target of German and Vichy repression. The communists went underground and formed the core of what became the key arms of the French Resistance inside Paris: the Forces Françaises de l'Intérieur (FFI), the Francs-Tireurs et Partisans (FTP), and the Comité Parisien de la Libération (CPL).[11]

Mass arrests of communists and laws banning Jews from public service soon followed. Anti-Semitic propaganda, such as that published in the right-wing journal *Je Suis Partout* and dramatized in films like *Le Juif Süss*, appeared across France. As they had done in Germany, the Nazis—with the help of their Vichy collaborators— forced French people to either acquiesce in the persecution of their fellow citizens or be exposed as Jewish or communist sympathizers. While some brave French people did hide Jews or wear yellow stars on their own clothes to protest the discrimination, most stood by, unable or unwilling to help.

The worst of the collaborators looked for ways to make money from the plight of their fellow citizens, buying and selling the possessions of the deported and often denouncing others for personal gain. In most cases, the Vichy state began its anti-Semitic actions well before the Germans did the same in the occupied zone, suggesting that indigenous French anti-Semitism, rather than German pressure, accounted for the hatred. Roundups of France's Jews began in May 1941 in both zones, starting with foreign-born Jews who had come to France in the 1930s seeking liberty, equality, and fraternity from Nazi tyranny. In July 1942 the Paris police rounded up 3,031 Jewish men, 5,802 Jewish women, and 4,051 Jewish children, almost all of them French citizens. They went first to a cramped indoor bicycle racetrack called the Vélodrome d'Hiver, or, as most Parisians called it, the Vel d'Hiv. From there they went to the notorious camp at Drancy, located in an unfinished housing complex in the northeast suburbs of Paris. Drancy had no heat in winter, no electricity, and just one working latrine for the entire complex. From Drancy, the Germans sent both French and foreign-born Jews to Auschwitz, where nearly all of them died in the gas chambers. Collaborationists not only looked the other way but were often eager participants. Political prisoners, too, increasingly went to jail and to concentration camps, most often starting at the squalid and unsanitary prison at Fresnes, located just south of Paris near Orly airport.[12]

The muscle for these operations came not just from Germans and the Paris police but also from the violent paramilitary Vichy force known as the *Milice* whose members swore a personal oath to Pétain. Its chief was a veteran of World War I named Joseph Darnand, described by one man who knew him as "exceptionally brave but completely unintelligent." Darnand, on the far right politically, was one of the truly despicable people of the new regime who saw in Vichy not the subjugation of France, but an opportunity to use the power of the new state to murder his real and perceived enemies. He had close links to France's most violent and vicious collaborators, including the man who nominated him to head the Milice, Xavier Vallat, Vichy's minister for Jewish questions. The Milice, 30,000 strong and largely funded by Germany, attracted thugs and dedicated fascists from a variety of backgrounds, including middle-class youths and members of the French aristocracy. They had in common a hatred for communism, Jews, and the members of the French Resistance, whom they labeled "terrorists." The Milice's oath included the words, "I swear to fight against democracy, against Gaullist insurrection, and against Jewish leprosy." The members of the Milice were active within occupied France as well as in Vichy itself, and most Frenchmen came to despise them even more than they despised the SS, the Gestapo, or the German Army.[13]

The second major change in the nature and character of the German occupation came in November 1942 in response to the Anglo-American landings in North Africa. The Germans reacted by taking formal control of the unoccupied zone, but they left most of the Vichy officials in power. Vichy politicians and functionaries now worked for, rather than with, the Germans in both the occupied and unoccupied zones. Consequently, Vichy officials looked less like independent, if unequal, partners with the Germans and more like their outright puppets. Soon Vichy leaders, such as Prime Minister Pierre Laval, were urging the French to volunteer to fight the Soviets on the Eastern Front and openly wishing for a German victory over the British and the Americans.

Fewer than 3,000 Frenchmen volunteered to fight on the Soviet front (those who did, however, received blessings at Notre Dame from the archbishop of Paris). Nevertheless, widespread anger at the British helped to reinforce the Vichy argument that France's future had to be tied to that of Germany. On July 3, 1940, fearful that the Vichy fleet might work with the Germans to interfere with British maritime operations in the Mediterranean and the Atlantic, the Royal Navy attacked the French fleet's main Mediterranean base at Mers-el-Kébir in Algeria. The attack killed 1,297 French sailors and led Laval to call Britain France's "inveterate enemy." Vichy propagandists noted that the British had thus killed more French than German sailors to that point in the war. In response to the attack, Laval claimed that there was "only one way to restore France . . . to the position to which she is entitled: namely, to ally ourselves resolutely with Germany and to confront England together." Although few Frenchmen wanted to go to war with Britain, the anger and suspicion that many Frenchmen felt toward their erstwhile allies later played an important role in generating suspicion over Anglo-American intentions for the future of France.[14]

Events that followed the Allied landings in North Africa laid bare Vichy's true character as little more than a German puppet. The Vichy Army did not resist the Germans when they violated the terms of the armistice and invaded the unoccupied zone. Nor did Vichy soldiers respond to the calls of Resistance groups to turn over or destroy their arms and equipment before the Germans seized them. Instead, they stood by meekly as the Germans took control of the whole of metropolitan France. Vichy soldiers in North Africa fired on Allied soldiers coming to liberate France, inflicting approximately 4,000 casualties on American and British forces. No longer could even the most obtuse Vichy supporter believe, as many had in 1940–1941, that the Vichy regime was working to pursue the interests of France. Vichy's true face as a German pawn was now obvious for all to see.[15]

The third, and probably most important, change in the relationship between the French people and their occupiers resulted from the introduction of the Service du Travail Obligatoire (STO) in February 1943. The STO required Frenchmen aged eighteen to sixty and childless women aged eighteen to forty-five to register for a two-year period of mandatory labor service in Germany if the occupiers so demanded. The STO constituted recognition on the part of the Germans that a previous policy, whereby French prisoners of war from 1940 could be traded for men voluntarily agreeing to work in Germany, had failed miserably. Although the Germans anticipated finding 250,000 skilled workers through this scheme, they got only a small fraction of that number, made up mostly of the desperate and chronically unemployed. The jobs these men did, moreover, were back-breaking and poorly compensated. Some of the deportees worked twenty hours a day in near slave conditions making weapons. Eventually, about 20 percent of all workers in Germany, or 5 million people, were foreigners there against their will.[16]

The STO, and its Paris chief, an SS general named Julius Ritter, were intensely unpopular. Applied arbitrarily and often unfairly, the STO reminded many Frenchmen of the despised *corvée*, or labor tax, during the feudal era, which had required citizens to devote a portion of their time to fixing roads and improving buildings on their master's estates. At least under the corvée, however, Frenchmen had stayed at home. Under the STO they were forcibly deported to Germany. Its unpopularity, even among many Vichy officials, who later claimed that they did all they could to reduce the number of men deported, made the power differential between the Germans and Vichy starkly obvious. While Vichy leaders chose to show their displeasure with the STO with empty words, the French Resistance had slightly more latitude; indeed, the Resistance scored one of its great successes in September 1943, when agents assassinated Ritter in broad daylight—symbolically, right in front of the Arc de Triomphe. The Germans reacted by executing fifty French political prisoners and threatening even wider reprisals if Resistance activities continued.

The STO was a German idea with a Vichy face on it; Laval became its chief public advocate, and the Milice was responsible for ensuring that men reported. But the program had an unintended consequence: Thousands of young men, afraid of the fate that awaited them in Germany, where they might die of overwork or Allied bombardment, escaped to the countryside. There they formed bands of men known as *maquis*, a Corsican word used to describe the thick woodlands of that island's interior. Many maquis cells had links to the French Resistance. Maurice Kriegel-Valrimont, an early member of the Resistance, called the STO "the greatest *coup de main* that the Germans could have given us."[17]

The defiance of these young men undermined the STO and infuriated an increasingly frustrated German occupation authority. In

March 1944, for example, only 13,000 men reported for the STO out of a German demand for 270,000. The Germans responded by threatening to deport every Frenchman under the age of twenty-five to Germany. Some men formed French Resistance cells instead, choosing to resist rather than accept deportation. Their efforts to defy the STO showed just how much the French had come to hate the occupation, even if there was little they could do about it without assistance from Britain or the United States.

The lack of help from the outside was the main impediment to the French Resistance becoming an important factor in the war. Hopes for an Allied invasion across the English Channel in 1942, and then again in 1943, came to naught as the Allies went to North Africa and then to Italy instead. French Resistance members, known as *résistants*, could point with great pride to the contribution of Free French troops to both theaters at places like Bir Hakeim in Libya and Monte Cassino in the Italian mountains, but they wanted to see French troops return to French soil as liberators. Only with the support of an Anglo-American army on the continent, furthermore, could the résistants stand any chance against the powerful German military. Until such an Allied force arrived, the Resistance's options remained limited to localized, small-scale engagements that could frustrate, but not overthrow, the occupiers.[18]

At first, most members of the Resistance were as interested in dodging the STO as in making political or patriotic statements, but over time they developed the capability to derail trains, blow up bridges, and deny the Germans unfettered access to large portions of France. The maquis mostly based themselves in the countryside, where they could melt away and conceal themselves from the Milice and from German Army patrols. Some of the maquis groups were highly successful and were able to depend on the active help of local farmers. They could also depend on more regular Allied air drops of ammunition and weapons than their comrades in the cities could. The most powerful such group ruled the so-called national redoubt on the Vercors plateau near Grenoble in the French Alps. This group, with 3,500 members of the maquis, declared the restoration of the French Republic and defied German authority until July 1944.

The maquis was a mostly provincial phenomenon. Inside Paris, the Resistance was mainly centered inside labor unions and led by members of the French Communist Party. Loosely organized into independent cells containing members of mutually antagonistic political groups, which ran the spectrum from monarchists to communists, the Resistance inside Paris had little choice but to stay underground. The Allies maintained a policy of not air-dropping weapons or other supplies into cities, leaving the Resistance with few means of self-defense. German and Vichy infiltration into the Resistance, moreover, was a constant problem, especially in the early years before the résistants learned how to cover their tracks by developing codes. They also devised a more professional military system of organization. Until 1943, the Resistance in Paris was less important and less active than the Resistance in Lyon, which sat in the unoccupied zone and therefore was spared the direct vigilance of the Germans, at least for the early phase of the war. In March 1943, however, shortly after the Germans took control of Vichy, the Gestapo and its Vichy allies broke the Lyon Resistance, arresting eighteen of its leaders and driving many others, such as the daring socialist Léo Hamon, to Paris. The main Resistance newspapers—*Franc-Tireur*, *Combat*, and *Libération*—all moved to Paris as well. Thereafter, the capital of France was also the capital of the Resistance.[19]

The German presence in Paris centered along the traditional power axes of the city. The headquarters of the German commander of the Military District of Greater Paris were in the luxurious Hôtel Meurice, located next to the Tuileries gardens and the Louvre. Just a short walk northwest along the famous arcades of the Rue de Rivoli would bring a traveler to the beautiful Place de la Concorde, the most famous buildings of which, the Hôtel Crillon and the French Navy Ministry, now served the German occupiers. Continuing north and west through this upscale section of Paris would bring a pedestrian to the heart of official Paris, the Place Beauvau, home to the

Élysée Palace, the residence of the French president, and the Hôtel Beauvau, the traditional place for foreign dignitaries to stay while in Paris.

As it is today, the Place Beauvau was then also home to the French Interior Ministry, accessible through an entrance on the narrow Rue des Saussaies. Inside the rather innocuous-looking building at number 9, the Gestapo had set up a torture chamber complete with meat hooks hanging from the wall and bath tubs in which to submerge their victims in icy water until they cooperated. The screams from the Rue des Saussaies kept neighbors awake at night and made most passersby cross the street to walk on the other side. Eventually, Parisians learned to avoid the street altogether unless absolutely necessary.[20]

Walking along the nearby Champs Élysées, in a neighborhood well-known for its collaboration and fascist sympathy, would bring a traveler to the Place de l'Étoile, home to the Arc de Triomphe, where the daily German changing of the guard ceremony took place. Although some Parisians feared that the Germans might destroy the monument, built by Napoleon to celebrate his victories, including those over Germans, it remained standing, dominating the wide avenues that radiated away from it. The Germans did, however, extinguish the flame of the tomb of the unknown soldier of World War I and conduct a daily victory march that enraged city residents. The Germans also banned the traditional flying of a French flag at the Arc. A march to the Étoile by French students in protest of Nazi policies on November 11, 1940, provided early inspiration to the nascent French Resistance. Although the Germans dispersed the march with minimal effort, it represented the first collective act of resistance by Parisians against the occupation.[21]

One of the wide avenues that radiates from the Étoile is the Avenue Foch, named for Ferdinand Foch, the marshal who led the coalition that defeated the Germans in 1918. Home to some of Paris's most graceful mansions, it had long been one of the streets of choice for Paris's most wealthy and conservative citizens; among those people were many of the industrialists and businessmen who profited handsomely from their collaboration with the new regime. After 1940, the Avenue Foch became an important axis of German and collaborationist power in the city. Along with the Boulevard de l'Amiral Bruix and the Avenue de Malakoff, the Avenue Foch formed the so-called Nazi Triangle, which housed most of the German leadership as well as the Gestapo headquarters. The headquarters were in a particularly stylish building on the Avenue Foch near the Bois de Boulogne, the enormous park on the city's western edge. Few Parisians could have had any doubts about the building's purpose, especially after the events of March 22, 1944. On that day, the journalist and Resistance leader Pierre Brossolette threw himself out of a fifth-floor window following three days of unimaginable torture so that he would not crack under the pressure and give his interrogators the names of his comrades.[22]

The neighborhood thus had two very different identities in wartime Paris. Saying that someone was "on the Avenue Foch" was wartime slang with two possible meanings: It could mean either that the person in question was attending an elegant dinner party in the home of a wealthy collaborationist, or that he was being tortured by the Gestapo. But despite their proximity to some of the regime's worst atrocities, the neighborhood's privileged residents experienced a different war from that endured by the rest of the city. Here Germans and wealthy collaborators dined on the best of the best, kept their servants, and led a life that sharply contrasted with the misery of the city's other residents. Adapting a disparaging French nickname for Germans, Parisians soon renamed the Avenue Foch the "Avenue Boche" to express their disdain not just for the Germans but for the rich lifestyle that some Parisians were enjoying while most Parisians went hungry. The stylish partygoers on the Avenue Foch were often among the first to be singled out after the liberation for retribution. In the eyes of the Resistance, it was a misdemeanor to work with the Germans out of dire necessity to feed one's starving family, but living the high life through the Germans while the rest of Paris starved was a clear felony that called out for punishment. As the day of the liberation approached, residents along the Avenue Foch received death warrants written in red ink and small coffins in their mailboxes—none too subtle warnings that a day of judgment for the collaborators of Paris was coming.[23]

A Métro or bicycle ride across Paris would put a traveler into an entirely different world. In the eastern neighborhoods around the working-class areas of La Chapelle, the Place de la République, and Belleville, communists and trade-union members dominated. In these neighborhoods the Germans were less visible and had far fewer contacts. Instead of the wide, flowery avenues around the Étoile, these neighborhoods featured small roads and blocks of crowded housing units. The Germans did not regularly patrol these areas, relying instead on informers and the Paris police for surveillance. These working-class districts, as well as the even more crowded areas around the Place St. Michel across the river from Notre Dame, became the centers of anti-German activity in the summer of 1944.

The locus of French power in Paris, such as it was, sat on the Île de la Cité, one of the two islands in the Seine River. In the center of the island stands the imposing Préfecture de Police, the headquarters of the Paris police force. The police represented the daily face of collaboration and, like most urban police forces, had traditionally had a tense relationship with the working-class residents of the city. While helping the occupiers keep the peace in working-class neighborhoods, they also made the regime's roundups of Jews and political foes possible. Without the police, the Germans could not possibly have hoped to hold Paris under anything but the most severe martial law. As a result, *"À bas les flics!"* (Down with the cops!) was a frequent phrase on posters and graffiti throughout Paris both before and during the war years.

Although they worked for the German occupiers, the police also had four separate clandestine groups that sympathized with the Free French under Charles de Gaulle in London or with the French Resistance inside Paris. They therefore held a crucial position. Despised for their role in helping the occupiers exploit Parisians, some of them were readying themselves to become a force for change inside the capital. In 1943 and 1944, they became less reliable to the Germans and to Vichy, even if most Parisians failed to see the difference in their own neighborhoods. Although few Parisians could have foreseen it, the eyes, ears, and feet of the Paris policemen held the keys to the insurrection that began in Paris in 1944. Their decisions in mid-August determined much of what followed.

Opposite the prefecture on the Île de la Cité stands one of Paris's most recognized and most famous buildings, the Cathédrale Notre Dame. For most of the occupation, Notre Dame and its cardinal-archbishop, Monsignor Emmanuel Célestin Suhard, symbolized collaboration even more than the police did. Suhard's cozy relationship with the Germans and his public support of Vichy's policies alienated him and much of the Catholic Church hierarchy in France from a working class already deeply suspicious of the church and its prerogatives. The day after the liberation, Notre Dame was to undergo a remarkable transformation, with Suhard kept away from celebrations in his own cathedral by an armed guard, while the hero of the hour, Charles de Gaulle, gave new meaning to the site through an astonishing act of theater from a career filled with astonishing theatrical acts.[24]

To Parisians in early 1944, these dramatic events still lay in the future. In the meantime, the residents of the city had to live their lives as best they could. Even during the height of the occupation Paris maintained a surface appearance of normality. For those not deported or imprisoned, the timeless rituals of Paris continued. Men still cast their fishing lines into the Seine hoping to find something to supplement their dinner, young people still sunbathed on the quays, and grandmothers still took their grandchildren for walks in the city's magnificent parks. Until the Allies landed in France, Paris could do little but suffer in silence—and wait.

THE BLOOD
of
FREE MEN

I

THE END OF
THIS NIGHTMARE

ON JUNE 6, 1944, AT 8:00 A.M., JACQUES BARDOUX'S telephone rang in his apartment near the Arc de Triomphe in the upscale sixteenth arrondissement of Paris. It had been a long night for Bardoux and his fellow Parisians. There had been six different air-raid alerts in the northwest section of the city, each marked by a piercing siren announcing the arrival of Allied bombers. The planes were attacking a wide variety of targets, but were especially focused on factories and transportation nodes like railroad stations, canals, and highway intersections in and around the city. For more than a year, such air raids had been a regular feature of life, sending Parisians scurrying into wine cellars and basements—but not into the Métro, which the Germans reserved for themselves, refusing to open it to city residents despite the safety its underground passageways and stations would have afforded.[1]

Bardoux, who had been a member of the French Senate in 1940, found the Allied bombings incomprehensible. Although the Allies, especially the Americans, touted the sophisticated technology of their aircraft, most bombs missed their targets because of bad weather, poor visibility, air crew error, or any one of a thousand other reasons. The bombs were thus just as likely to fall on residential areas with no military importance at all as they were to hit a target of value to the Germans. The attacks had nevertheless become routine in an already tortured occupied Paris, except for those blessed nights when heavy cloud cover or rain kept the Allied planes away and allowed the residents to get a few hours of uninterrupted sleep.

Bardoux wore a black necktie all through the occupation in a silent act of protest as he kept a careful eye on events. He guessed that the increasing number of air raids probably meant that an Allied landing in France was imminent. A young adolescent in the city named Gilles Perrault also thought that "the ever-increasing number of bombers in the Paris sky" indicated that something big was afoot. "We were spending at least half the school day down in the shelters," he noted with decidedly mixed emotions, the danger of the bombs contrasting with the excitement at the thought of the Allies coming to France at long last. Bardoux was better informed than Perrault, a friend with military training in amphibious operations having told him that June 4 to 10 presented the Allies with the optimal moon phases and tides for a landing on the French coast. Still, Paris had had many nights with six (or more) air raids before. Bardoux's sleepless night, and Perrault's days in the school shelter, might not necessarily mean that anything unusual was going to happen soon.[2]

The phone call changed Bardoux's thinking in an instant. The man on the other end of the line said, "My mother in law has arrived," then, after a few words of meaningless chatter, hung up. The message was part of a prearranged code informing Bardoux that the Allies had landed in Normandy. Although he was not part of the Resistance, Bardoux had been working behind the scenes to organize the members of the French Senate of 1940 in the hopes that they could return to their seats as soon as the city was once again free. In his eyes, the Vichy government had wrongly and illegally robbed the French people of their freely elected representatives. Despite his hope that the Allies might attempt a landing that week, Bardoux could hardly believe what he heard. Nor did he fully understand what the long-anticipated landings meant for France or, more immediately, for Paris. He spent much of the day wandering the streets of his neighborhood trying to gauge the reactions of Parisians as rumors of the landings slowly spread across the city. He found his neighbors' faces hard to read and wondered why they were not showing more emotion. Had these men and women developed a habit of suppressing their feelings after four arduous years of occupation? Were they afraid to show any happiness in public out of fear of attracting unwanted attention from the Germans? Or did they think that the landings would simply mean more deadly air raids and greater German repression?[3]

Parisians, whom the novelist Marguerite Duras thought were simply dumbfounded by the momentous news of the landing, might also have been waiting for some reliable information to confirm the rumors, which were flying fast and furious that day. Duras noted that few of her friends believed the initial reports of a landing, although both she and the Parisian journalist Jean Galtier-Boissière noted a "sweet joy" in the subtle smiles that Parisians cautiously exchanged on the streets and in the cafés that day. The increasingly agitated behavior of the Germans in Paris indicated that there was some truth to the rumors, although the possibility of reprisals from anxious German soldiers tempered the enthusiasm of most of the city's residents.[4]

At 1:00 p.m., those Parisians with clandestine radios heard the voice of Winston Churchill himself on BBC radio, confirming that the Allies had landed. The British prime minister told the world that a landing "on a scale far larger than anything there has been so far in the world" was proceeding "in a thoroughly satisfactory manner." To Pierre Bourget, one of those Parisians huddled around a radio playing at low volume, Churchill's voice meant that the war had entered a new phase, possibly its last. Jacqueline Gaussen-Salmon, a young painter, noted the fear of the unknown that the news provoked in many of her acquaintances, although she hoped desperately that the news meant "the end of this nightmare." To the memoirist Charles Braibant, the voice of the British leader meant that "it really is the Landing, with a capital L," and was thus a cause for cautious excitement. "People are hopeful," he wrote in his journal, "but they are afraid of getting carried away." Yves Cazaux, a professor who had kept a detailed journal since 1940, too, was hopeful—he even started a new journal to mark "this historic day." Still, Braibant was right to be cautious and to guard his optimism. The beaches of Normandy were a long way from Paris.[5]

Early reports were contradictory. Although the German and collaborationist radio stations said nothing at first about the landings, they soon had no choice but to confirm the news being broadcast into Paris by the BBC and the recently established pro-Allied Radio Rome. The Germans had initially announced that the invasion had failed and that "the protective forces of the German Army annihilated the invaders in a matter of a few hours." Through its newspaper *Le Franciste*, the regime tried to turn the city's residents against the landing, calling the Allies "the valets of Stalin" and warning Parisians that the Allies were acting as the tools of world Jewry and communists, bringing with them only death and Soviet tyranny. The Germans warned the city's residents against doing anything that might interfere with German military activity as units moved through Paris to the fighting fronts. They also put posters up around the city warning that anyone suspected of resistance activity would be shot on sight.[6]

Ernst Jünger, the famous author of the World War I memoir *Storm of Steel*, was then based in Paris and assigned to the German cultural ministry. He noted that most German generals in the city, although expecting a landing at some point, were nevertheless surprised that it had actually occurred. "Why that place? Why this time?" he recalled them thinking. Still, he reported no sense of fear or panic inside Paris headquarters and wrote in his diary for June 7 that the city was calm, displaying its usual "serenity and melancholy." On June 8, he noted that the Paris stock market was rising and the city was operating as normal. The D-Day landings, seen today as such a dramatic turning point in the war, did not cause any major changes to daily life in Paris under occupation.[7]

The Vichy government tried to depict the landings as only another phase in the victimization of a France that did not seek a direct role in the battle between Germany and the Allies. Vichy's formulation took on the view of the Germans: The British and Americans were the unwitting dupes of a Jewish-Soviet worldwide conspiracy. "We are not in this war," declared the Vichy prime minister, the increasingly detested Pierre Laval, who urged his countrymen not to choose sides and not to interfere with German military movements. Pétain, the head of the Vichy state, urged his countrymen to remain neutral, warning them "not to aggravate our misfortune by deeds that risk bringing upon you tragic acts of reprisal. It will be the innocent people of France who will suffer the consequences."[8]

The Allies were aware of the potential power that the French Resistance held. An uprising by the many groups that constituted the French Resistance formed a key element of the planning of General Dwight D. Eisenhower's staff for the operations in Normandy and beyond. Churchill, too, placed great faith in the French Resistance. One of his pet projects, the British Special Operations Executive (SOE), had established a network of agents inside France and had parachuted weapons, radios, and other supplies to them. The SOE flew daring agents in and out of France on extremely risky missions. These brave agents distributed code books to allow members of the Resistance to understand messages dropped by parachute or broadcast over the BBC. The SOE also worked with the rural Resistance group known as the *maquis* to recover downed Allied air crewmen, dozens of whom secretly passed through Paris during the war.

As the day for the landings approached, the SOE and the American Office of Strategic Services increased their activities inside France to prepare the Resistance to play an active supporting role. Through their networks, British and American agents notified their contacts throughout France to listen carefully to the BBC for three lines from

Paul Verlaine's nineteenth-century poem "Chanson d'Automne." The lines, *"Blessent mon coeur / D'une longuer / Monotone,"* were the signal for the members of the Resistance to go into action. They were to blow up rail lines, cut telephone and telegraph communications, and do anything else they could to confuse and disorient the Germans, thus giving the landings their best chance at success. Unfortunately, these lines were also the signal for the Germans to go on high alert, as their agents had already broken the code through torture and interrogation of captured French Resistance fighters. German Supreme Command West, the army headquarters responsible for the defense of France, went on high alert just thirty minutes after the broadcast. Many important German commanders and intelligence operatives nevertheless refused to believe that the broadcast was truly the signal that an invasion was imminent, especially given the poor weather conditions in Normandy that night.[9]

Soon after the poem went out over the BBC airwaves, another message went out, this one from General Marie-Pierre Koenig, the London-based leader of the Forces Françaises de l'Intérieur (FFI). Koenig urged the members of the FFI, known inside France by their nickname the "Fifis," and at least nominally under the control of the French government-in-exile in London, to rise up. These men and women were among the best organized members of the French Resistance, even if for reasons of necessity and security they were diffuse and hard to command. Koenig's message urged them to begin a guerrilla uprising in support of the landings and to act as a fifth column for the Allies. Members of the FFI anxiously and eagerly joined the fight that they hoped would lead to the liberation of their homeland. Despite the Germans having cracked the code, the FFI succeeded in carrying out many acts of sabotage. Besides dynamiting railroads and cutting telegraph lines, in isolated instances FFI agents targeted German officials for assassination.

Rising up in Normandy, where confusion reigned and FFI members could melt into the countryside, was easier than rising up in Paris, which was honeycombed with informers. French agents also ran risks if they tried to move around Paris without proper papers. Nevertheless, many members of the Resistance tried to organize an uprising inside the city. The Comité Parisien de la Libération (CPL), a communist-dominated Resistance group headed by a thirty-one-year-old artisan, labor organizer, and lifelong resident of Paris named André Tollet, ordered its men into action on June 8. Tollet, who had survived fifteen months in a German prison before escaping in June 1942, was one of the many tough, determined communist leaders of the Resistance who both gave the movement its energy and terrified the opponents of communism in Paris, London, and Washington. From him came an order, plastered overnight on kiosks and walls across Paris, that read:

> The landing of the Allies, so long desired by the population of Paris, has occurred. . . . Sabotage, destroy, or burn anything that can be of use to the enemy. Disrupt his transportation and his production. Paris, capital of combat and capital of insurrection, Paris, capital of liberty, must have the full mobilization of its people.[10]

The CPL thus represented a way to organize the working class of Paris—but a working class aligned with communism could be a new potential rival as well as a potential weapon. Consequently, Allied agents tried to have little to do with the CPL and its followers.

Good news seemed to follow in the first few days and weeks after the landings. Word quickly spread throughout Paris that Charles de Gaulle had arrived in Bayeux to a rapturous welcome. The leader of Free France, operating as the head of a Provisional Government of the Republic of France, was on French soil. At least a small part of France was back under French control. Parisians also knew that an elite Free French naval commando unit had landed in the first wave of the D-Day assault and had participated in the liberation of the town of Ouistreham on the eastern edge of the Allied lodgment area. It hardly mattered to most Parisians that the unit was small or that its overall contribution to the events of June 6 was minimal. The unit's appearance meant that French soldiers were fighting the Germans inside France.

But, as Charles Braibant and many others had correctly guessed, the people of Paris would have to wait for the Allied landings to have a positive impact on them. Although the Allies had overcome stiff resistance in places and had liberated the beautiful medieval town of Bayeux within a few hours, the Normandy landings had not been a complete success. The five Allied landing forces did not achieve the linkage envisioned for the first day, meaning that critical gaps existed between them that the Germans might be able to exploit. More importantly, the vital rail and road juncture of Caen, a target for day one of the operation, remained in German hands until July 18.

Parisians quietly tried to learn as much as they could. They emptied bookstores of maps of Normandy and followed the progress of the Allies as closely as they could. Real news was often hard to come by, forcing Parisians to sort out rumor and propaganda from fact, all the while wondering if the Allied forces moving slowly across Normandy would reach Paris in the near future or if they would stall as the Allied advance into Italy had done. Some also recalled the failed Allied raid on Dieppe in August 1942, which cost the Allies 3,600 casualties but did nothing to change the situation in France. They feared that the landings might in the end be nothing more than a repeat of that disaster on a far larger scale. If the landings should fail, moreover, the Allies might not be in a position to try again for several years.[11]

The BBC and Radio Rome kept Parisians reasonably well informed, as did the informal grapevines and rumor networks that ran through the city. Anyone who could get near a radio and had a means to power it tuned in, hoping to learn what the Allies were saying about the latest events. Listening to the BBC and Radio Rome was illegal but widespread nevertheless. Every night at 9, the BBC broadcast in French. The thirty minutes of news and entertainment included coded messages to the French Resistance as well as a nightly address from Charles de Gaulle. The BBC made de Gaulle something more than just a name; his voice was a nightly reminder to France that an alternative to Pétain and Vichy existed. So many people were listening to the BBC that a grim joke circulated around Paris that a Jew had killed a German soldier and eaten his heart at 9:20 p.m. "Impossible for three reasons," ran the punch line: "A German has no heart. A Jew eats no pork. And at 9:20 everyone is listening to the BBC."[12]

Largely because of the BBC's nightly updates, the journals and letters of Parisians from these weeks show a remarkably accurate picture of the overall military situation despite the torrent of lies and misinformation that the Germans and Vichy authorities released. Not all of the news was good. The slow Allied advance off the beaches led Charles Braibant to wonder if the landings, rather than being the start of a liberation that "had filled our hearts with hope," instead were "a new Anzio," a reference to the frustrating Allied landings south of Rome that had stalled on the beaches from January to May. A repeat of that disaster might delay liberation for months.

Parisians also learned, with mixed emotions, that the Allies had turned their main effort toward the major port city of Cherbourg on June 20. The obvious value of seizing one of the largest ports on the English Channel was evident to all—to Braibant it represented "an enormous step on the road to victory"—but it also meant that the Allies were moving their strategic axis west and therefore away from Paris. Allied progress through the rough hedgerow country that began just inside the coast was painfully slow, forcing the Allies to regroup and rethink their operations and tactics. Supply also remained a problem. Allied inability to capture Cherbourg until June 27 (giving the Germans enough time to do serious damage to its facilities), combined with a storm that destroyed one of the two artificial ports custom-designed for the operation, caused massive logistical problems that continued to haunt the Allies until the end of the war. A lack of supplies and reinforcements and the slow progress through the hedgerows worried not only anxious people in Paris but the officers in Eisenhower's headquarters as well.[13]

While Allied operations in Normandy slowed, the Germans reacted savagely to the newfound threat, rounding up any Parisian they
suspected of having been involved in resistance activities since the
landings. Increased German surveillance sent Resistance leaders in
the city even farther underground. The Germans arrested hundreds
of men, many of them, the young Gilles Perrault noted, for no crime
other than being "caught outside the cinema without papers." Many
such men disappeared into prisons like Fresnes or onto trucks bound
for prisons or work camps in Germany.[14]

The slow pace of the Allied advance thus had direct implications
for the members of the FFI in and around Paris who were bearing the
lion's share of the fighting. Just a few days after the landings, Koenig
reluctantly ordered an end to FFI sabotage activity because the Allies
were still stuck near the beaches; any further sabotage outside the
battle area, he felt, only risked exposure and death for FFI agents.
His telegram of June 10 read:

```
PUT MAXIMUM BRAKE ON GUERRILLA ACTIONS   STOP
CURRENTLY IMPOSSIBLE TO SUPPLY ARMS AND AMMUNITION
IN SUFFICIENT QUANTITIES   STOP   WHEREVER POSSIBLE
BREAK OFF ATTACKS TO ALLOW REORGANIZATION   STOP
AVOID LARGE GROUPINGS FORM SMALL ISOLATED GROUPS
```

Although the order made tactical sense, it alienated members of
the FFI inside France who had risked their lives for what they believed was a final fight to the finish for the liberation of France. One
FFI leader compared it to the surrender of 1940; another warned
that it would lead to mass arrests of French Resistance agents. The
order created mistrust between the FFI in France and its nominal
chiefs in London.[15]

While the Allies stalled, the Germans and their Vichy allies increased the repression and harassment of résistants. On June 21
came news of the German killing of thirty young unarmed Parisians
in cold blood, their bodies left near the waterfall in the Bois de

Boulogne. They had been looking for weapons to purchase but had been betrayed and led to their deaths by a Frenchman they trusted, who was in fact on the payroll of the Gestapo. Because of this and other crackdowns, Parisians quickly retreated back into the scared silence that had marked the city and its inhabitants for four long years; it was the same silence that had led its German occupiers to give Paris the nickname "the city that never looks back."[16]

Parisians had to deal with much more than just increased vigilance on the part of the Germans. The air attacks that so terrified Parisians before June 6 intensified as the Allies sought all possible means to help get their troops out of the Normandy beachhead. The attacks, part of the Anglo-American Combined Bomber Offensive, aimed to cripple Germany's ability to move men and supplies through northern France. Since 1943 the bomber offensive had been striking industrial targets in Europe and forcing German fighters to engage Allied fighters on Allied terms. Because Paris was both the vital center of all communications in northern France and the node through which the vast majority of German rail and road traffic passed, the city was a prime target of this campaign. From a strategic perspective, the transportation network of Paris and its suburbs was the single most important military asset of the capital. Eisenhower's staff estimated that each of the 59 German divisions in France needed 350 tons of supplies per day plus the operational mobility that the railroads gave them. The airmen concluded that destroying 80 to 90 percent of the French rail network would immobilize those divisions and render them militarily ineffective.

In the months prior to the landings, therefore, Eisenhower ordered his air forces to reduce the amount of bomb tonnage they were dropping on German industry and increase the tonnage of bombs dropped on the French transportation network, especially on the giant roundhouse that Paris represented. The damage to factories caused by an air raid against industrial targets and marshaling yards in the Paris suburb of Trappes in early March inspired confidence in Allied air commanders, who had long believed that air power alone might bring Germany to its knees. Although some of them were reluctant to slow the bombardment of German industry, others saw a chance for air power to make a direct contribution to the success of the cross-channel invasion. Eisenhower, also impressed by the results of the Trappes raid, made the French railway network a high priority for Allied bombers from April to June.[17]

Given the notorious inaccuracy of aerial bombardment, the so-called Transportation Plan faced enormous odds. The partial success at Trappes did not change the estimates of British analysts who thought that the goal of destroying 90 percent of the French rail network was absurdly optimistic; they estimated that, at best, aerial interdiction could disrupt 30 percent of German supplies, not nearly enough to debilitate enemy operations in Normandy. The Allies nevertheless increased the bombings, dropping more than 500,000 tons of bombs on France in 1943 and 1944. The damage that these operations inflicted was often far less than the airmen had promised, and the Germans more than made good their losses of rolling stock by seizing almost 60 percent of French rolling stock.[18]

Most of the important French rail yards and stations, of course, were located in urban areas, presenting a conundrum to Allied planners. Paris, the unquestioned center of the French rail system, had eight large stations and a number of smaller substations as well as important stations in the suburbs. Many of these stations were dedicated to moving heavy cargo and equipment and were obvious targets for air operations. The British and Americans, however, were well aware that the Transportation Plan involved bombing not an enemy country, but an occupied nation that they were hoping to liberate. Some of the planners agonized over the estimated 160,000 French casualties to be expected (half of whom they guessed would be fatalities), not to mention the immense damage the bombing would cause to the very same rail network that they would prefer to maintain in order to feed and supply France in the first winter after the liberation. Churchill and the British foreign secretary, Anthony Eden, also worried that the air campaign—which they described as "criminal" and "murderous"—

would give German and Vichy propagandists enough material to turn the French against their liberators, not just during the war but for years thereafter.

Eisenhower, while hoping to spare the city by prohibiting the use of incendiary bombs and promising to do "everything possible to avoid loss of life among our friends," nevertheless criticized as "sheer folly" any objections that might reduce the Normandy campaign's chance of success. Admiral Sir Andrew Cunningham, a senior British strategist, dismissed concerns about French civilian casualties as "sob stuff about children with legs blown off and blinded old ladies" that he believed was insignificant when compared to "the saving of risk to our young soldiers landing on a hostile shore." President Roosevelt, to whom Churchill also appealed, refused to second-guess his military commander. Consequently, Churchill got nothing more for his efforts than an empty promise from the air force commanders that they would take greater care in aiming their bombs around Paris. Given the inability of air forces to drop their bombs with anything that remotely approached accuracy, this promise accounted for precious little.[19]

Thus the bombs kept falling on Paris and across northern France. And they kept killing. German soldiers, who had access to solid shelters, rarely suffered, but the French people suffered terribly. Allied bombardments killed 67,078 French citizens in all, 35,317 of them in 1944 alone. One raid, on May 30, killed 5,358 Frenchmen, wounded 7,075 more, and left thousands of men, women, and children homeless. Even when the Americans tried to reduce casualties, people still died needlessly, often because of the inherent inaccuracy of aerial bombardment. One raid, aimed at the Paris suburbs of St. Cloud and Sèvres, attacked factories on a Sunday. The commanders had hoped to damage the buildings without killing the workers. But the bombs missed their targets, killing 380 and wounding 446; it was a beautiful spring day, and many of these people had been out for a walk in a nearby park. Another raid in April destroyed the city's main Red Cross warehouse along with its irreplaceable stores of badly needed medical supplies. Each air raid warning (six on the night of May 28, three more on the night of May 29) kept the city on a razor's edge and suggested momentous events in the days ahead. The raids also filled Paris's badly stretched hospitals, leading Jacques Bardoux to wonder "if the military advantages can possibly compensate for their political and moral effects."[20]

Allied air strategists, many of whom were contemptuous of French military performance in 1940, thought little of France's suffering. Concerned with minimizing their own casualties, they saw the air campaign as a legitimate form of warfare even if civilians died. For Parisians, however, the raids seemed a terrible price for people already suffering under German occupation. They left even dedicated résistants furious at what they called the "criminal imbecility" of a policy that killed Frenchmen by the hundreds and thousands but rarely did even moderate damage to German positions. Some on the French Left even wondered if the attacks were part of a larger plan to destroy French industry in order to render it incapable of competing with the British and Americans after the war. André Tollet and others in the Communist Party were stupefied and infuriated at the Allied willingness to drop bombs by the ton on innocent civilians, while simultaneously refusing to drop badly needed weapons to the Resistance from those same airplanes for fear of the weapons ending up in German or communist hands.[21]

The bombings were foremost on the minds of the Frenchmen who talked to the courageous American journalist Alice Moats shortly before the Normandy landings. Based in Madrid for much of the war and tired of hearing about the situation in France from people who had not been there since 1940, she snuck across the Pyrenees on foot and caught a train into Paris, arriving in April 1944. She stayed for a remarkable three weeks before she decided it was too dangerous to remain any longer, but in that time she saw just how badly the Transportation Plan had failed. The Germans, she found, were able to rebuild rail yards almost as quickly as Allied planes destroyed them. Meanwhile, the people of Paris continued to suffer from both the direct and indirect effects of the bombings. Neither the Germans nor the collaborationist government of the city of Paris provided any aid to those rendered homeless or unemployed by the bombings. On her arrival in Paris, Moats went to the scene of a raid in the La Chapelle neighborhood (near the rail yards of the Gare du Nord and the Gare de l'Est) that had killed 565 people a few weeks earlier. Residents were still digging bodies out of the rubble, and the locals she saw all wore "the same dazed look of suffering."[22]

Parisians tried to understand the bombings as a tragic but necessary prelude to their freedom, but the slow Allied progress across Normandy made it harder and harder for them to see any direct connection between their immediate suffering and their eventual liberation. One Frenchman told Moats, "What a terrible thing it is, Madame, to be slaughtered by the very people who are coming to liberate us," although he believed that Parisians would quickly forgive the Allies if they liberated the city soon. Some, however, feared that there might not be anything left to liberate if the bombing campaign continued. The expatriate English journalist Sisley Huddleston undertook a dangerous trip from his home in the south of France to Paris because he wanted to see the city he loved one last time before, he feared, Allied bombers destroyed it as they had already destroyed Hamburg, Cologne, and Rouen. Jacques Bardoux was also fearful about what might happen if the Allies did not arrive quickly, writing in his journal, "We ask ourselves anxiously what will be left of France if the Anglo-Americans only reconquer it meter by meter all the way to Lorraine!" Bardoux talked with other members of the French Senate of 1940 about ways of appealing to the Americans and the British to warn them that the air attacks were "radicalizing" public opinion against the Allies; they also discussed asking the Vatican to step in and demand that the Allies stop the attacks on humanitarian grounds.[23]

The air attacks gave the Germans the only possible public relations boon they could have hoped for after four years of occupation. Few Parisians believed the most outrageous claims of German and Vichy propagandists: that the Germans were protecting Paris from an

"Allied army of crime" that was in the pay of the Jews and the Soviets. But the air raids did give some credence to the claims of Vichy
supporters that the policy of collaboration served as the only viable
option for a nation stuck between two warring parties, neither of
which had France's best interests at heart. Huddleston noted that
Parisians were angry and resentful about the bombings, which "defi-
nitely did harm to the Allied cause."[24]

Vichy leaders moved quickly to take advantage of the growing
anti-Allied sentiment. Pétain, the living symbol of collaboration and
the man who coined the term, came to Paris in late April for a mass
at Notre Dame in memory of the dead from the La Chapelle bombings. It was his first appearance in Paris since 1940, and the city
gave an ecstatic reception to the man who had once been France's
greatest hero. Pétain played the role for all it was worth, posing for
photographs near bomb craters in Montmartre and in front of the
damaged outer walls of the Sacré Coeur basilica, his eyes filled with
tears for the cameras to record. Appearing without bodyguards or
uniformed security as he moved through bombed-out areas, he
basked in the reception the capital gave him. One sympathetic observer noted that "never in the palmiest days of Hitler, in the most
triumphant days of Stalin, has a chief been better received than
Pétain was in Paris."

While many in the Resistance might have found comparisons to
Hitler a bit too close for comfort, there was little doubt that Pétain's
popularity offered a potential counterweight to the efforts of de
Gaulle and the FFI to win over the hearts of Parisians. Even among
members of the Resistance, however, there was surprisingly little animosity toward Pétain personally. One Resistance leader told Alice
Moats that "the patriots among us hate the Vichy government, but
few of us can bring ourselves to hate Pétain." Moats, who risked
exposure and arrest to see Pétain's arrival at Notre Dame, heard
Parisians discussing the hope that Pétain might return to Paris permanently, take control of the government as he had in 1940, and sign a
deal with the Americans to end the air attacks. Such hopes were un-

realistic, but they spoke to the desires of Parisians for an end to the war and the bombings under almost any conditions.[25]

Although the bombings continued relentlessly, the Transportation Plan came nowhere near to achieving its goals. It failed to stop German units from getting to Normandy from other parts of France. The German 12th SS Panzer and Panzer Lehr divisions, for example, experienced delays of less than twenty-four hours as a result of transportation problems around Paris. In fact, the Germans did not suffer a single insurmountable supply problem; their supply lines were more secure than those of the Allies, which suffered from a lack of appropriate port facilities. The Germans responded to the damage caused by Allied bombing by taking over more of the French civilian rail network's capacity. As a result, the Germans made up the difference, while the residents of Paris had to make do with even less. The Transportation Plan harmed French civilians much more than it harmed the Germans. Seen from French eyes, the plan was more than simply inefficient; it was murderous.[26]

The air attacks were terrifying enough on their own, but they also aggravated the single most important problem facing Paris in the days after the landings: a dangerous shortage of food. As early as the occupation's first winter Parisians had begun to feel the sting of privation. Those with connections in the countryside wrote to their friends and relatives asking them to send anything edible to the increasingly malnourished city. As the war dragged on and as German requisitions from the French countryside increased, meat virtually disappeared from the Parisian diet, reducing the city's residents to what one Parisian called "the level of beasts" as they scoured Paris for food. As early as the spring of 1943, Parisians began to suffer from a host of diseases associated with poor nutrition. One visitor to the city that year found the food situation in Paris much worse than in the countryside or in smaller French cities. Huddleston confided to his diary that he "could not understand how the ordinary Frenchman lived at all. The insipid and unnutritive vegetables, the small portion of horrible bread, which was about all he could get, reduced him to a skeleton."[27] A report prepared by a Swiss Red Cross official estimated that Paris had 25,000 severely malnourished babies and toddlers. The supposedly nutritious *biscuits Pétain* fed to students at school could not stop the wartime trend of declining average weight and height among French children.[28]

In another of the tragic ironies of war, the food situation in Paris grew markedly worse as a direct result of Allied efforts to liberate France. Not only did Paris need fully functioning rail lines to bring food into the city, but the landings had also cut Paris off from the fertile agricultural lands of Normandy, the city's primary source of milk, meat, and vegetables. Even before the landings, milk deliveries had fallen 50 percent and meat deliveries 40 percent because of the extensive damage to the rail network of northern France. Many truck drivers and railroad workers refused to go north of the capital because of the dangers involved. With much of Normandy in Allied hands, moreover, the region's ample food stocks went more often to England, which also badly needed them, than to Paris. As a result, food prices in Paris were as much as eight times higher than those in the countryside.[29]

The arrival of 350,000 more German soldiers after the landings and the German requisitioning of 25,000 French cows per month to feed them severely aggravated the food problem. The Germans also seized approximately three-fourths of the available trucks in Normandy, severely depleting the only viable alternative to rail supply. Paris badly needed the trucks, because two-thirds of the French railway network's rolling stock not requisitioned by the Germans had been damaged or destroyed by the Allied bombardments. The result was a virtual end to regular food shipments into the capital. In July 1943, an average of five hundred railcars had brought food to the city every day; by July 1944, that figure had plummeted to just twenty. Charles Braibant thought that although the city had been hungry for many months, "the real start of the famine" dated to mid-June 1944.[30]

His observation was accurate. Weekly rations, which even in the early years of the occupation amounted to barely enough to sustain the city's 2.5 million people, fell precipitously throughout 1944 and again after the landings. By the time of the liberation, a Parisian's weekly ration included one-half pound of unappetizing meat, often of indeterminable origin and in the form of a grayish sausage; three-fifths of a pound of butter or equivalent fats; and a handful of fresh vegetables, most often rutabagas. Only fruit and locally caught fish were available in reasonable, if not ample, supply. It could take as long as five hours to get to the front of a bread line, and on any given day, as many as three-fourths of the city's bakeries were closed because of a lack of flour or fuel for the ovens. Parisians Janet Flanner and Gilbert Reynaud Rémy, who both lived in Paris during the occupation, independently estimated that the average Parisian lost forty pounds. Rémy had seen people die in the streets of hunger in the city's poorest neighborhoods.[31]

Parisians did what they could to amass enough food to survive, but life became increasingly precarious in the spring of 1944. The semiregular shipments of food from friends and relatives in the countryside had stopped, owing both to shortages in the provinces and the difficulty of transporting what little extra food was available. One city resident celebrated his ability to save his ration coupons for several days and thereby hoard enough radishes, peas, potatoes, and pasta to form something resembling a regular meal. His joy was tempered, however, when he found himself hungry again after just two hours. Two weeks later, he recorded in his journal, "not a cat to be seen on the streets."[32]

Alice Moats, the American journalist who had sneaked into France in April, almost blew her own cover because she was not accustomed to the near-starvation diet of Parisians. In a restaurant near the Gare de Lyon, she was served "a cold, disgusting mess" of "gray and lumpy" mashed potatoes that she found too unappetizing to eat. She left the potatoes sitting on the plate, hoping that the waiter would take them away. The waiter, "unable to believe that a person could possibly leave a portion of potatoes uneaten," would not clear her plate, and she did not want to ask him again for fear of him noticing her foreign accent. Soon, all the diners in the restaurant were staring at her, wondering what kind of person would leave food of any kind uneaten. She chose to leave the restaurant as quietly as she could, but she felt the eyes of the others in the restaurant follow her as she did.[33]

The city authorities in Paris tried to deal with the food shortages by establishing communal kitchens within individual neighborhoods. Like ration cards, tickets for meals in so-called "national restaurants" were not valid outside a family's neighborhood of residence. This system controlled movement inside the city and limited formal connections between people living in different parts of the city. It therefore made neighbors dependent upon one another through a barter system that often functioned much more effectively than the traditional cash system. The communal kitchens rarely offered much beyond a thin, watery soup and some hard cakes made from second-grade flour. Often they did not have nearly enough food to meet the needs of the neighborhood. Paris authorities also tried to sell sugar, milk, and coffee substitutes as "patriotic" alternatives to goods no longer available, but they rarely succeeded because of the obvious low quality of those goods.

Even when Parisians could find food, they often had no fuel with which to cook it. Gas and electricity were normally available only intermittently, sometimes for as little as thirty minutes per day. Andrzej Bobkowski, an expatriate Pole living in Paris, had so little gas that it took the meager flame on his stove more than two hours to boil a small cup of water for a "patriotic" tea made from dried herbs. Shipments of coal and wood had long since stopped coming into the city, leading residents to search out alternative fuels. They even burned sawdust. Electricity came on only at night, and usually, only then, for an hour or two. The city's cinemas compensated by hooking generators to groups of bicycles, whose teenaged riders provided the power to run the projectors.[34]

There was not even enough power in the city to run the Métro, which operated with unpredictable hours. City authorities looked to save power by closing some of the stations. On some nights, less than half of the stations were fully functioning. Parisians learned to adapt by relying on their feet and the city's ubiquitous bicycles. A joke even went around the city that the Métro closures were not that important, as Paris would need just four stations for the liberation: Bienvenüe ("welcome") for the Allies; Cambronne (Parisian slang meaning "shit") for the Germans; Concorde ("agreement") for the various elements of the Resistance; and Père Lachaise (named for the city's most famous cemetery) for the collaborators.[35]

As such bitterness attests, not all Parisians suffered equally. A thriving black market operated in the city for those with the cash to afford it. Luxuries like butter, eggs, and meat were available but at exorbitant prices well out of the reach of all but the wealthiest Parisians and for those with close connections to the Germans. Before the war, butter cost 15 francs per kilogram. By mid-1943 it cost 1,500 francs per kilogram on the black market. By July 1944, prices had skyrocketed so much that 1 kilogram of butter cost 13,000 francs. Bread, officially listed at 3.75 francs per kilogram, sold on the black market for almost ten times that amount. The Normandy landings only exacerbated the problem. The price of a kilogram of black-market meat rose from 250 francs to 450 francs in the week following D-Day.[36]

Most Parisians depicted the black market as a place frequented by the rich and the collaborators, although most residents turned to it on occasion in a desperate search for food. They had little choice, as official rations were not enough to feed most families. By one estimate, more than 20 percent of the food coming into the city ended up in the hands of black marketers. Some Parisians even rationalized that shopping on the black market was a patriotic activity, because the food at least stayed in France rather than being shipped back to Germany, as so much of French produce was.[37]

But if the black market was out of reach for most Parisians, it did not necessarily operate in the shadows. Some restaurants had concealed back rooms and secret menus, but others operated openly, making money selling fine foods to those few who could afford them. Such restaurants posted signs saying that they operated *sans tickets* or *hors catégoire*, meaning that the food inside could not be obtained by ration coupons, but by cash only. Alice Moats observed that such restaurants, mainly frequented by Germans and collaborators, had "butter on the tables, fresh cream overflowing in every dish, juicy meat," and even unheard of luxuries like pâté, steak, cheese, and vintage wines. For most Parisians, wine and liquor were rare luxuries, being available only in poor quality and sold in restaurants and cafés only three days a week.[38]

Moats recorded two dinners she attended in her time in Paris in April and May 1944. They tell the tale of the two ways of life in wartime Paris. The first dinner, which she attended under an assumed name at the invitation of an old friend, was in the home of one of Paris's most famous collaborationist families on the Avenue Foch. There she was welcomed with martinis and a full five-course meal, which was served and prepared by the family's staff. The meal featured champagne, white wine, red wine, brandy, and the only real coffee she drank during her extraordinary trip. Over dinner the guests spoke openly and with no shame about the best places in the city to find black-market goods of all kinds. Little wonder that the guests expressed their fear of the city's communists, and little wonder, too, that Moats left that night aware that the small but rich group of collaborators was the only segment of the Parisian population not going hungry during these difficult times.

The other dinner she wrote about was in the small Left Bank apartment of a key Resistance leader, whom she never identified by name. That meal was cabbage followed not by brandy but by the passing of coarse cigarettes to curb hunger. The conversation that accompanied the meal revolved around impressions of the Americans and British, who they hoped would soon liberate France, as well as the desire of working-class Parisians for vengeance against the collaborators. One of the résistants at the meal told Moats that he was far from alone in having "a long list of people he was planning to shoot and there wasn't a German name on the list."[39]

Food remained the city's main problem. Jacques Bardoux feared an open battle in the city less than he feared starvation. On June 26, he wrote, "Paris *might* know a disaster [caused by a battle in the city], but it *will* know famine," unless something happened soon to change its fate. Jacqueline Gaussen-Salmon, the painter, thought that the city was too hungry even to dream about liberation. On July 12 she wrote in her journal that "the great fear of famine crushes all our spirits. No one thinks of anything but food."[40]

But if most Parisians were hungry, at least they still had a bit of freedom. Some Parisians lost much more than their prewar material comforts. In June and July the Gestapo increased its arrests of suspected Resistance members, presumed political opponents, and labor leaders. More and more Parisians found themselves in the torture chambers of the Rue des Saussaies and on the Avenue Foch. The terrible prison at Fresnes overflowed with political enemies of the Reich, most of whom the Germans deported to camps in the east. Roundups of Paris's few remaining Jews continued as well, with 240 Jewish children being sent to the squalid suburban camp at Drancy on July 21, followed by another 400 children ten days later, and a final roundup of Jewish children on August 17, the day that the last trains left Drancy for Auschwitz. With them went the last Jews to remain in a city that had had a thriving Jewish population before the war. In 1940, some 140,000 Jews had lived in Paris, and two-thirds of them had been born in France.[41]

If there was any kind of silver lining in these terrible events, it was in the behavior of the Paris police. Since the Allied landings, some Parisians had noted that the police seemed less willing to work with the Germans and had, in fact, stopped arresting Parisians for their political views alone. This refusal on the part of the Paris police may help to explain the increased activity by the Gestapo, which now had to do more of its own dirty work. Jacques Bardoux was one of the Parisians who noted a new attitude among the police. He asked a policeman he knew about this turnabout and recorded his impressions in his journal that night. The policeman told him that the vast majority of the Paris police force was "against the Germans." He added, "We want very much to have the opportunity to set things right with the odious and rotten Nazi regime. We are for the Republic, although not a communist Republic." The Paris police had, in fact, begun to unite the force's four separate Resistance groups, pledging their allegiance to Charles de Gaulle. The prefect of the Paris police, however, remained loyal to the collaborationist city administration of the right-wing and anti-Semitic Pierre Taittinger, founder of both a successful champagne-making house and the Jeunesse Patriotique (The Young Patriots), a fascist youth movement of the interwar years. And if Parisians detected a change within the police force itself, it was a minor one, as even the most militant members limited their resistance to passive acts.[42]

The Allied landings, which had inspired so much hope on June 6, had therefore made Paris an even more desperate and anxious place. Streams of alternatively bad news and good news arrived in the city constantly, adding to the fears and uncertainty so many felt. On June 18, Parisians learned of a massacre that had taken place a week earlier in the town of Oradur sur Glane, near Limoges. There, members of the 2nd SS Panzer Division had rounded up the town's inhabitants into churches and barns then set those buildings on fire, burning 425 men, women, and children alive. Only 17 people survived. The Germans defended their actions by claiming that locals had thrown rocks at them, using this excuse to justify their decision not to punish a single German for the atrocity. The horrors of Oradur were too much even for the officials in Vichy, who demanded that the Germans at least apologize. One German general did go to Oradur to make amends; the local bishop told him, "God may forgive you, but France never will."[43]

Oradur was far from the only place that suffered the wrath of the Nazis in the wake of the Normandy landings. At the end of July, the Germans landed glider planes filled with SS troops in Vercors, a southern stronghold of the rural maquis. The Allies had in fact dropped supplies into Vercors in July; tragically, though, these supply drops were enough to rouse the Germans into taking action without giving the *maquisards* sufficient arms to defend themselves. At the end of July, the Germans wiped out Vercors, killing 830 people amid atrocities that rivaled in brutality those committed at Oradur. The Allies ignored the final desperate pleas of the men and women in Vercors for more arms, reinforcing the view in Paris and elsewhere that the Resistance could not count on help from de Gaulle, the Americans, or the British. One of those final messages read, "If no aid [arrives] we and population will consider [the Free France government] criminal and cowardly." The Allied abandonment of Vercors underscored to the FFI in Paris the dangers of rising against the Germans prematurely. Similarly, the Resistance, responding to the Allied landings in Normandy, managed to liberate the town of Tulle in central France for a few hours on June 7 and 8. The Germans responded by hanging ninety-nine people in the town square.[44]

Fierce fighting erupted in many places. St. Lô, Caen, and many other towns and cities suffered near total destruction. Some became sites of intentional German atrocities; others were simply caught in the middle. FFI commander Raymond Massiet was among those who saw in the fates of those towns, "caught mercilessly between two armies fighting on soil that was not theirs," a terrible omen for Paris. The Germans had already shown themselves capable of committing mass atrocities in Oradur, Tulle, and Vercors. Other cities, like Stalingrad in southwestern Russia, which had been directly on the front lines in 1942–1943, had been completely destroyed. Parisians knew that their city sat at the edge of an abyss and that calamity was just as likely as liberation. One resident noted that "the Paris air is more highly charged with menace than at any time since the French Revolution. Invasion, civil war, siege, famine, prison—whatever the future may take—Parisians are ominously expecting the deadliest phase of the war."[45]

Before she left Paris, Moats talked to an FFI member about the future that awaited Paris. He compared Paris, and France more generally, to a woman in labor: "At the moment . . . she doesn't say to herself 'This is going to be a boy, and I shall educate him to be an engineer.' All she can think of is getting rid of the burden she has carried for so many months and having the pain stop." If the pain did not stop soon, he feared, Paris itself might die from the labor it was then suffering. Another Parisian later recalled, "We just could not go on any longer. There was absolutely nothing left. We had thought we had reached the end so many times, yet the finish line kept on moving further back." With its population depleted both physically and psychologically, the city seemed close to the breaking point. As a symptom of this decline, street violence also began to increase.

While most of Paris was engaged in a desperate struggle for survival, a small but determined band of Parisians planned and prepared to move that finish line forward. They hoped not just to end the German occupation, but to settle old scores and give France a future of security and safety from enemies inside and out. The Resistance had waited for years for this moment and now would attempt to seize it.[46]

2

RESISTANCE

I N OCTOBER 1941, A HANDSOME FORTY-TWO-YEAR-OLD MAN
arrived in London to meet with Charles de Gaulle. With the help
of British agents, de Gaulle's visitor had managed to travel from
Marseilles to Barcelona to Lisbon, with the original intention of going to America. While living in Lisbon, he had used fake names and
changed residences frequently, trying to avoid both German agents
and the Portuguese police. He had also begun to write down his observations of the nascent Resistance movement developing in France.
The British agents with whom he worked in Lisbon read those notes
and, convinced that he was too valuable to leave Europe, insisted
that he go instead to London. When he met de Gaulle for the first
time, the charismatic fugitive was wearing the silk scarf around his
neck that soon became his trademark. It hid a telltale scar that resulted from a failed suicide attempt following his torture at the hands
of France's new German masters.

The man's name was Jean Moulin, and just a year earlier he had
been the youngest prefect in France and a fast-rising star in French
politics. Now he had arrived in England with news for de Gaulle that
promised to transform the nature of French resistance to the Nazis
and Vichy. Moulin had already showed a deep reservoir of courage.

After the German takeover of Chartres, the city outside Paris where he was based, Moulin had refused to sign a Nazi document that falsely blamed Senegalese soldiers in the French Army for the deaths of civilians that had obviously resulted from German artillery. For his refusal, the Germans tortured him, only reaffirming in his mind the necessity of opposing the new regime and its vicious racism. After his failed suicide attempt, the Germans, figuring that he had learned his lesson, released him, but they refused him permission to return to Chartres. With the help of an American consul in Marseilles, he boarded a train for Barcelona under an assumed name. Then, finding Francisco Franco's Spain too dangerous, he carefully made his way to the British embassy in Lisbon.

It took Moulin almost six weeks to convince British diplomats to put him on a plane to London, probably because the information he wanted to bring to de Gaulle seemed too fantastic to be believed. When at last they met, Moulin told de Gaulle that he had spoken to the leaders of three different Resistance groups in France and they had given him authorization to speak on their behalf. They were willing, Moulin said, to swear their allegiance to de Gaulle and join his movement. The Free France movement in London and the French Resistance in France itself now had their first true linkage. Despite his discomfort with Moulin's socialist politics, de Gaulle immediately saw the value in Moulin's offer of alliance. He gave him the title of delegate-general to the occupied territories, making him a kind of ambassador to the various Resistance groups within France. Knowing that Moulin's politics and his heroism gave him a legitimacy in the eyes of French socialists and communists that he himself did not have, de Gaulle assigned Moulin to fuse together the various elements of the French Resistance and, more importantly, to find a way to tie them to the movement de Gaulle was building in London.[1]

De Gaulle badly needed Moulin because his own support inside France was thin. Before the war, de Gaulle had been a tank commander and undersecretary of defense who had made a name in French military circles by criticizing the Maginot Line and advocating

the development of a modern mechanized army. Well known, but far
from universally admired, inside the French Army for his prewar cri-
tiques, he was almost completely unknown to those outside the army.
Having led well in the early battles of the war, he had left France in a
British airplane on June 17, 1940, rather than accept the armistice
that Pétain had signed with Germany. The following day, de Gaulle
tried to rally his countrymen with an appeal broadcast over BBC
Radio. He said, in part:

> Believe me, I who am speaking to you with full knowledge of the
> facts, and who tells you that nothing is lost for France. The same
> means that overcame us can bring us victory one day. For France
> is not alone! She is not alone! She is not alone! She has a vast Em-
> pire behind her. She can align with the British Empire that holds
> the sea and continues the fight. She can, like England, use without
> limit the immense industry of the United States.
>
> This war is not limited to the unfortunate territory of our
> country. This war is not over as a result of the Battle of France.
> This war is a worldwide war. All the mistakes, all the delays, all
> the suffering, do not alter the fact that there are, in the world, all
> the means necessary to crush our enemies one day. Vanquished
> today by mechanical force, in the future we will be able to over-
> come by a superior mechanical force. The fate of the world
> depends on it.

The appeal of 18 June, touted as the start of the Resistance movement that eventually led to the liberation of France under de Gaulle's
leadership, became an important part of the Gaullist legend. According to this legend, de Gaulle, France's man of destiny, had divined the
general outlines of the next four years of war and had developed a
strategy for leading his countrymen to victory. After the war, the
French government printed copies on metal placards and affixed them
to public buildings across the country to remind Frenchmen of this
historic moment. De Gaulle's words also appear on a tablet under the

Arc de Triomphe as a testimony to his foresight during his country's darkest hour.

The acclaim came later. In 1940 de Gaulle was virtually alone in London with his small handful of supporters. His words did inspire some, such as Agnès Humbert, a courageous woman who helped to form Paris's first major Resistance cell before her arrest and deportation to a German labor camp. Although she did not know who de Gaulle was, she listened carefully to the "jerky and peremptory" broadcast that moved her to chase away the thoughts of suicide plaguing her mind. Even by the end of the broadcast she still did not know who the voice belonged to, but the words had deeply moved her. "I feel I have come back to life," she wrote. "A feeling I thought had died forever stirs within me again: hope. There is one man after all—one alone, perhaps—who understands what I feel in my heart: 'It's not over yet.'" Days later she marveled at having been so inspired by a man whose photograph she had never seen and who was being dismissed by most Parisians as some kind of crackpot.[2]

The British put so little faith in de Gaulle that they did not even bother to record the appeal, which happened to fall on the 125th anniversary of the Battle of Waterloo, an unfortunate omen for Franco-British cooperation. Rather than rally to de Gaulle, most of France came to terms with the new collaborationist regime under Pétain. Thousands of French soldiers who had been evacuated as part of the Dunkirk operation, who might have formed the core of a Free French Army based in Britain, instead went back to France under an amnesty provided for in the armistice. Known as "de Gaulle le Seul" (de Gaulle the Lonely), the self-styled leader of Free France was then little more than another defeated soldier in a humbled army. He was in fact the most junior general in the French Army, having been promoted just before the armistice. Sentenced to death in absentia by a Vichy court for treason, de Gaulle also saw his property seized by the Vichy state. He was literally a man without a country.

The only resources de Gaulle had in 1940 were a dedication to a vision of a France cleansed of its occupiers and a relationship, however tenuous, with the British government. He certainly did not hold much influence with his hosts. Although he was a determined enemy of Germany and Vichy, and the British could have used him for propaganda purposes, de Gaulle had no real power and little influence outside his small circle of followers. He struggled in vain to get the British, and later the Americans, to recognize and empower him as a leader of Free France, which was then still much more a vague idea than a political entity. The Americans infuriated him by refusing to allow Free France to open an embassy in Washington, choosing instead to exchange ambassadors with Vichy. Not seeing him as a leader in exile or a military commander in anything but a nominal sense, both the British and the Americans largely kept him in the dark on matters pertaining to France. Nor did they seek his advice.

Both Roosevelt and Churchill mistrusted de Gaulle's ambitions and disliked his arrogance. Acting as if he were the legitimate head of the government of France in exile, de Gaulle had a way of infuriating the same people on whose support he so deeply depended. In return, the Allies infuriated de Gaulle by, for example, landing troops in Madagascar (then part of the French empire) without informing him and, worse still, retaining the pro-Vichy governor there rather than replacing him with a representative of Free France. Later, they invited de Gaulle to attend the Casablanca conference, which, held in the nominal French protectorate of Morocco, de Gaulle felt he should have hosted. He almost refused to attend because of the slight he felt to his, and to France's, honor. The relationship between de Gaulle and the Allies improved over time and became functional, but it was never warm. At one point, de Gaulle threatened to move his headquarters to Moscow; at another, Churchill threatened to send the obstinate Frenchman to Algiers—"in chains if necessary"—to get him out of London.[3]

Moreover, de Gaulle was not the only French leader trying to gain recognition as the face of opposition to the Germans. General Henri Giraud, who had led a French Army Group before being captured by the Germans in 1940, also sought the mantle of leadership for Free

France. In April 1942, a group of right-wing but anti-German (and also anti–de Gaulle) army officers from a prewar paramilitary group known as the "Cagoule" sent French commandos into Germany to free the sixty-three-year-old Giraud from the prison at Koenigstein. Giraud scaled down a 350-foot cliff to escape the hilltop fortress and dodged German assassins all the way to Algiers. He briefly became a folk hero for this daring exploit and the obvious embarrassment it caused the Germans. Hoping to lead the new state's army, he came to Vichy, but his presence there proved to be too politically charged for Laval and Pétain. They could neither allow him to remain in Vichy nor turn him back to the Germans. Giraud refused to go to London despite British attempts to lure him there, largely out of his disgust for de Gaulle, whom he saw as a disobedient subordinate. Eventually he decided to go back to Algeria.

Despite Giraud's right-wing politics and his close personal and political connections to Pétain, the Americans initially saw him as a viable alternative to the difficult and ambitious de Gaulle. The need for a reliable partner increased after the Allies landed in North Africa, because the Americans hoped to turn civil administration over to French officials as quickly as possible. President Roosevelt and General Eisenhower, who came to think of Giraud as a friend, both much preferred to work with Giraud instead of de Gaulle. They got their chance when a monarchist French student assassinated Admiral Jean Darlan, the head of Vichy's armed forces, during a visit to Algiers to see his ailing son. The Americans had been working with Darlan, much to de Gaulle's ire, but they disliked him even more than they disliked de Gaulle. Needing a Frenchman with whom they could work, the Americans named Giraud as Darlan's replacement and gave him authority over the civil and military affairs of the French colonies in North Africa.

Giraud proved to be a disappointment. His ultraconservative politics and disdain toward democracy offended both the Allies and the French people whom he would need to inspire. He also refused to repeal the anti-Semitic laws Vichy had put in place in North Africa and demanded the right to command all Allied forces, including British and American forces, deployed anywhere in the French empire. His views on the conduct of modern war, moreover, resembled "a sort of strategic delirium," according to one of his own intelligence liaisons to Allied headquarters. Whatever courage he had displayed as a soldier, he was obviously unsuited to the world of politics and civil government. His feuds with de Gaulle only intensified as the two men postured for control over the nascent Free France movement.[4]

Still, the Americans needed French allies, and they wanted above all to avoid a wasteful power struggle that could tear apart the small but growing Free French movement. In early 1943, under American pressure, de Gaulle and Giraud reached a compromise. Giraud agreed to serve as a copresident alongside de Gaulle, even though the animosity between the two men had intensified. The Americans insisted on the arrangement, which they cemented with an awkward handshake in front of cameras at the Casablanca conference in January. The plan to share power never stood a chance of success, and de Gaulle soon proved to be the more skilled operator of the two, slowly edging his rival out of the political picture. Giraud eventually tired of the infighting and the politics and went back to a field command instead. He led the liberation of Corsica in September, then disappeared from the picture altogether. Thereafter, de Gaulle became the unquestioned leader of Free France. The Americans and the British would need to work with him whether they liked it or not.

Neither de Gaulle, based in London, nor Giraud, based largely in North Africa, had much impact in Paris. Neither had any power to change conditions on the ground in the capital, and neither could provide material support to those who wanted to lead a Resistance movement. Nor was it obvious, as late as 1943, that de Gaulle even wanted to help establish a major Resistance movement inside France. In part, de Gaulle feared such a movement would develop into a rival that could challenge his own claims to speak for and lead France. As a professional officer, de Gaulle also tended to discount the military value of civilians in arms, especially lightly armed civilians trying to fight the most powerful army in the world. He much preferred to liberate France with a regular military force armed with planes and tanks and led by skilled professionals like himself.

De Gaulle also recognized that the various Resistance groups did not form a single, unified movement. Coming from diverse political backgrounds and necessarily operating under the strictest security, they had few links between them. They also lacked common goals, other than the obvious one of getting the Germans out of France and the collaborators out of power. Some were communist based; others, like those who supported Giraud, favored the restoration of the French monarchy or the imposition of an authoritarian form of government. In mid-May 1943, there were no fewer than sixteen Resistance groups operating in Paris, and de Gaulle only had tenuous links to a few of them.

Nor was it clear that the resistance movements spoke for the majority of the city's population. In mid-1943, less than 10 percent of France could even loosely be classified as pro-Resistance, and an even smaller number was active in any of the various Resistance groups. It is, of course, extremely difficult to assess with any accuracy what was in the hearts and minds of Parisians, but it is clear, understandably enough, that absent any realistic hope of help from the outside world, few Parisians were willing to challenge the German Army and its well-armed allies in the Vichy French administration.[5]

Thus Moulin's appearance at de Gaulle's London headquarters promised to solve a number of problems. Moulin could bring the various arms of the French Resistance together under de Gaulle's nominal authority and, in doing so, could help to build a power base for de Gaulle inside France. Given new code names, Moulin soon became the most important asset de Gaulle had in France itself. In exchange for their cooperation, Moulin could promise the French Resistance money, arms, and links to the British.

Moulin parachuted into France twice to organize and build a cohesive French Resistance. He spent months living a clandestine life and meeting with Resistance leaders across the country. In January 1943, he presided over the fusing of three provincial Resistance groups that together pledged their loyalty to de Gaulle. In March, de Gaulle sent him to Paris despite the danger and the enormous challenges he faced in fusing a movement together in the much more difficult political environment of the capital. Moulin knew that if he was betrayed or captured, he would face torture and a painful death.

In March, Moulin and two of the most important Parisian Resistance leaders met in the Bois de Boulogne, the sprawling park on the western edge of the city, for a tense and confrontational discussion. Moulin insisted that the Resistance could only function effectively if it operated under central command and control, an idea that rankled the two résistants. Constantly walking through the park in order not to be too closely observed, the independent-minded leaders of the mostly left-leaning Resistance movements refused to submit to the authority of de Gaulle or anyone else based outside the city.

Moulin stayed in Paris to break the logjam despite the increasing risks he knew he was running; the longer he remained in the city, the greater the likelihood that his activities would be noticed by the Germans. But, using his own powers of persuasion and promises of money and weapons from London, he managed to bring the various parties together. At a tense and often acrimonious meeting in a small apartment in the St. Sulpice neighborhood of Paris, Moulin finally achieved his aim through the formation of the Conseil National de la Résistance (CNR), to which all of the major groups pledged their allegiance. The CNR stated as its three main purposes the reestablishment of a republican form of government guaranteeing the rights of the people of France; full support of the Allies in their war against Germany; and the complete repudiation of Vichy. The CNR also agreed to recognize de Gaulle as the head of the Free French government-in-exile and Giraud as commander in chief of its army. In return, the leaders of the CNR insisted that de Gaulle accept the return of a republican form of government after the war and that he provide them with weapons and other supplies.

Moulin had achieved the impossible, creating a political structure that mutually suspicious groups would accept and that would allow them to work together toward their common goals. He had even persuaded the communists, who held much of the real power in Paris, to accept de Gaulle as their nominal political leader in exchange for a promise of their participation in a postwar government. These decisions had enormous implications for the development of the Resistance movement and for events in Paris in the months that followed. Working in extraordinarily dangerous conditions, Moulin had made a critical contribution to the liberation of Paris. Tragically, though, Moulin never saw the fruits of his labors. A victim of the jealousy of his own comrades and an intensive Gestapo manhunt, he was living on borrowed time. Less than a month after the meeting in Paris, the Germans caught him near Lyon and tortured him in a railroad car bound for Germany until he succumbed to their brutality. He maintained his silence until his violent end, taking all his many secrets about the members of the French Resistance with him to his grave.[6]

The French Resistance thus had a hero and a martyr in Moulin. But without his leadership and skillful diplomacy, the various elements of the Resistance had a difficult time staying together. In reality, they were only connected through mutual hatred of their common foes, the Germans and Vichy. The constant presence of German and Vichy surveillance also made working together difficult, especially given the widespread fears that rival Resistance organizations contained informers. Moulin's own death served as a warning: Most members of the Resistance believed, with good reason, that the Gestapo and the "Butcher of Lyon," the dreaded Klaus Barbie, had only been able to find Moulin because of critical intelligence provided by an informer inside their ranks.[7]

As 1944 began, the Resistance was becoming a more important force within France, but the Germans still held most of the cards. There had been no Allied invasion of France in 1943; nor had the Allies changed their minds on either the bombing of French industry or the policy of not dropping arms to the French Resistance, which they still did not fully trust despite the promises of the CNR. Both de Gaulle and Allied headquarters remained ambivalent about supporting any kind of uprising inside France until it could be coordinated with, and subordinated to, a major Allied military operation. Nevertheless, anger at the Germans and Vichy was clearly on the rise inside France. The numbers of men escaping to the forests to join the rural maquis continued to increase, providing the Resistance with a pool of potential manpower, although most of it was dispersed throughout the countryside.

To those inside Paris, Allied and Gaullist indifference to the Resistance only fueled a growing sense that those in London had forgotten about them and did not care about their suffering. Those on the Left, especially the communists, saw a more nefarious scheme at work. Many believed that de Gaulle and the Allies were intentionally exposing them to grave danger in order to weaken them numerically—and thus politically—in the postwar years. These fears reflected the left vs. right tensions inside France still left over from the 1930s. Most on the Left respected de Gaulle for accepting Frenchmen of all political viewpoints into his movement. They understood how important his links to the Americans and British were for the future of France. Nevertheless, they often remained suspicious of his motives, seeing him as a representative of the same rotten system that had collapsed in 1940. Some, like the writer Marguerite Duras, noted de Gaulle's conservative politics and saw little real difference between a France led by de Gaulle or one led by Pétain.[8]

The communists, who held most of the real power in the Paris Resistance movement, had the worst relationship with de Gaulle. One French underground newspaper, *Le Franc-Tireur*, summed up the relationship in terms similar to those used by Duras: "We have previously stated, and we repeat it here, that we are entirely with General de Gaulle in his struggle to liberate the country; but we will be against him once liberation has occurred if, against all his previous declarations, he considers setting up a dictatorship[,] which we would not be any better able to accept from a General than we have been from a Marshal [Pétain]."[9]

The communists thus revealed the great tension in their own thinking about the liberation. They knew that they needed to work with de Gaulle and, through him, with the Americans and the British. But at the same time they saw the risks of fighting and dying for France only to see de Gaulle impose a postliberation government that would shut them out of power. As future events were to reveal, they had reason to worry.

Members of all Resistance groups saw their activities against the Germans and Vichy as the first stage in a larger struggle to remake France in the postwar years. Even before the Allied landing in Normandy, the Russians had broken the back of the German Army in the east at the Battle of Kursk, and Benito Mussolini's fascist Italy had surrendered following an Allied invasion there. Both events augured a new future for Europe, one that Resistance members hoped to help shape. In Paris, the unquestioned political heart of France, Resistance leaders began to think more concretely about their own visions for France's future in the spring and summer of 1944. Almost all Resistance members agreed on the need to reform or dismantle the Third Republic that had governed France since the 1870s. French political parties blamed its inherent weaknesses for the tensions of the 1930s and the collapse of 1940. Furthermore, they were in general agreement that France needed a republican form of government in which all French citizens could participate equally.

The liberation of France, therefore, was about more than the present; it was also about the future. In contrast to the analogy of the FFI member who likened France's suffering to that of a woman in labor, Resistance leaders were in fact beginning to think about the kind of child they wanted to raise. They knew, however, that they would need to prove to their countrymen that they deserved a voice in that future. Resistance leaders therefore pledged that their activities would not end with the liberation. The end of the occupation would be only the first stage in a new political future for France—

one in which economic and social structures would be radically re-
formed. A new Fourth Republic would correct the mistakes of the
past, including, in their eyes, an inequitable prewar concentration of
wealth and power.[10]

Resistance leaders of all political stripes also insisted that France,
an occupied nation, not be treated like Italy, a conquered nation.
France, they contended, should have the right to determine its own
leaders through immediate and free elections, a right denied to Italy
after Mussolini's collapse. The prospect of fighting and dying to liberate France, only to be shut out afterward by an imposed government
led by de Gaulle or some other anointed choice of the Americans,
was for them a nightmarish scenario.[11]

For his own reasons, de Gaulle agreed that the Allies had no right
to treat France as a conquered nation. He threatened not to come to
France in mid-June 1944, following the Allied landings, after hearing
that the Americans had retained a mayor who had Vichy connections
in one of the liberated towns in Normandy and had begun to assemble 5.5 billion francs in U.S. military scrip for use in occupied France.
He argued that both the selection of local officials and the printing of
currency were prerogatives of Free French officials and therefore the
American actions were an infringement of French sovereignty. Moreover, he argued, with some justification, that the Americans could not
issue money for which they were unwilling to assume responsibility
after the war because of the risk to France's future financial stability.

This kind of behavior struck the Americans as ungrateful and ar-
rogant in the extreme, but de Gaulle held firmly to his own vision of
postwar France. At the cost of increased acrimony with Eisenhower's
headquarters, he succeeded in getting the Americans to recall most of
the scrip, which had the blue, white, and red colors of France, but
was in the shape of the U.S. dollar and prominently featured the
words "US Army." Still furious with de Gaulle, Churchill warned him
not to expect "the title deeds to France" as soon as the Normandy
landings were over. Roosevelt, who disliked de Gaulle even more
than Churchill did, told him that the United States was not bound to

recognize any government not chosen by the French people. De Gaulle would need to win enough support inside France to make clear that he did indeed have a mandate to represent the wishes of his countrymen. On June 3, 1944, the Americans agreed to treat de Gaulle as head of the provisional French government, but, for these reasons, they stopped short of making a formal announcement to that effect. They also refused to recognize this provisional government as the legitimate government of France.[12]

De Gaulle and the Americans may have disagreed about the extent of French sovereignty, but they agreed on the potential threat the French Left might pose to postwar stability. The Americans and British, in fact, presumed that the Resistance was full of communist elements anxious to start a civil war as soon as the Germans left France. De Gaulle and many of his followers blamed the French Communist Party's foolish support of the Nazi-Soviet Pact of 1939 for allowing the Germans to focus the full weight of their military might in the west. Now, they feared that the communists were plotting to turn France over to a regime led by the French Communist Party leader Maurice Thorez, who had spent the war years in Moscow after deserting from the French Army in 1939 and subsequently having his citizenship revoked.[13]

De Gaulle thus warned the Allies against supporting the Resistance for fear of helping them grow too powerful at the end of the war. In doing so he was walking a fine line between courting the support of the Resistance and ensuring that its communist elements did not grow powerful enough to challenge him. In other words, he wanted the Resistance to serve as an extension of his own power. On this point the Americans and de Gaulle were in full agreement. Although the Americans had their doubts about de Gaulle, they surely preferred him to the revolution that they feared was the goal of the members of the French Resistance, especially those of the working class inside Paris. Memories of the dreadful Paris Commune in 1871 still hung over the heads of decision makers in 1944, laying before all of them the specter of a French civil war once the Germans left. As the FFI had surmised, fear of communist power was indeed the main reason for the Allied policy of not air-dropping weapons into Paris.[14]

The Allies had agreed to recognize de Gaulle as head of a provisional French government in part to head off the possibility of such a revolution. Roosevelt also went out of his way to tell Eisenhower that he was not bound by the agreement to recognize de Gaulle's authority inside France if doing so conflicted with military operations. De Gaulle had worn out his welcome in both Eisenhower's headquarters and at No. 10 Downing Street because of his repeated insistence on Allied recognition of his authority, but he was at long last the recognized head of a provisional French state, even if he did not yet control any of its territory. De Gaulle, never shy about reaching for whatever he could, saw the creation of the provisional government as recognition not only of his coequal status with President Roosevelt and Prime Minister Churchill, but also as recognition of his authority over the French Resistance. The move certainly helped to solidify de Gaulle's nominal standing as the leader of a future French government, although it remained to be seen if the French themselves would respect him as such.

The Allies also looked the other way as de Gaulle began to set up the structure of a permanent government. He carefully and quietly selected men whose politics he shared and whose loyalty he valued to join a nascent state that could take power in Paris as soon as the Germans left, but before the Allies could establish a government of occupation. Most of those officials were based in Algiers, not London, giving them room to operate away from the peering eyes of Allied political and military leadership. Whether the communists would accept the new government or fight to prevent its implementation no one knew, nor did de Gaulle know if the Americans would endorse his plan. He did, however, know that he needed to be in a position to control France, even against the wishes of some of his Allies and some of his countrymen, even at the risk of civil war.[15]

De Gaulle did have some tangible assets, including approximately 100,000 men in the Free French Army. Armed, trained, and clothed by the Americans, most of the men were the descendants of Europeans who had migrated to North Africa or African subjects of the French Empire; very few of them had come directly from France itself. These men formed the heart of the French Expeditionary Corps under General Alphonse Juin that had helped to open the Allied route into Rome just days before the landings in Normandy. Another French unit, the Deuxième Division Blindée (Second Armored Division) under General Philippe Leclerc, had been fighting its way across Africa in the name of Free France since 1940; in June and July 1944, it was in England training for operations on the continent. These highly esteemed units had made important contributions on the battlefield and helped to give de Gaulle and Free France respect within Allied military circles. Exactly who commanded them remained an issue of some ambiguity. They were formally a part of the Allied command structure that reached back to Eisenhower, and they were fully dependent on the Americans for their arms and equipment, but de Gaulle was, after the creation of the provisional government, their head of state.

While the military value of these French units was considerable, their symbolic importance was even greater, as Allied commanders were well aware. As early as May 1943, Eisenhower and his staff had concluded that it would be of paramount importance to the postwar political picture to have regular French forces commanded by a French officer liberate Paris. Eisenhower had no interest in governing France after the Liberation, but he had even less interest in seeing civil disorder break out along his lines of supply as he pursued the German Army to the Rhine. He therefore saw the value of a restoration of order, although he did not necessarily believe that only de Gaulle could provide that order, as his retention of several Vichy officials in Normandy suggests.[16]

To those in Paris, however, the formation of the provisional government changed nothing but the heading on de Gaulle's London stationery. Mutual suspicions between de Gaulle's supporters and the communist heart of the Resistance in Paris remained deep, almost tearing the Resistance apart before it could have any impact on the liberation of France. De Gaulle and his supporters had no intention of liberating France only to see a communist uprising assume power thereafter. For its part, the Left had no intention of fighting to rid France of Vichy only to see another unrepresentative and authoritarian government, led by a soldier, replace it. As Albert Camus put it in the pages of the clandestine left-wing newspaper *Combat*, the liberation of France would mean nothing if it did not also liberate the nation from the moneyed interests that had so badly failed "in all its duties" in the prewar years. "We want without delay," Camus wrote, "to institute a true peoples' and workers' democracy. . . . We believe that any politics that cuts itself off from the working class is futile. The France of tomorrow will be what its working class becomes."[17]

The potential for class violence after the liberation frightened all but the most bloodthirsty résistants. Resistance groups, anxious to avenge the crimes of Vichy, kept "a bewildering catalogue [listing] prominent collaborators" and promised to punish them once the opportunity presented itself. "There [soon] comes a *règlement des comptes*," one French Resistance member told a downed American pilot hiding in Paris, "a settling of accounts. You will see." The enemies against whom he planned revenge were French, not German. A tired, hungry, and desperate city with a long history of political violence might see another chapter in that history unfold if the liberation turned into a civil war between Frenchmen.[18]

To head off such a crisis, the Americans developed plans to impose an American Military Government (AMGOT) on France as it had done on parts of Italy. Eisenhower saw AMGOT as a last resort only, preferring instead to transfer authority to a government selected by the French people themselves. The difficulty lay in finding a way for the fractured and divided French polity to agree on a form of government and a leadership to run it. The AMGOT proposal, even as an emergency measure, predictably infuriated de Gaulle, who saw the plan as an American attempt to assert sovereignty over liberated France. Jacques Soustelle, de Gaulle's chief of intelligence, recalled that he and de Gaulle had decided to reject AMGOT "no matter what the cost." Soustelle believed that Roosevelt and his cabinet neither understood nor respected France. He also feared that the Americans were planning a special occupation force to grab and hold the reins of power with help from Vichy officials anxious to cut a deal, as they had in North Africa two years earlier.[19]

When rumors of an AMGOT reached Paris, the leaders of the FFI were as angry as de Gaulle. They assumed, ironically, that AMGOT would serve as a cover for the imposition of an authoritarian regime under de Gaulle. They feared that de Gaulle and the Americans were plotting together to deny them a political voice after the war. Most could accept de Gaulle as a temporary head of a provisional government, pending elections, but none of them wanted de Gaulle imposed from the outside and supported by the presence of American occupation troops. They therefore pledged to increase their efforts to present a liberated Paris to de Gaulle and the Americans as a fait accompli, thus demonstrating to the world the political and military power of a people in arms. Only by fighting, they believed, could they assume a role in determining the political future of France.[20]

If there was to be an uprising in Paris, it would undoubtedly be led by one of the most powerful and indomitable Resistance leaders in the city, Henri Tanguy, better known by his nom de guerre, Colonel Rol. Then thirty-six years old, Rol's police file described him as "a dangerous militant communist [and] one of the chiefs of the central terrorist organization." Rol was a metalworker and labor organizer who saw himself more as an antifascist than as a communist, although he did not shrink from the latter label either. He was a hardnosed veteran of the antifascist International Brigades, which had fought against Franco's armies in Spain. Wounded in that war, he came back to France in 1938 as an organizer for France's largest trade union syndicate, the Confédération Générale du Travail (General Trade Union). Fired from both the Citroën and Renault companies for his labor agitation, Rol never abandoned his beliefs in leftist politics or in the potential of working-class France to serve as a model for Europe. Mobilized in 1939 to serve as an antitank gunner (training that later served him and his fighters well during the liberation), he refused to accept France's defeat without a fight.[21]

Rol's connections in the trade unions and his experiences in Spain made him a natural leader for the emerging Resistance inside Paris. He did not speak much, but when he did it was with an intensity and determination that inspired fanatical devotion from his followers. As early as October 1940 he had begun to organize Resistance cells inside French labor unions. In 1942, he was a founding member of the Francs-Tireurs et Partisans, who derived their name from the guerrilla fighters who had opposed the Prussians in 1870 and 1871. Under Rol's guidance, they grew to become one of the most powerful left-leaning Resistance groups based in Paris, dedicating themselves to stopping the deportations and arrests of political prisoners as well as helping men evade the German labor drafts. In September 1943, following the arrest of its commander, the FFI nominated Rol to assume command of its operations in Paris and its immediate suburbs. Rol now had leadership positions in the city's two most powerful Resistance groups. He quickly put his stamp on both, merging them under his authority and the collective designation of the FFI. The day before the landings in Normandy, Rol assumed command of all FFI forces in the Île de France, the larger region encompassing Paris, its suburbs, and the four surrounding departments.

Rol faced the challenge of recruiting men into the FFI while simultaneously protecting it from police and Gestapo informants who might try to infiltrate it. He preferred to rely on men with prewar training in the French Army, and he established a hierarchy and organization in the FFI that mirrored one found in a regular army unit. He thus created bureaus for operations, intelligence, and supply, each of which submitted regular reports of its activity as if it were a fully functioning military unit. Because of the need for secrecy, however, the FFI had to function in the shadows. Not even Rol knew the names of all of the leaders of the various cells in the Paris region. Although still nominally under Koenig and de Gaulle, Rol was not the

kind of man to take orders from men hundreds of miles away whom
he had never met and whose goals he mistrusted.

Rol claimed that the FFI in and around Paris had more than
42,000 members in April 1944. Of that number, 17,000 were in reserve, with orders not to report for duty until a full insurrection in
Paris had begun. Another 25,000 were trained but lacked arms. Undoubtedly the biggest shortcoming of the FFI was a lack of weapons.
Rol counted only 155 men in the Paris region as fully armed and
trained. Many men were fighting with obsolete weapons and precious little ammunition. Rol repeatedly begged London for arms
drops only to be refused time and again on the grounds that air drops
were too inaccurate, a logic that must have infuriated Parisian FFI
leaders suffering under deadly Allied bombing runs that regularly
missed their targets.[22]

Not one to be easily deterred, Rol responded to the Allied landings in Normandy by ordering the FFI to seize arms from the Germans if the Allies would not air-drop them. In his vision, the FFI
would liberate Paris by itself without waiting for the Allies to approach with regular forces. A strong FFI presence in Paris would help
the group assert itself politically in the wake of the liberation. It
would also help the Allies advance to Paris by preventing the Germans from using the city to move forces forward to the combat
zones. An uprising might even force the Allies to increase their efforts to break out of Normandy in order to get to Paris more
quickly. In addition to giving his men instructions to capture German arms, Rol ordered FFI agents to seize money from black-market
dealers and known collaborators to fund the movement's operations. His actions made the FFI a respected (or feared, depending on
one's point of view) force in the city; the FFI's trademark symbol of
the Cross of Lorraine soon became synonymous inside Paris with
guerrilla activity. By Rol's own admission, however, the arms his
men had seized by mid-July "were hardly Ali Baba's cave." Paris's
seventh arrondissement, for example, had 700 active FFI members
but just 3 submachine guns, 20 rifles, and a handful of revolvers.[23]

Through agreements like the one Moulin had negotiated, the FFI owed its ultimate allegiance to General Marie-Pierre Koenig and, through him, de Gaulle, both based in London until they transferred their headquarters to France at the end of June. Rol saw the need to work with and through Koenig, but he suspected, rightly, that the conservative Koenig did not share the political goals of his fighters inside Paris. Rol thus reacted angrily to Koenig's June 10 order to stop guerrilla activity because of the slow progress of operations in Normandy. Once unleashed, Rol felt, an insurrection was not easy to stop. Many of his men had also come out from hiding and were now dangerously exposed. Nor were the Germans, who had already declared that the FFI was a group of outlaws, not soldiers (and therefore not protected by the laws of war), likely to ease their pressure. Koenig's order meant that members of the FFI would be targets but could not fight back.

Both Koenig and de Gaulle saw the FFI not as an insurrectionary force in itself, but as an adjunct of the Free French Army, to be used or not as needed. As a result, they saw the uprising of the FFI as a strictly military issue. Rol and his men, who had lived under the Germans and seen their horrors firsthand, saw the uprising as a moral and political issue. They also felt, even more strongly than de Gaulle, that only by rising up and liberating Paris themselves could Parisians earn the right to govern themselves once the Germans left. Thus did underground newspapers like the communist *L'Humanité* argue that the liberation of Paris need not depend on the arrival of Allied forces. Rol knew better, but he also suspected that de Gaulle and Koenig did not share his goals or those of most of the men in the FFI.[24]

In an attempt to impose some measure of control over the FFI, de Gaulle sent Jacques Delmas (code-named Chaban to protect his family from any repercussions that the Germans or Vichy authorities might mete out) into Paris as his military representative. Chaban, who had found his way to de Gaulle in London after leaving Paris in 1940, had quickly become one of de Gaulle's biggest admirers. Before dispatching him to Paris, de Gaulle promoted Chaban to brigadier general, making him, at just twenty-nine years old, the youngest general in the French Army. The promotion gave the handsome, charismatic former rugby player the gravitas de Gaulle thought he needed to face down Rol, a colonel. Chaban's mission was to sneak into the capital, bring order and discipline to the FFI, and ensure that its members understood the need to follow instructions from a regular command structure that ended with de Gaulle at its head.[25]

De Gaulle also wanted Chaban to delay any FFI insurrection until the Allies could support it with regular military operations near Paris. Chaban was to make it clear that Rol was not to begin an insurrection unless and until he got the order from de Gaulle. But Chaban soon found that the star de Gaulle had given him to outrank Rol mattered for precious little inside Paris. While the colonel understood and respected the need for a chain of command, he nevertheless argued that an insurrection should precede an Allied advance on Paris, both to show the power of the people of Paris to liberate themselves and to make it clear that the FFI was more than a military afterthought to the armies of General Eisenhower. Rol did, however, reluctantly agree to obey Koenig's order to stop overt guerrilla activity.

Chaban was de Gaulle's military representative in Paris; Alexandre Parodi, who had assumed the post once held by Jean Moulin, was de Gaulle's political representative in the occupied city. De Gaulle told Parodi that the "various forms of the Resistance are but means" subordinated to the state. This statement reflected de Gaulle's conviction that, while the Resistance was a branch of the Free French Army, the military itself ultimately answered to the provisional French government, with de Gaulle at its top. Parodi was to "always speak out loudly and clearly in the name of the state" in his dealings with local Resistance leaders. His advocacy for the Free French government had one paramount aim: Parodi, who feared that the FFI might begin a communist revolution during the confusion that would accompany a liberation of Paris, was to try to delay any insurrectionary activity until the Allied and Free French armies could both support it and contain it. Only thus could the FFI serve the needs of the provisional government.[26]

Parodi and de Gaulle were not the only ones who feared what the FFI might do in the wake of Paris's liberation. Although they were heroes to some of their fellow Frenchmen, to others the members of the French Resistance resembled outlaws and troublemakers who lacked the requisite skills to govern in the wake of the liberation. Even many of their admirers saw the members of the FFI as men of the streets unfit for roles in a postwar civil government. What they might do if they actually acquired power was an open question, even to their own leaders. Memories of past revolutions and class warfare in the city hung over Paris in June and July 1944, clouding the prospects for a bloodless outcome of any uprising. Few doubted that a power struggle would follow the liberation of the city. Whether or not it turned violent was still an unknown.[27]

Rol was a military man, and he knew that he had little choice but to operate within the general structure of the provisional government in order to keep everyone's attention focused on the common enemies at hand. After the tense first few days after the Allied landings in Normandy, therefore, the FFI went reluctantly back underground in accordance with Koenig's order and the urgings of Chaban and Parodi. The orders from Rol's headquarters stopped calling for insurrection and called instead for renewed vigilance and intelligence gathering. Rol reluctantly acknowledged that until the military situation in Normandy changed in favor of the Allies, he had no choice but to take Chaban's advice and halt active operations. Rol nevertheless urged Chaban to endorse the resumption of the insurrection at the earliest possible moment, regardless of the orders coming from London. He also begged Chaban to use his influence in London to arrange for arms drops, without which the FFI could not hope to make a difference inside Paris. Chaban could do little other than tell Rol that his orders came from de Gaulle and de Gaulle alone.

Even as they were debating future strategy, however, the leaders of the Resistance had to come to terms with the reality that their liberation might still be a long time away. The military situation in France remained in Germany's favor for weeks after the landings. Germans inside Paris regained their confidence in late June as the FFI stopped active resistance, the Allies remained stuck near the beaches, and the Germans unleashed their new V-1 rockets against targets inside Great Britain. Press releases in Paris in mid-June noted that London was on fire from the new weapons that, the Germans claimed, would turn the tide of the war. In June 1944 alone, the Germans launched 2,452 V-1s at Britain, approximately 800 of which hit Greater London. Ernst Jünger, the famous writer assigned to the German cultural ministry in Paris, wrote in his diary that few Parisians seemed bothered by a German propaganda report that the V-1s had destroyed much of London, an indication of the bitterness toward Britain that remained. The Germans boasted that the weapons would bring Britain to its knees and end the war in the west on German terms. The Germans promised even greater levels of destruction when the more sophisticated V-2 and V-3 weapons were ready for operations, assuming that the British and the Americans had not yet surrendered.[28]

Adding to the frustrations of the Resistance, as late as mid-July the fate of the Allied landings in Normandy remained very much in doubt. Consequently, the Germans in Paris in late June and early July displayed what one German field commander called an "incredibly indifferent serenity" to the events in Normandy. Paris once again became a place where German officers wore their formal dress uniforms for elegant dinners followed by nights at the opera or the theater. Jünger noted that German officers in Paris put their faith in the new weapons, the supposed disunity of the Allies, and the belief that Germany's "favorable destiny, which had always gotten it out of dead-end situations in the past, would somehow reappear." Even at this late date, the Germans were reluctant to ruin the relatively comfortable position they had in the city. Paris may have had the atmosphere of a city under occupation, but it did not have the atmosphere of a city on the front lines.[29]

One incident in the city in late June led to heightened tensions, if only temporarily. On June 28, fifteen FFI agents disguised as members of the Milice assassinated Vichy propagandist Philippe Henriot in his home. A former right-wing deputy from Bordeaux and an early and enthusiastic supporter of Vichy, Henriot's voice on Radio Paris spewed out some of the regime's most vituperatively anti-Semitic and anti-leftist propaganda. To many Frenchmen, Henriot was the French equivalent of Joseph Goebbels, Hitler's propaganda minister. They blamed him for having done more than anyone else to turn Frenchmen against one another. His assassination, planned by a professional hit man, had long been a goal of the Resistance and showed that even if it was underground, the French Resistance could strike against the most inveterate enemies of France.[30]

The assassination led to a momentary increase of tensions inside Paris. The Germans responded to Henriot's death by turning Georges Mandel, a Jewish and anti-Vichy politician whom they had imprisoned at Buchenwald, over to the Milice. While supposedly taking him from one prison to another, the *miliciens* drove him into the forest of Fontainebleau, where they shot and killed him. The Milice also carried out a series of politically motivated killings in the south, sparking a new round of political violence outside Paris. Inside Paris, however, the tensions following the two assassinations soon faded, leaving the city reasonably calm once again.

The military situation in Normandy slowed so much that many Parisians, especially on the Left, began to follow the results of the massive Russian offensive in Belarus. Indeed, some followed it more closely than they followed events within France itself. On June 22 (the third anniversary of the German invasion of the USSR), the Russians launched the massive Operation Bagration. Dwarfing the D-Day landings, the Soviet operation involved 2.6 million Soviet soldiers supported by 26,000 artillery pieces and more than 5,000 tanks. Bagration crushed an entire German army group, leading to the capture of German soldiers by the tens of thousands and the recovery of lost ground by hundreds of miles a week. Such success stood in stark contrast to the slow and grinding progress of the Allies in Normandy. Communist and other left-leaning underground newspapers sang the praises of the Soviets. One of the largest clandestine newspapers, *La Défense de la France*, spoke of the Red Army, not the Allies, as the force that would crush German power. It also spoke of the historic Franco-Russian alliance of the pre–World War I years and proposed that a renewal of that partnership would form the basis of a new European order of stability and peace.[31]

The slow approach of the Allies made many Resistance leaders fear that the Germans would break them before the Americans and British could get close enough to give an uprising a reasonable chance of success. Others continued to worry about the risk of widespread famine if the Allies did not get to the city by the end of August. Some Parisians on the Left half-jokingly observed that if current operations proceeded at the pace of late June and early July, the Russians might even get to Paris before the Americans. Most Parisians failed to see the humor, although another joke at German expense spread through the city in the wake of Bagration. In this joke, four men are sitting at a dinner in Paris when one, obviously a German, asks another where he is from. The man replies that he is Polish, to which the German says, "Nonsense! Poland is now part of the German Empire, you are German." He asks the third man where he is from. The man replies that he is Danish, to which the German says, "Nonsense! You are also now German." He then turns to the last man, who says, "Well, I was raised in Paris, but since we are all Germans here, isn't it a hell of a beating those Russians are giving us!" All jokes aside, given the threat that communism posed to the return of democracy in Europe, neither de Gaulle nor the Americans welcomed the idea of the French people looking to the Soviet Union as a viable postwar partner.[32]

Parisians in June and late July remained for the most part spectators to the great global dramas unfolding around them. Most remained obsessed by the daily need to find food for themselves and their families. A few found ways to show their patriotism, such as the old men who played patriotic French songs, or even a John Philip Sousa march remembered from World War I, in the corridors of Parisian Métro stations. "No French person," Alice Moats noted, "passed without giving [them] some money." Others wore the French national colors of blue, white, and red in some combination, but these were all silent, passive, and largely futile acts of resistance from a powerless citizenry. None of them posed even a remote threat to German control of the city.[33]

The communist Resistance leaders of the CPL found the inaction of Paris unacceptable. Praising the effort of the Soviets, they put up posters across the city urging Parisians to begin a major uprising on July 14, Bastille Day, the national holiday commemorating the French Revolution, which had been banned by Vichy. The French had not celebrated the holiday since 1939. Chaban and Parodi opposed the idea, saying that the insurrection was premature and would only result in needless bloodshed. Rol, too, was against it. Through his contacts in his intelligence network, Rol knew that the Allies were still hopelessly stuck in Normandy. He therefore also knew that an insurrection on July 14 was unlikely to succeed. Consequently, he did not lift the order to remain underground.

Rol may not have backed the plan for a July 14 uprising, but he had not given up the idea of a preemptive strike against the occupiers. He had told his men that in his mind a free Paris was worth 200,000 dead. If the Allies were not willing to make the sacrifice, perhaps the people of Paris would be.

3

BERLIN, WASHINGTON, LONDON, AND PARIS

"EVERYBODY, IT SEEMED, WANTED TO LIBERATE PARIS," AMERICAN general Omar N. Bradley recalled after the war. "Everybody, that is, except me." Bradley was the commander of the American First Army that landed on Omaha and Utah beaches on D-Day, a role that gave him tremendous influence over Allied operations in Europe thereafter. Because of his reputation for honesty and integrity, he had the trust not only of his former West Point classmate Dwight Eisenhower but of almost everyone in his command. More than anyone else except maybe Eisenhower, he represented American power and authority in France. And in his eyes Paris counted for almost nothing.[1]

Bradley, fifty-one at the time of the liberation, was not quite as alone in dismissing the strategic value of Paris as he later made it seem. The city did not figure highly on the list of priorities for almost anyone inside Eisenhower's Allied headquarters in June and July 1944. While war correspondents wrote wistfully about the antici- pated liberation of a city they had known and loved before the war, and while war-weary GIs dreamed of the luxuries that Paris might of- fer, serious strategists in the American command structure barely gave the city a second thought. Paris mattered even less to the British and the Canadians. To British general Sir Bernard Montgomery, commander of Allied ground forces in France, the city might as well have been on the other end of the earth as he cast his eyes toward the German V-1 launch sites on the English Channel that were threatening London and the large port at Antwerp, which was capable of supplying Allied armies deep into Germany.

Nor did Paris figure highly in German strategic thinking. The difficulties of defending the city against a determined attack led most German strategists to assume that any battle for northern France would need to be fought and won in Normandy, not in the Seine valley. German forces were not equipped or designed for urban fighting, which required a specialized kind of fighting at close quarters. Any battle for Paris, moreover, would take place among a hostile population and with tenuous supply lines that ran through areas vulnerable to attack by the French Resistance.

Ironically, the City of Light, whose liberation became such a symbol of freedom to the entire world, was an afterthought in the minds of most senior decision makers in the American, British, and German high commands. Nevertheless, leaders in all of the armies fighting in France would have to rethink the importance of Paris, in large part because of the actions of the Parisians themselves. As the British, Americans, and Germans came to learn, Paris was too important to be ignored.

For the strategists behind Operation Overlord, the code name for the Battle of Normandy, Paris was simply too far from Normandy to merit much attention. Eisenhower, Montgomery, Bradley, and the planners of the Normandy landings devoted most of their efforts to dealing with the immediate problems of how to land and sustain their infantry divisions on the French coastline. The major obstacles they identified were the neutralization of German air power over the beaches, the need to support the initial waves of Allied soldiers with heavy weapons, and the overwhelming problem of supplying hundreds of thousands of troops in the days that followed. The enormous stakes that were riding on Overlord understandably led them to focus most of their energies on the problems of the first few days of the landings. Paris, more than 150 miles of bombed-out roads away, did not figure into their thinking much at all. To the extent that it did, Paris was largely a problem for the Allied bomber commanders who hoped to neutralize its role as a German transportation hub.

Nor did the Allies have a clear sense of when they might be in a position to take the city. The original Overlord plans did not call for the Allies to be in Paris until mid-October, by which time they expected to have cleared the Île de France region around the city of all serious German opposition. Even that timetable struck many Allied strategists as overly optimistic. Winston Churchill, with his sharp political and historical eye, clearly understood the political and symbolic significance of the city. He nevertheless told Eisenhower before the landings that no one could reasonably ask any more of him if the Allies managed to liberate Paris before Christmas. Even Charles de Gaulle put thoughts of Paris to one side while he focused on establishing political control of Normandy once the Allied armies moved through.[2]

After the landings, when the Allies found themselves stuck near the beaches, the problem of Paris receded ever farther from the planners' minds. To Eisenhower and the staff officers of his headquarters, Paris must have seemed a million miles away from Normandy. The immediate goal for the Allies remained the capture of ports like Cherbourg and Le Havre in order to supply Allied soldiers in France with the enormous quantities of arms, fuel, and other supplies that they needed. The fighting in the rough hedgerow country known as the *bocage* also occupied planners as they struggled to devise new ways to fight in unfamiliar terrain. The bocage featured sunken roads, thick earthen embankments, and dense hedges that surrounded the farms of Normandy. The hedges turned each bucolic corner of the French countryside into a small fortress with excellent defensive cover. The nature of the fighting in the area caught Allied commanders badly by surprise. American and British officers, new to combat in northern France, had little experience fighting in anything like it. Remarkably, none of the one hundred junior officers involved in the Overlord operation and interviewed by a board of inquiry afterward had received any training at all for dealing with these challenges.[3]

Although the Allies were primarily concerned with the stalled offensive in Normandy, they had other strategic issues to consider as well. They were still fighting a frustrating and inconclusive war in Italy that devoured resources at an alarming rate. Eisenhower had to think not just about France, but about how to divide Allied resources across all of Europe. Allied headquarters were also in the process of planning an invasion of southern France (code-named Operation Anvil or Operation Dragoon), in part to gain control of the large Mediterranean ports of Toulon and Marseilles. Although southern France was far from Normandy and Paris, an invasion there, some of the planners hoped, would create a second French front for the Germans and open up badly needed alternative supply routes for a drive into Germany before winter complicated military operations.

Moreover, the south of France, especially the areas controlled by the rural maquis, offered much greater opportunity for coordination with the French Resistance than operations toward Paris did. Thanks to the efforts of Allied special operations personnel who spent time in the relatively safe countryside, the Allies had much better contacts with the maquis than they did with résistants in Paris. Thus, to the extent that planners were thinking about the French Resistance, they were thinking about building working relationships with groups in the south, such as those in Vercors that could contribute directly to the success of the landings in that area.

Given all of the demands on the time and energy of Allied planners, it is perhaps not surprising that they hardly thought about Paris at all. But while this lack of attention may be understandable, it later had dramatic consequences. The FFI lost confidence in the Allies and pledged to liberate the city themselves, if necessary without regard to the plans of Eisenhower, Bradley, Montgomery, or de Gaulle. American pilot Thomas Childers, hiding in the city until the

Resistance could smuggle him to safety in Spain, saw firsthand how discouraging the slow Allied progress was to the FFI. Every night FFI agents listened to the BBC hoping to hear news of Allied progress, and every night "they muttered and swore as the program came to an end" with little good news to report. The communists both honored the Soviet Union and took a slap at the western Allies at the end of July in a poster that read, "We gratefully and enthusiastically salute the glorious Red Army and its chief, Marshal Stalin. The people of Paris will never forget that the Red Army crushed the German Army thanks to the heroic resistance of the people of Moscow in the dark days of 1941." The Comité Parisien de Libération, calling itself the legal authority in the city, urged Parisians to be ready to fight and sacrifice as Moscow had. "The simple and sacred duty of all Parisians is to fight," read one of its posters. "Paris liberated by Parisians will welcome the Allies."[4]

Still, the Allies were in no hurry to be welcomed, especially not by the communists. Occupied by the landings and subsequent operations in Normandy, they preferred to postpone any discussion about the future of Paris and France until the military situation improved. Not without reason, moreover, they wanted to delay planning for military operations near Paris until they had a clearer picture of how the fighting in Normandy evolved. Even as that picture developed, however, Eisenhower and his staff stubbornly refused to think seriously about military operations in and around the city. When the need to do so suddenly arrived, Eisenhower, the consummate military planner, had to improvise a solution to the problem of liberating Paris.

Nor were the Americans and British ready to think seriously about the postwar political status of France, beyond the vague notion that the nation needed to be returned to the folds of democracy. De Gaulle wrote to a colleague in Algiers in mid-July that he was impressed by the American desire to win a total military victory over Germany, but that he also saw in the American political and military leaders "a great uncertainty in regards to finding a solution to postwar problems." This uncertainty led the Allies to begin planning for the possible implementation of a postwar American military government. That such a government would only have stayed in place until the political situation within France stabilized itself did not, of course, make it any more popular with its intended subjects. The furious opposition to it by virtually all French political groups made it unlikely that the plan could succeed, a reality to which the Americans themselves gradually awakened. Without an alternative, the Allies had no real plan for governing France, and thus gave no political guidance to the Resistance. This lack of attention gave the various political interests in France room to maneuver—not least among them de Gaulle, who planned for his provisional government to become the legitimate authority in France the instant the Germans left. For his plan to work, however, he needed to be able to demonstrate to both the Allies and the French themselves that he had the support of his countrymen. He also needed to control Paris, his country's capital and its clear center of power.[5]

De Gaulle's relationship with the Americans remained as tense and unsettled as ever in the wake of the Normandy landings. President Roosevelt invited de Gaulle to come to the United States in early July, but de Gaulle initially refused because Roosevelt did not invite him in his capacity as the head of the French state. Nor did Roosevelt agree to reopen the French embassy under de Gaulle's aegis. Only after the Americans agreed to recognize de Gaulle as the provisional head of civil authority in France did de Gaulle make the trip, spending July 6 to 10 in Washington and New York City. In his meetings with Roosevelt, Secretary of State Cordell Hull, and other high-ranking American officials, de Gaulle stressed that Paris "was the center point of strategy and the heart of politics in France." He also warned that "insurrection in the capital would surely tend towards setting up a power dominated by the Third International," the international revolutionary movement begun by the Soviet Union to propagate communism.[6]

For their part, the Germans were not worried about a threat to Paris from communists, Americans, or the Resistance. If anything, the German high command in the west devoted even less serious strategic thinking to Paris than the Allies did. Before the landings, strategic debates inside the German high command had centered on the best way to defeat an Allied invasion of the European continent, albeit one whose exact place and time were necessarily unknown. Some German officers argued that given the strength of Allied air power, the only way to defeat the Allies was by throwing the invasion back into the sea. Once the Allies were ashore, their air and sea supremacy would ensure that the Germans stood no chance of winning. The Allied landings at Anzio earlier in the year seemed to prove the point. There the Germans proved temporarily capable of containing the Allied troops coming ashore but had no long-term answer for the awesome firepower of Allied battleships and airplanes. Thus, although the Germans had been able at first to contain the Allies to a large beachhead, eventually they broke through. The Germans used this line of thinking to justify building the Atlantic Wall across northern France, a complex network of coastal bunkers, gun emplacements, and other obstacles. A massive effort to stop the Allied landings on the beaches, its construction relied upon the forced labor of thousands of Frenchmen.

Other German commanders argued that because the Germans did not know when or where the Allies would land, the best strategy was to create a powerful mobile reserve that could react to a variety of contingencies. German intelligence officials thought that the Allies were most likely to target the Pas de Calais region because it offered good ports and the most direct route into Germany, but they could not be certain that Calais was where Eisenhower would aim his *Schwerpunkt*, or decisive blow. The Allies did their best to confuse the Germans with an elaborate series of deceptions and ruses. Those operations may have helped to distract and mislead the Germans, but German commanders were still confident that they could defeat the Allies long before they threatened Paris. Given the poor performance of Allied amphibious operations in Italy, the Germans expected to have time to design counterattacks. The Germans therefore wanted their forces to be in a position to take advantage of the operational mistakes they expected the Allies to make. If the Americans and

British advanced off the beaches too quickly, the Germans wanted to have infantry and armor ready to strike with enough combat power to deal the Allies a decisive defeat.

The Germans never did fully reconcile the differences in these two visions of how to defeat an Allied landing in France. To the extent that Paris was involved at all in their thinking, the Germans saw it as a critical supply and transportation node. Simply put, the Germans could not move sufficient numbers of men and supplies anywhere in northern France without control of Paris. The Île de France region contained more than one hundred bridges over the Seine and its tributaries as well as most of the main highways and railways in the region. The Germans needed Paris to remain as calm as it had been throughout most of the war in order to guarantee smooth logistical and transportation routes through the region. Consequently, they did not want to change the security situation in the city if they did not need to do so.

The Allied landings in Normandy posed no immediate threat to German control of the Île de France. The commander of the Greater Paris Military District, Lieutenant General Wilhelm von Boineburg, had even excluded the capital region from the original alert order on June 6. He had seen no reason to risk a panic among either the city's residents or its German garrisons. The Paris district had approximately 30,000 German soldiers divided into three sectors: the northwest sector, with 10,000 men; the southeastern sector, with 8,000 men; and the St. Cloud sector, with 12,000 men, located just west of the city. The most powerful German unit in the area was the 325th Security Division, composed of four regiments and belonging to the St. Cloud sector. Boineburg dedicated one of those regiments to patrolling the *ceinture*, the beltway that rings Paris, and the Paris district lost another regiment to security duty in Normandy in June, leaving just half of the 325th dedicated to the security of Paris itself.

Because most of the German combat power was needed in Normandy, arms and equipment were also in short supply for the troops in the Île de France. The troops in the Paris district were armed

mostly with light weapons such as rifles and pistols. Heavy arma-
ment was almost completely lacking: Greater Paris had just 14 tanks,
mostly former French tanks and obsolete Panther 1s. The demands of
the Normandy effort put other strains on the city's defenders as well.
Troops rotated in and out of Paris frequently, making training and
unit cooperation almost impossible to develop. Perhaps most alarmingly, a disproportionate number of men in the Paris garrison were
non-Germans, including large numbers of Alsatians and Poles, whose
reliability and willingness to fight for the Nazis their German commanders had good reason to doubt.[7]

Given this disposition of forces, Boineburg knew that he could not
hold Paris against a determined attack from the outside. Nor was he
expected to do so. Rather, he understood his mission to be the "maintenance of peace, security, and order" in Paris so that the Germans
could continue to use the roads, bridges, rail lines, and canals that Allied aircraft had not destroyed.[8]

Given the massive problems he faced, Boineburg knew that he
lacked the resources to defend the city against a determined attack
should the Allies attempt one. The German defensive lines, as
Wehrmacht officer Kurt Hold knew, "could not possibly suffice for a
successful defense of Paris." Their units were too small and too
widely dispersed to offer mutual assistance and protection. Nor did
the Germans have any answer to the increasing power of Allied air
forces. For more than four years the Germans had had no reason to
think about the defense of Paris from an outside attack. In the circumstances of June 1944, there was precious little time and too few
resources to develop a new strategy. If the Allies got close to Paris,
Boineburg believed, they would have little trouble taking it.[9]

But if the Germans lacked the confidence to hold Paris from the
outside, they still expected to be able to maintain its internal security.
Kurt Hesse, a senior officer in the German First Army, was dismayed
by the resources available for the security of Paris. He thought that
the units assigned to defend German positions inside Paris were
weak, "significantly smaller than . . . an active division," and filled

with second- and third-rate soldiers who were "only conditionally suitable for fighting purposes." Hesse judged that the only serious internal threat came from the French Resistance, but he counted on their lack of weapons and severe internal divisions to keep them from becoming too big a threat. Like many German officers, he had greatly underestimated the military potential of the Resistance and had grown complacent in a city where active opposition to German authority had been a rare phenomenon.

The German authorities in Paris also knew that they could depend on the notorious brutality of the paramilitary forces in the city to maintain order. Even if the Paris police were proving to be less and less reliable, and even if more and more of the German Army's regular units were being transferred to the fighting fronts, especially as the demands of combat in Normandy increased, the Germans could still use the SS, the Gestapo, and the paramilitary Vichy Milice to keep order in the city. As the internal security of Paris increasingly became the responsibility of the paramilitary units, their brutality increased as well. By July there were 10,000 political prisoners in Parisian jails, more and more of whom the Germans were deporting or executing without even the formality of pressing charges. German officials remained confident that these methods could ensure internal security against the Resistance, which they presumed was poorly armed and poorly organized. Still believing that their main job was to keep the Parisian lines of communication open for German activity, they downplayed the need for a large regular army presence in the city itself.[10]

Hesse and others within the German military establishment had also begun to deduce that Paris was not a part of the long-term plans of the Allies. If the Allies had wanted to make Paris an offensive base of operations, German strategists reasoned, they would not have targeted its bridges and rail lines so ferociously. The more damage the Allies did to Paris and its surrounding region, the more costly and time-consuming its reconstruction would be. Nor did German strategists think that the Allies had the stomach for a bitter fight inside the city, when so much good tank country existed to the north and south of Paris. Rather than sending troops into the city, surely the Allies would try to bypass it, thus cutting off the German garrison in the Île de France and isolating it from outside help.[11]

Some German generals, including Erwin Rommel, thought Paris could best serve their interests as a hostage. Holding Paris would give the Germans an important bargaining chip should their positions in Normandy collapse. They could blackmail the Allies by threatening to destroy Paris, or they could promise to surrender it intact as a bargaining chip. Such plans betrayed a growing desperation within the German military. Many German generals had already come to the conclusion that the war had turned irrevocably against them. This belief led some to support an assassination attempt by disillusioned German generals against Hitler in late July; others continued to hold out hope that the German Army could delay the Allies in the west long enough to give diplomats time to cut a deal that might allow Germany to keep some of its gains. The most delusional of them envisioned the British and Americans joining the German Army in a new anti-Soviet alliance.[12]

In public at least, German generals displayed an air of calm, confidence, and loyalty, but as German misgivings increased, so too did their estimation of Paris's importance. On July 1, Hitler sent them a reminder of the need for loyalty, firing Army Group West commander General Gerd von Rundstedt for merely suggesting that the Germans seek a negotiated peace with the American and British. In private, though, some generals (including Rundstedt's replacement, Guenther von Kluge) had concluded that once they lost Paris they would also lose any remaining bargaining strength they had. The Germans therefore had to hold Paris as long as they could, and they had to be able to threaten to do serious damage to it in order to force the Allies into negotiations.

The Germans had gauged Allied intentions for Paris accurately. In mid-July, about the time the Germans were making their estimates of Allied strategy toward the city, Eisenhower's planners concluded that

"Paris will be a tempting bait, and for political and morale reasons strong pressure will doubtless be exerted to capture it easily." But they had already determined that they would resist those pressures and bypass the city instead. In part, this decision came from the American presumption that taking Paris would entail unacceptable losses. The Germans would have no choice but to fight for the city. Paris, they feared, might become the site of Germany's last stand in the west, for both political and military reasons. The prospect of losing Paris would be embarrassing enough to the Germans to compel them to try to hold the city for as long as possible.[13]

A battle in the streets of Paris was a nightmarish scenario for Allied commanders. Their forces were no more trained for urban fighting than the Germans. A battle inside the city would neutralize two of the most important tactical advantages the Allies possessed, their airplanes and their tanks. Moreover, the Germans could use the streets and alleys of Paris to draw Allied forces in and pin them down, incurring disproportionate casualties while also causing widespread damage to the city, its infrastructure, its people, and its irreplaceable artistic and architectural treasures. One study done at Eisenhower's headquarters foresaw "prolonged and heavy street fighting similar to that in Stalingrad" that would inevitably lead to the "destruction of the French capital," an eventuality that everyone hoped to avoid at all costs. Although Paris featured lightly in the Allies' strategic thinking, the city's precious cultural and historical landmarks did not— nor did the dangers that Allied troops would encounter if they attempted to take the city by force.[14]

Furthermore, if the Allies did get drawn into an urban battle and the Germans fought a successful delaying action inside Paris, the Germans could use the time they were buying to establish a strong defensive position on the Rhine River, or, in the worst-case scenario, along the ridges, fortresses, and forests of the western front from the last war. For a generation of leaders, especially British leaders, who had been enlisted men and junior officers in that war, a repetition of static war on the 1914–1918 battlefields was too horrifying a possibility to consider. The Germans also had at their disposal the prepared defensive positions of the Maginot Line (which, using forced labor, they had already begun to reorient to face west) and their own Siegfried Line. If they were given the fall and winter to improve those defensive lines, the Germans could turn them into formidable positions along the model of the imposing Hindenburg Line that had inflicted thousands of Allied casualties in 1917 and 1918.[15]

These military reasons were sound, but Allied planners had other reasons for not wanting to drive on Paris. Foremost among them were the liability and potential supply problems that Allied logisticians saw in a liberated Paris. They estimated that feeding and supplying the city would require the enormous figure of 4,000 tons of goods a day (as it turned out, this number proved to be far too small). Allied logistics were already operating on a shoestring that went all the way back to a badly damaged Cherbourg; the port required six weeks of intensive work by engineers and construction crews to make it usable after the widespread damage the Germans did before surrendering. Even if the Allies could push those badly needed supplies forward to Paris, they would have to come out of the needs of the army units actively engaged in fighting the Germans. Supplying Paris would also mean an enormous diversion of the precious gasoline upon which Allied divisions depended for mobility and supply.[16]

Better, the Allies thought, to force the problem of feeding the city onto the Germans for as long as possible before having to assume that burden themselves. Callous though this line of thinking may have been, the Allies were reluctant to assume the responsibility of feeding a city of 2.5 million people if they did not have the supplies needed to do so. Nor, it should be noted, did the Allies have a clear picture of just how bad the food problem in Paris really was until late August. Thus did Eisenhower take a larger risk than he knew by deferring "actual capture of the city" unless he "received evidence of starvation or distress among its citizens." That evidence was clear to those inside the city, but much harder to discern for Allied planners outside the city, who still tried not to think about Paris if they did not have to do so.[17]

The example of Rome exemplified many of the Allies' fears about launching a direct assault on Paris. Eisenhower, Bradley, and their staffs were acutely aware of the controversy then raging over Lieutenant General Mark Clark's handling of the liberation of Rome. As commander of the U.S. Fifth Army, Clark had been in charge of the slow, bloody march of Allied troops through central Italy. Along the mountains and narrow roads of that country, the fighting—complete with infantry attacks on trenches and a supply system that relied on mules as often as it did on trucks—had often resembled the operational environment of 1914 more than 1944. In early May 1944, Clark's forces, with the French Expeditionary Corps in the lead, broke through the stubborn German defense position known as the Gustav Line, leaving Rome open. Clark was mesmerized by the possibility of being its liberator.

Clark had received clear guidance (although, he later pointed out, no direct orders) to cut off the elements of the German Tenth Army that were retreating north, but on May 25 he dropped a "bombshell" of an order on Major General Lucian Truscott to move instead on Rome. Truscott was stunned by the order, which he knew would force his men to disengage from the fleeing Germans and make a hasty advance toward Rome. Even so great a prize as the Italian capital, Truscott thought, "was poor compensation for [the] lost opportunity" of destroying the retreating German units. French Expeditionary Corps commander Lieutenant General Alphonse Juin agreed, writing that "questions of prestige are shaping events." He warned that "history will not fail to pass severe sentence" on the decision to make a hasty march on Rome.[18]

Juin had judged correctly. As a result of Clark's decision, tens of thousands of German soldiers escaped what should have been an Allied noose and established a new defensive line, the Gothic Line, which was fifteen miles deep and ran from Massa on the Ligurian Sea to Pesaro on the Adriatic. The Germans held the Allies on that line for months, and most of northern Italy remained in German hands until the end of the war in May 1945. Equally as tragically, more than four thousand Allied soldiers died making the ill-planned and ill-supported move on Rome. Even Clark's close friends, including Eisenhower, saw that he had made a critical mistake. By going for the glory of capturing the Eternal City and the first Axis capital of the war, he had allowed an entire German army to live to fight another day.

Clark has come in for widespread criticism, both then and now, for the decision to focus on Rome, which was by then a lightly defended city. He could have taken Rome with far fewer casualties after completing the encirclement of the retreating Germans. His toughest critics have accused him of wanting to get his name and picture in the newspaper to feed his own ample ego. That his well-photographed entry into Rome happened just hours before Overlord began has only served to fuel criticism. His detractors saw him as vain and hungry for the publicity that he feared others would soon get. Both Eisenhower and Bradley were well aware of the aspersion being heaped on their friend and fellow commander. Neither wanted to make the same strategic mistake Clark had made, and neither wanted to face accusations of having liberated Paris to feed their egos while the Germans escaped to better defensive ground, thus prolonging the war.

Another omen from the Italian campaign also haunted Allied planners. The Allies, especially the Americans, had come in for criticism in Italy for bombing the sixth-century Benedictine abbey of Monte Cassino. The abbey, an architectural, religious, and historical jewel, sat atop a mountain along the Gustav Line. Its defenders had been bitterly resisting Allied troops well before Clark broke through in May 1944. After a series of hard-fought battles, the Allies decided to bomb the abbey despite the protests of the Vatican and the outspoken opposition of many American Catholics. On February 15, 1944, more than 200 bombers dropped 1,500 tons of explosives on the abbey, reducing it to ruins, only to find that the rubble afforded the German defenders (who had had no troops in the abbey and therefore suffered no casualties) excellent cover to continue repelling Allied attacks. The attack on Monte Cassino was an operational and public relations disaster, with even many Allied governments voicing their displeasure.

Paris, of course, was home to any number of treasures as valuable as Monte Cassino. Although the air attacks on the city had already caused widespread damage, the focus of Allied operations was still on the factories and rail yards. Planners hoped to spare the city's other districts. A full-scale offensive on Paris could require the mass targeting of the city itself. As a result, the city's monuments, churches, and cathedrals were sure to suffer as Monte Cassino had. For all these reasons, Eisenhower had already decided "to avoid making Paris a battleground" unless it became absolutely unavoidable.[19]

With all of these considerations in mind, Bradley responded to a reporter's question about the safety of the city by announcing that the U.S. Army "would not damage so much as a cobblestone in its streets." The fact that American and British bombers had already done significant damage to much more than Paris's cobblestones seems to have escaped Bradley's attention. The reporter, moreover, could be forgiven for thinking that Bradley was talking about a quick liberation of Paris, not about bypassing the city altogether, in part out of an aversion for assuming the burden of feeding its residents. Bradley and his staff were so focused on the German Army that they had all but put aside the welfare of the people they were supposed to be rescuing.[20]

The Allies had concluded, to use Bradley's words, that Paris "represented nothing more than an ink spot on our maps to be by-passed as we headed toward the Rhine." To those few Parisians who either knew of or guessed at Allied plans, the decision came as something akin to a death sentence. One Parisian who was in the know was Colonel Claude Ollivier, code-named "Jade Amicol," an intelligence officer working with the British who was hiding in southern Paris. On August 2, a British agent snuck into the city and told Ollivier not to expect outside help because the Allied armies were planning to bypass the city. "My God," he said upon hearing the news, "this is a catastrophe!" FFI leader Maurice Kriegel-Valrimont also knew that Churchill was willing to wait until Christmas to liberate Paris; such a delay, Kriegel-Valrimont concluded, would result in mass starvation.[21]

Unaware of these discussions at the highest levels of Allied and German strategy, Parisians themselves had continued their clandestine activities and their planning for the future. Despite Rol's refusal to endorse an uprising until the Allies were in a position to provide direct help, plans for massive workers' strikes on July 14, Bastille Day, continued. In the eyes of the FFI, by denying Germany a workforce, the strikes had far more potential to disrupt German industry than the Allied bombings did. Throughout June and July strikes had become more commonplace, as had industrial sabotage and work slowdowns. *L'Humanité*, one of the most important clandestine communist newspapers, urged Parisians to see the strikes as the start of a full insurrection. But the FFI was still too weak for such an uprising to succeed, and the Allies were too far away to come to the city's rescue. Nevertheless, strikes on July 10 in the Paris suburbs of St. Denis provided a positive omen for the larger strikes planned for July 14.

Although the Germans had warned Parisians not to strike, on Bastille Day tens of thousands of people took to the streets in the largest demonstrations Paris had seen since before the war. Estimates vary, but it seems clear that the strikes, which were mainly centered in the working-class districts of eastern Paris, drew at least 100,000 people. Some neighborhoods, like Belleville, St. Antoine, and La Chapelle, shut down entirely, although in most middle-class neighborhoods the strikes and demonstrations had little impact. In the western parts of Paris, around the Avenue Foch, there were no strikes and no disturbances. Jacques Bardoux, a resident of that neighborhood, recorded his impressions of a day that had been "sad and quiet, calm and chilling. No strikes. . . . Paris remains sad, savagely decimated by the Germans and Vichy, crushed by Allied bombardments, [and] starved by famine." Yves Cazaux agreed, bemoaning a "sad and heavy day" for a nation "that does not even have the right to fly its own flag."[22]

Some Parisians were more optimistic, seeing in the strikes a signal that their deliverance was near. Benoît Frachon, the head of the Confédération Générale du Travail, the French labor syndicate responsible for organizing the Bastille Day strikes, saw them in grandiose, historic terms: "In Paris today, the inspiration of our ancestors of 1792 is in the air. Paris, ravaged for four years, has started to make its torturers pay for their crimes." Another Parisian sympathetic to the strikers recorded in her diary that night: "No, Paris has not become a dead and resigned city." Even if they did not directly threaten the German position inside the city, the strikes were proof to this diarist and others that Paris was still alive.[23]

Rol was pleased by the strikes, as they demonstrated to him that the people of Paris would support a wider insurrection. Given that the Allies were still stuck in the Norman hedgerows, Rol thought that a general uprising was weeks away. Other, smaller signs of support could be seen in the city, however. A large number of Parisians wore blue, white, and red; some young Parisian girls, dressed as smartly as they could be given the wartime shortages, took to walking in groups of three, with the one on the left wearing a blue dress, the one in the center wearing a white dress, and the one on the right wearing a red dress. It may have been a small and ineffective act of resistance, but it was a symbol of a new mood developing in the city.[24]

A much more important message came from the Paris police, who were conspicuous by their inactivity. Despite their reputation in past years for violently breaking up marches, the police made no effort at all to disrupt the demonstrations. Some police officers stood on the streets with their arms folded; others sat in cafés and watched the unfolding spectacle like any other city resident. The strikers received the message: The police supported them, at least tacitly. The attitude of the police encouraged Rol and others. They were starting to see a shift in the balance of power in Paris. Even before the strikes, the police had begun to show significant restraint; of the 400 arrests made in the first two weeks of July in Paris, only 46 had been made by Paris policemen.[25]

The events of July 14 inspired the FFI and the French Communist Party leadership. Although still suspicious of the police, they drew confidence and momentum from the strikes. Some suspected the police of trying to atone for their odious behavior under the occupation, while others were afraid that the police were pulling some sort of a trick. The communist leader André Tollet was among those who remained deeply suspicious of the police, but he began to think about repeating the strikes on a much larger scale. He considered whether it might be possible to retake the city from the Germans even if the Allies could not provide any immediate help: If the Paris police could be convinced to join the Resistance, an even broader uprising might stand a fighting chance.[26]

The Paris police may have sat idle, but the Germans did not. Unable to rely on the police, the Germans rapidly took matters into their own hands. With the willing assistance of the Milice, they arrested more than 1,000 people, including several members of the French Senate whom they erroneously believed had been involved in planning the strikes. Many of the arrests were arbitrary, and few formal charges were filed. But the already overcrowded prisons of Fresnes and Cherche-Midi filled with more and more people. By the end of the month there were more than 10,000 political prisoners in Paris's jails facing uncertain futures. The Milice also carried out 37 summary executions on July 14 and 15. The mood in Paris grew more tense by the day. "The massacre of the French population continues at an even faster pace," noted Jacques Bardoux in his diary on July 15. "What will be left of France?" Three days later, he wrote, "Slowly but surely, without Algiers, Moscow, London, or Washington seeming to care, France is falling deeper and deeper into ruin, blood, and famine."[27]

In the week following the strikes and the German reprisals, events began to accelerate. On July 20, Claus von Stauffenberg, a German officer who hoped to remove Hitler and then open peace negotiations with the Allies, placed a bomb under the table at Hitler's "Wolf's Lair" headquarters in Rastenburg, in modern-day Poland. The plot was part of wide conspiracy on the part of German officers, who had a variety of motivations. Some, like Stauffenberg, came from the old Prussian aristocracy, with whom the Nazis had always had a difficult relationship. The most common thread uniting the conspirators was a belief that Hitler and his coterie were unable to realize that Germany was being crushed on two fronts. The conspirators believed that they could negotiate more effectively with the western Allies if Hitler were out of the picture. An armistice with Britain and the United States would then allow the German Army to focus its efforts on the eastern front, where the Soviet Union had already entered Poland on its menacing drive toward the heart of the Reich.[28]

The Gestapo suspected that a cabal of German generals whom they called the Black Orchestra was responsible for the Rastenburg attack. They also suspected that a disproportionate number of the plotters were based in Paris, where the desire for a separate peace with the Americans and British had wide support from generals who had concluded that the German forces in France were, in the words of one of them, "badly trained and frequently ill people who were only fit for office work." With the best of the German Army in the east, such generals saw an armistice as the only viable option for Germany. Still in possession of Paris, the western commanders thought that their position was stronger than it would be once the Allies finally did break through. Thus their support for the bomb plot was based on a desire to get what they could from a rapidly deteriorating military situation. Only a small minority were motivated by a sense of moral revulsion at the behavior of the German Army, the SS, and the Gestapo.[29]

The Gestapo was right to suspect the Paris high command of being involved in the plot. General Karl-Heinrich von Stülpnagel, another old-line Prussian aristocrat who mistrusted the Nazis but did their genocidal bidding until the war began to turn against Germany, was a senior member of the plot. He had been closely involved in the negotiations over the 1940 armistice with France before going to the eastern front, where he had worked closely with the notorious Nazi death squads known as the *Einsatzgruppen*. Stülpnagel had then returned to France, where he had served as the military commander of the country since the spring of 1942. He pursued a consistent policy of brutality toward the French Resistance, often arresting the relatives of Resistance members in the hopes of influencing them to reduce their activities; Rol's father-in-law, deported to Auschwitz, was one such hostage.

The Gestapo knew that some of the members of the Black Orchestra group had begun secret talks with the Allies through neutral intermediaries and diplomatic channels.[30] They did not, however, know the identities of the conspirators with any certainty. Nor did they have enough information to prevent Stauffenberg from placing a briefcase bomb inside the room where Hitler was hosting his morning conference. The bomb that exploded in Rastenburg in fact represented the group's fourth attempt to kill Hitler and some of his closest advisers. It contained a kilogram of explosives and a ten-minute timer to allow Stauffenberg to get away safely. Unfortunately for the plotters, Stauffenberg had not had the time to put a second kilogram of explosives in the briefcase; if he had, the bomb would surely have killed everyone in the room. Nevertheless, Stauffenberg was at first certain that the bomb had done its job. Unaware that Hitler had in fact survived, he left Rastenburg to put the pieces of the plot in motion. Generals sympathetic to the plot were ready to assume civil and military command in key places, including Berlin, Vienna, and Paris, as soon as they received word that Hitler was dead.

Stülpnagel received a call from Stauffenberg himself at 5:00 p.m. announcing prematurely that the first phase of the bomb plot had succeeded and that Hitler was dead. Stülpnagel then put in place his part of the plot, ordering the arrest of Paris's 1,200 Gestapo and SS officers to prevent Nazi loyalists from foiling the unfolding plan. Stülpnagel also contacted another conspirator, General Guenther von Kluge, the man who had replaced Rundstedt as commander of German forces in the west just a few weeks earlier. Kluge, however, had more current information than Stülpnagel. He told Stülpnagel that, contrary to early reports, Hitler was wounded, but still alive. He then advised Stülpnagel to go underground and told him that, in an effort to stay in Hitler's good graces, he would have no choice but to order the release of the Gestapo and SS officers that Stülpnagel had arrested.

The Paris garrison also contained hundreds of officers who disliked the Nazi regime but had been unaware of the plot. One of them was Gerhard Heller, a francophile who worked with French writers in the Nazi propaganda office. While hosting a party for French authors at the Institut Allemand, he received a phone call telling him that Hitler was dead. Heller grabbed a waiter and told him to fill some champagne glasses. He was preparing to announce the good news with the words that Goethe had used at Valmy in 1792: "From this place and from this day forth commences a new era in the world's history and you can all say that you were present at its birth." Suddenly, a friend pulled Heller aside and told him that he had just received a call warning that Hitler might not be dead after all. Heller just had time to stop the waiter, who had his trays of champagne ready in the kitchen. Heller recalled his first thought being that the Nazis would execute five thousand people in response to the assassination attempt.[31]

Parisians heard rumors of the plot but hardly knew what to make of them. Jacques Bardoux correctly deduced that the plot signaled Germany's desire to cut a deal in the west before it was too late to prevent the Russians from entering Germany with a thirst for revenge. Of course, neither he nor anyone else could have hazarded a guess about what the terms of such a deal might entail for Paris or for France. In 1943, the Allies had committed to fight until the Germans surrendered unconditionally, but now they were stuck in the bocage, and they still had a war with Japan to conclude. Might the Allies and Germans negotiate a deal that would leave the Germans in control of Paris?[32]

Around midnight, Parisians heard the voice of Hitler himself on loudspeakers across the city and on the collaborationist Radio Paris, an event for which the Germans had made electricity temporarily available. "A very small clique of ambitious, wicked, and stupidly criminal officers forged a plot to eliminate me and, along with me, virtually the entire leadership of the Wehrmacht," Hitler thundered. "We will settle accounts the way we National Socialists are accustomed to settling them." Released from their jail cells with the thin explanation that the whole operation had been a training exercise, Gestapo and SS officials quickly resumed their places in the Rue des Saussaies and on the Avenue Foch. Pro-Nazi authorities were firmly back in charge, and the day's events passed so quickly that neither the Paris police nor the Resistance had any time to react to them.[33]

The fallout from the bomb plot shook the German high command in Paris deeply. Virtually all of the senior officers in the city at least knew about the plot to take control of the army in the west after Hitler's assassination; many of them were either sympathetic or actively supportive. Boineburg, a fast rising star in the German Army and the man directly in charge of Paris, had lost faith in Germany's ability to win the war after the Battle of Stalingrad. He had been responsible for executing the arrest order, and in all likelihood he knew the details of the plot intimately. He heard Hitler's voice on loudspeakers outside the Hôtel Raphaël and knew that the failure of the plot and his close association with Stülpnagel would place him under intense suspicion. Boineburg was relieved of command of the Greater Paris garrison on August 3 but was not arrested, and he survived the war.

The SS and the Gestapo, furious at the plot and their arrests, opened investigations on more than a thousand German officers in France alone. They executed ten officers and arrested hundreds more, removing from Paris what Ernst Jünger called "the last gentlemen, the last free spirits," although that characterization is debatable and relative to the SS and Gestapo thugs in the city. Stülpnagel was among those suspected of being involved and ordered back to Germany for interrogation. While in Verdun, where he had fought in 1916, he managed to get a gun and tried to commit suicide, but he only succeeded in blinding himself. The Gestapo refused to give him medical attention and sent him to Berlin, where he died under interrogation while

attached to meat hooks. Kluge at first thought he had managed to escape suspicion, but months later, as the Gestapo closed in, he obtained
a cyanide capsule. He committed suicide with the pill after failing to
contact American general George Patton in one final effort to negotiate a separate peace with the western Allies.[34]

Thereafter, the Gestapo and SS insisted on German troops in Paris
using the Nazi salute, which up to then had been a rare gesture in the
city, to show their loyalty to Hitler. The atmosphere in the city under-
went a rapid change as the manifest tensions between the Gestapo
and the SS, on one side, and infantrymen of the German Army, on the
other, became obvious to all Parisians. The morale of the soldiers of
the German Army in Paris also dropped precipitously. An FFI intelligence report on July 24 noted that the morale of German soldiers in
the city was at its lowest point of the war, with many soldiers fighting
on simply out of fear of the SS. Rumors quickly spread that the Germans were sending more SS troops into the city, including those units
that had been responsible for the massacres at Oradur and Tulle.[35]

Fear of the SS, combined with the new attitude of German soldiers, created a strange new mood in the city. For the first time in the
occupation, the frailties of the Germans were becoming clear to all.
One Parisian could barely believe his eyes when he saw a German
soldier turn to his comrades in a public place and say "Normandy!
Germany! Kapout!" He was even more amazed to see the soldier's
comrades "make small gestures to show that they were in perfect
agreement." Such gestures had never before been in evidence in the
city. Marguerite Duras heard from a Resistance friend code-named
Morland (who was, in fact, the future president of France, François
Mitterrand) that "the Germans are starting to get frightened, . . .
some of them are deserting." Charles Braibant recorded in his journal
that German soldiers were buying or stealing the clothes of French
civilians in an effort "to avoid the vengeance of the French after Germany's capitulation." Braibant noted, however, that their plans were
unlikely to succeed, because German soldiers looked too well fed to
blend in with the emaciated Paris crowds.[36]

The decline in German morale was not the only problem faced by the Paris garrison. The confusion caused by the bomb plot and the disorientation created by the turnover in the German officer corps further impeded any attempt to prepare proper defenses for the city. Two of the city's four regimental commanders were among those arrested, and Kluge, under heavy suspicion for his role in the bomb plot, was perhaps understandably seized by frequent bouts of fear and indecisiveness. After the war, Boineburg gave American interrogators his strategic assessment of the condition of Paris at the moment that he handed over his command on August 3, saying: "Against an enemy attacking from the outside . . . there was no chance of success. . . . A battle for the open city of Paris would have been senseless for operational and tactical reasons. But it also would have been irresponsible in view of the destruction of irreplaceable art treasures."

Boineburg was not the last German general who would claim humanitarian reasons for his army's failure to keep Paris out of Allied hands. Whether he was telling the truth or telling his American captors what he thought they might like to hear, he knew perfectly well that all he had the resources to do if the Allies attacked was to delay the inevitable. His men knew it, too. They did not need to be generals themselves to figure out that Germany had too few troops, far too few heavy weapons, and an antiaircraft system that would not be sufficient to stop the Allies if they attacked. As another German officer later noted, "construction of a coherent defensive front had become impossible," because the Paris garrison lacked proper soldiers, weapons, and leadership.[37]

German morale, already low, suffered yet another blow just days after the failure of the bomb plot, when the Americans finally broke out of Normandy. The Allied plan, code-named Operation Cobra, got off to a miserable start on July 24, when bad weather and poor coordination led to a premature air attack that resulted in more than two dozen friendly-fire deaths. The next day, 1,850 Allied bombers dropped more than 4,000 tons of bombs, as well as napalm and antipersonnel weapons, in a ten-square-mile area just west of the town of St. Lô. The official U.S. Army historian of the campaign undoubtedly understated the impact of this massive use of bombers in a tactical role when he wrote that "the earth shook." Nevertheless, accuracy remained a problem. Poor coordination at St. Lô again caused heavy friendly-fire casualties, including the death of Lieutenant General Lesley J. McNair, the highest-ranking American officer killed in World War II.

The inaccuracy of the air assault notwithstanding, the sheer weight of Cobra stunned and shocked the Germans who felt its full force. The entire German left flank collapsed, opening the route to the town of Avranches and then the gateways into Brittany, where the Allies intended to shut down German U-boat bases on the Atlantic coast. Although supply problems continued to slow the Allied advance, Cobra had changed the momentum of the war in northern France. General Dietrich von Choltitz, whose 84th Army Corps had suffered terribly near St. Lô, called the fighting in Normandy a "monstrous bloodbath," the likes of which he had never seen. Choltitz soon received notification that he was being reassigned away from Normandy and given a new, potentially even more challenging assignment, but for the moment he had his hands full simply holding together the collapsing German defense. To Guenther von Kluge, his commander, the campaign in Normandy was devolving into "an awful mess" that the German Army could not contain with the resources it then had on hand.[38]

Although the Americans initially turned west into Brittany, the breakout had implications for Paris as well. By the end of July, it appeared as though the Germans were either retreating into their fortifications in Brittany or beginning to stream east in a state of disorganization. This new operational environment meant that the Allies could reduce the number of units they dedicated to the liberation of Brittany and focus more effort on the Seine River basin, which suddenly appeared to be within reach. As Eisenhower told

General George Marshall, the U.S. Army chief of staff, on July 30, "The prospects for the future were unlimited."[39]

Astonishingly, however, Paris still formed no part of those prospects. Allied planners continued to think in terms of bypassing the city to push the Germans as far east as possible. The most optimistic among them hoped for victory in the west in 1944 in order to allow the Allies to begin to move units to the Pacific theater for a spring campaign against Japan. Paris was still, in their eyes, a distraction and an unnecessary diversion of resources.

But circumstances soon forced Allied commanders to reconsider. Events were about to move much more rapidly, beginning with the arrival of a new German commander for Paris, a man known throughout the German high command as the "smasher of cities."

4

THE SMASHER OF CITIES

On August 7, Dietrich von Choltitz arrived at the "Wolf's Lair" in Rastenburg in modern-day Poland for a meeting with Adolf Hitler. Choltitz, the heavy-set fifty-year-old general who had recently been mired in St. Lô, was a career soldier. He had been one of the four thousand officers who had served in the interwar German Army, which had been limited in size by the Versailles Treaty. Although he had met Hitler only once, he had, like most German generals of his generation, followed him loyally since 1933. He had received orders to come to Hitler's headquarters, which was under unusually heavy security in the wake of the recent bomb plot, to discuss a new assignment. In the back of his mind, however, he wondered if he was going to be chastised for the collapse of his corps outside St. Lô during Operation Cobra or, worse still, if he had been incorrectly implicated in the assassination plot.

The area where the bomb had exploded still showed evidence of the attack, and the atmosphere at Rastenburg was tense. The fear and anxiety there could not have done much to alleviate Choltitz's own anxiety. The rapidly advancing Red Army was just sixty miles away, exacerbating the already edgy environment among Hitler's lieutenants. The impending arrival of the vengeful Russians on German soil was the main topic of conversation; Hitler's daily briefings began with the situation on the eastern front no matter what was happening elsewhere. Rastenburg hardly looked like a headquarters ready to deal with the many crises Germany faced. Hitler could not even shake Choltitz's hand firmly because of wounds suffered in the bomb blast.

The meeting unnerved Choltitz from the beginning. Hitler appeared, Choltitz later recalled, as an "old, stooped, and swollen man . . . a trembling being [who was] physically broken." Choltitz recalled Hitler raging on about "the clique of Prussian generals" who tried to "prevent me, Adolf Hitler, from continuing my work, from fulfilling my destiny of leading the German people." Dozens of those generals, Hitler reminded Choltitz unnecessarily, now "bounced at the end of a rope." Choltitz realized that Hitler was a "soul filled with hate" against his own generals; that rage, he believed, prevented Hitler from seeing the true situation facing Germany. "I found myself in the presence of a madman," he concluded. Even before the meeting went much further, Choltitz realized that Hitler had an unrealistic view of the true military situation in the west, which, Choltitz believed, was on the verge of complete and irrevocable collapse.[1]

During their meeting, Hitler gave Choltitz command of the Paris Military District with a demand that he reform it and make it more effective. Hitler railed against what he saw as the unmilitary and lax attitude of the officers in Paris, telling Choltitz that "the fighting going on [in Paris] is over the seats in the officers mess" rather than against the enemy. He wanted Choltitz to make Paris "a frontline city" and prepare it for a proper defense while restoring "discipline among troops accustomed to easy living." Hitler offered Choltitz no new resources and left him no opportunity to ask questions. He then surprised Choltitz by telling him that a major counteroffensive would begin immediately that would change the military situation in the west in Germany's favor. The announcement only further undermined Choltitz's opinion of the strategic vision of the German high command. Hitler ended the meeting by telling Choltitz that he was extending his command authority, essentially making Choltitz an independent commander with powers akin to those of a fortress commander under siege. Choltitz would therefore have virtually unlimited control over German Army units in the city, although, in line with new security measures after the bomb plot, he would have no control over the Gestapo or the SS.[2]

Hitler and the German high command had chosen Choltitz as the new commander of Paris in large part for his presumed reliability in the wake of the bomb plot. He was one of the few German generals in France whose name had not come up in the Gestapo investigations following the assassination attempt, leading Hitler to believe that Choltitz could be trusted. He was also, in the words of the man he replaced, "a devoted Nazi and an unshakably obedient Prussian" who had always done what he was told without thinking about the consequences. Choltitz did indeed have a well-deserved reputation inside the German Army for never refusing an order. After the war, while sitting in an Allied prison and being secretly recorded by his British captors, he told another German officer that "the most difficult order of [his] life" had been the order he received in Russia to liquidate all Jews in his area of responsibility. He had nevertheless followed the order in its entirety and without any hesitation whatsoever.[3]

Ominously for his new assignment, Choltitz also had a reputation for ferocity in urban warfare. He had been responsible for the German Army's ruthless devastation of several city centers, most notably Rotterdam in 1940 and Sevastopol in 1942. In Rotterdam, Choltitz's aggressiveness resulted in almost a thousand civilian deaths after the surrender of the city, mostly from air raids he ordered that also left eighty thousand people in the city homeless. Operations in Sevastopol were far nastier, killing tens of thousands of noncombatants. Choltitz's nickname, "the Smasher of Cities," reflected his unusual area of specialty. So widespread was this reputation inside the German Army that he was often believed to be the man who had overseen the destruction of the fortifications of Warsaw in 1939, even though he had in fact not been involved. Part of his fearsome reputation came from the brutal way that Choltitz had treated civilians in the cities he devastated. Like many of his German comrades, he held irregular combatants in utter contempt. In his eyes, any fighter not wearing a uniform was a terrorist unworthy of any protections under the conventions of war. The communities that harbored these civilian fighters were also open to any form of collective retribution necessary to ensure order.

Choltitz is one of the most difficult personalities in the history of the liberation of Paris to understand. After the war, he granted many contradictory interviews in which he alternatively revealed his disgust at Paris (and Parisians) and boasted that he, and he alone, had saved a Paris he had come to love from complete destruction. His memoirs, like all memoirs from Nazi generals, need to be corroborated by other sources and read with great care, as they are an obvious mixture of truths, half-truths, and convenient fictions. Choltitz, like most of his colleagues in their later recollections, tried to blame as much as he could on Hitler and the German high command, thus absolving himself of responsibilities for war crimes and fatal errors of judgment. In 1955, an interviewer wrote that "one must ask at what point, if ever, General Choltitz was sincere. This is a point that History might one day clarify." Such clarification remains difficult to achieve decades later.[4]

Whatever the level of his sincerity, however, by 1944 Choltitz was clearly not the same aggressive general he had been in 1940–1942. Raoul Nordling, the Paris-born Swedish consul with whom Choltitz came to work closely, described him as "the very incarnation of Prussia . . . corpulent, powerful and broad-shouldered, extremely stiff, imposing, and, it seemed to me, of an overbearing Prussian demeanor." Like many of his fellow generals, he had lost faith that Germany would win the war after the disaster at Stalingrad, and by the time of the Paris liberation he was badly disillusioned with the army's leadership, a belief strongly reinforced by the meeting with Hitler at Rastenburg. Although there is no evidence linking him with the bomb plot, he shared the beliefs of the plotters that the best hope for Germany's future rested in signing a favorable armistice with the Americans and the British. He was also suffering from heart problems, which had evidently sapped much of his customary energy.[5]

Choltitz left Rastenburg more demoralized than reenergized. He saw more clearly than ever that Germany would lose the war. "I asked myself," he later wrote, "the difficult question of whether a general, a leader of men, can in his soul and in his conscience take the responsibility of sacrificing his poor soldiers for a cause that had lost all hope." Evidently, he answered yes to that question, because he took the Paris assignment despite his belief that the orders had come from a man he described as a lunatic. He had come to the conclusion that both Hitler and his staff were delusional. Conveniently for him, however, Choltitz had concluded that this state of affairs "relieved [his] conscience as a soldier" if he decided not to follow their orders.[6]

Choltitz arrived in Paris on August 9 and quickly saw that the city was in no position to defend itself or to help the retreating German forces in France. It took him more than four days just to straighten out the confused and ever-changing command structure in the city. He found most of the newly assigned officers to the area anxious to use Paris as a base for offensive operations, but he knew that the necessary facilities and personnel did not exist. He was surprised to learn that the troops in Paris were in even worse condition than he had feared. Poorly armed and badly trained, they could not, he knew, "keep the enemy at bay outside the city for very long" if attacked. Some of the troops in the Paris Military District were using World War I–vintage rifles, and others had received little to no training in the use of heavy weapons. Most alarmingly, he found the morale of the Paris garrison beyond rehabilitation. In his mind, years of service in "beautiful France, with its magnificent climate and its charming inhabitants," had sapped the "wild resolution" that had enabled German soldiers to win the Reich's early victories.[7]

The francophile German officer Gerhard Heller recalled Paris at the time Choltitz arrived as a place where parties continued as a means for most German officials to avoid the unpleasant reality that their side would lose the war. "We tried to forget the hazards that weighed on us, keeping in our minds our sweet memories of Paris," he recalled wistfully. Heller did note, however, that the Gestapo and the SS still contained diehard believers in the Nazi cause whose "hate, [and] whose thirst for destruction and death[,] had never been greater." They spoke of any retreat from the city as being temporary and believed it would be followed by a new victory march "into a Paris even more beaten and submissive." Dangerous though they could be, such men were in the minority. Most German officials, fully aware that their time in Paris was coming to an end, spent their days figuring out how many items from the city they could ship home on the limited transportation available.[8]

Garrison service in *La Belle France* was not the only reason for the decline in the fighting ability of the German Army. The effects of five years of trying to conquer Europe in the name of a morally bankrupt ideology, combined with the recent impacts of brutal combat in Normandy, had reduced the German Army in the west to a shell of its former self. Many of the German Army's units in France, moreover, were still recovering from the frightful and murderous beatings they had taken on the eastern front. For Parisians like Gilles Perrault, the degradation of the German Army meant that the men of the Paris district were no longer "the splendid specimens of humanity" that had marched triumphantly into the city in 1940. Instead, they appeared to Perrault as "gray-haired old men . . . and lanky boys, dwarves, bandy-legs, hunchbacks—a whole army of ragged men. They reeked of disaster." For Choltitz, a veteran of the prewar army and recently a corps commander of a frontline unit, the sight of so many men in such a poor physical and moral state must have come as quite an unpleasant surprise.[9]

Based on these observations, Choltitz quickly abandoned any thought of Paris serving as a major German stronghold. He decided instead on a strategy of keeping the city open for as long as possible as a German communication and transportation node. Doing so would allow the Germans to move troops and equipment west to assist with the counterattack the German headquarters was preparing at the very moment that Choltitz arrived at his new assignment. If, as Choltitz expected, the counterattack failed, then the German Army would need a secure Paris to move as many men as possible to a new defensive line east of the city. Given the resources he had at hand, Choltitz did not believe that he could accomplish much more.

Choltitz disliked the idea of being the man who would leave Paris in ruins, even though he knew that Hitler wanted him to do so. He may have had humanitarian reasons for his desire to save Paris, but he also had no wish to see his name forever associated with the destruction of the city unless doing so would help the German Army in some significant way. There is little evidence to suggest that Choltitz had ruled out destroying large parts of the city under any circumstances; although his attitude toward the war may have changed, he was still the same man who had decimated Rotterdam and Sevastopol earlier in the war. In August 1944, however, Choltitz had more reasons to keep Paris intact than he did to inflict intentional damage on the city. Given that the Germans already knew that the Allies did not have Paris in their short-term plans, denying it to them would not slow them down enough to justify its demolition. It would, however, make the safe withdrawal of German troops in northern France much more difficult. From a purely operational perspective, therefore, damaging Paris was senseless. Most importantly, destroying Paris would not put the Allies in a positive frame of mind to sign an armistice that might be relatively favorable to Germany. Obtaining such an armistice was the only strategic goal the German command in the west could envision.

Choltitz also knew that if it became evident that the Germans were preparing major demolitions inside Paris, it would likely lead the Resistance to rise in opposition and the majority of Parisians to become actively anti-German. An uprising in the city was Choltitz's worst nightmare, because it would make control of the city's transportation nodes virtually impossible. It would also involve his troops in the kind of guerrilla warfare for which they were untrained and unprepared.

He therefore decided to implement a less risky defense plan for Paris that envisioned holding thirty-six mutually supporting strongpoints, including the Place de la Concorde near his headquarters in the Hôtel Meurice, the Luftwaffe headquarters in the Palais du Luxembourg, the large German barracks on the Place de la République, and critical infrastructure points, such as the main telephone exchange on the Rue de Grenelle and the city's gas and water works. The plan also allowed for strongpoints to provide security for the main boulevards and avenues in the city in order to ensure smooth circulation for German mobile forces.

Despite his fears of an urban uprising, Choltitz seems not to have thought that the Resistance posed a serious threat to German control of the city. At least, he was relatively sanguine about this point during his first week as commander of Paris. Army Group B's weekly reports at this time dismissed the Resistance as only capable of fighting what it called "miniature warfare," noting that "the Resistance movement has been crippled by the capture of almost all of its leaders." Choltitz was concerned that a new round of strikes, similar to those of July 14, could cause disruptions to German activity in the city, but he downplayed the possibility that the Resistance was capable of organizing operations on a large scale. Nor did he worry about the increasing unwillingness of the Paris police to assist German authorities.[10]

Choltitz did, however, make a priority of building a strong working relationship with several collaborationist officials, including Pierre Taittinger, Paris's right-wing mayor. The two men shared a mutual dislike of the FFI and the city's communist leaders, whom they both suspected of planning an insurrection and civil war that could destroy the city from within. At this point, Choltitz was still confident of his ability to break up any attempt by the FFI to disrupt order in the city, but he needed French allies to ensure that matters did not get out of hand. The Paris police were nominally under Taittinger's authority and subject to his orders. For his part, Taittinger saw Choltitz as a powerful ally against his own political enemies. He also saw him as a viable alternative to the SS commanders in the city, whom he feared far more than he feared the German Army. Choltitz and Taittinger formed a tight bond that outlived their working relationship. Before leaving Paris, Choltitz gave Taittinger an autographed photo of himself as a parting gift, citing the "Christian and European" spirit that had "united their efforts" to save Paris from civil war and destruction. Taittinger later wrote the introduction to the French edition of Choltitz's memoirs, calling him "chivalrous" and "humane." Their relationship typified the collaboration between German and Vichy authorities that had served the interests of the occupiers at the expense of the people of Paris for four long years.[11]

Despite his downplaying of the Resistance's ability to pose a serious threat to German positions in Paris, there is little doubt that Choltitz feared Parisians more than he feared the approaching armies of the Allies. He hoped to deal with any trouble from civilians in the city by imposing a harsh regime. Although he may have been disappointed in the resources at his disposal for controlling Paris, he had little doubt that he had enough force to intimidate the FFI, for whom he had nothing but disdain. In his first few days in his new command, Choltitz gave an interview to the *Petit Parisien* newspaper in which he said that he "would not hesitate to use the most brutal measures of repression" at his disposal to put down an uprising in the city. On the same day, he made an official statement that read: "It is important to stress that order shall be maintained at all costs. The Military Governor of Paris has resolved to respond to cases of sabotage, attacks, or riots with the most severe and most brutal measures. The proximity of the front gives German military authorities particular responsibilities which justify this harsh attitude. Any and all measures that can deal with disorder, no matter how severe, will be used."[12]

Choltitz also threatened to level any city block from which a single shot was fired at a German soldier. German authorities tried to take some of the sting out of these harsh declarations by claiming that they were necessary to guarantee the steady supply of food into the city, but Parisians, most of whom knew of Choltitz's reputation, understood his message.

From his hideout on the Rue de Meaux in northeast Paris, Rol care-fully observed the new German garrison and its actions. He studied the German dispositions for the city and saw nothing original or creative about them. As Rol later wrote, they suggested that the new German commander "didn't understand that the situation had changed" in the past few weeks. The strikes of July 14 and the refusal of the Paris po-lice to intervene, he concluded, had turned the tide in the city to the FFI's favor. The strategic outlook for the Resistance was good. In the event of a major uprising, the German strongpoints would become isolated and unable to assist one another. The FFI could surround and attack them one by one, especially if by doing so they could deny the Germans easy movement through the streets.[13]

Rol developed a new plan for seizing control of the city once the opportunity presented itself. The main impediment remained the lack of weapons. Rol begged and pleaded with his contacts in London to air-drop or smuggle weapons into the city. Without weapons, there would be little that Rol's dedicated band of FFI agents could do. To him, the dilemma was obvious, and the need for weapons even more so. The continued silence from London frustrated him and made him suspect the motives of de Gaulle and the Allies. "Can the Military Delegation [in London] be ignorant of this situation?" he demanded in a message to French officials, but still he got no answer and no weapons. Maurice Kriegel-Valrimont assumed that the Allied refusal to air-drop weapons was part of a larger plan to impose an American military government on a prostrate and beaten France. But whatever its cause, the implications were clear: If the FFI was going to fight the Germans, they would have to take the extreme risk of doing so with-out outside help.[14]

Events outside the city, and not just in London, continued to have a dramatic impact on Paris. As Choltitz was leaving Rastenburg to as-sume command of Paris, the Germans launched the counteroffensive that Hitler had mentioned. German forces attacked the advancing Al-lies in the region directly south of the Normandy beaches around the strategically important town of Mortain. Hitler hoped that the attack would delay the Allies for six to ten weeks. German forces could then redeploy their infantry units east of Paris along defensive lines that they could build on the same lines where German forces had held off the Allies in 1916 and 1917. These positions had bought time for the Germans, which allowed them to design the Ludendorff Offensives for the spring of 1918. Those offensives had experienced temporary success but had ultimately failed, leading to German defeat, but this important detail seems not to have influenced German strategists.

Although Hitler held out high hopes for the August 7 attack, the Allies knew it was coming thanks to the cryptographers involved in the Ultra project, a top-secret effort that broke the German codes. On the appointed day, three armored divisions advanced more than seven miles and retook Mortain, and the Germans at first thought they had won a great victory. The Allies, however, had been ready; they had carefully retreated to high ground in good order, leaving the Germans with a *salient*, or bulge, in their lines that looked like a finger poking into Allied positions. Now surrounded on three sides, the German advance had become a trap with Allied units in place to threaten the only route of escape. Bradley quickly moved forces to the base of the salient, hoping to pinch it off simultaneously from the north and south, thereby trapping the Germans inside what became known as the Falaise-Argentan pocket, named after the two French towns on either side of the gap.[15]

With one drive coming from the north and another coming from the south, the Allies had to proceed with great care, lest they either allow the Germans to slip away or accidentally fire upon one another. Although the Allies possessed many advantages, the situation was still precarious. It occupied the full attention of the Allied (and German) commanders for two weeks, further diverting their eyes from the situation in Paris. A debate began in Allied circles about whether a short hook that cut off the main roads or a complete encirclement of the pocket was the best way to capitalize on the precarious German position. Allied commanders saw a chance to win a major victory and possibly open the routes to the east if they acted quickly and carefully. Intensive planning began for a counterattack to be launched on August 14. Little wonder, then, that Rol had trouble getting Eisenhower and his staff to focus their energies on the FFI's lack of weapons inside Paris.

The Falaise pocket proved to be more difficult to eliminate than Eisenhower had hoped. In military terms, the Allies possessed exterior lines, meaning that the Germans could move forces inside the pocket more easily than the Allies could move them outside the pocket. Although the Allies held the tremendous advantage of being able to fly over the pocket and destroy German armor and infantry formations from the air, they knew that the Germans would fight tenaciously out of their fear of being surrounded and trapped. Fierce fighting began inside the pocket shortly after the Germans reached Mortain as the Allies tried to close the noose and prevent German troops from escaping to the east.

Inside the pocket sat twenty-one German divisions whose only line of communication to the rest of the German Army was a tenuous fourteen-mile gap in the line. Almost as soon as the German offensive began, Eisenhower and his staff started moving units behind the German divisions to cut off the pocket. The Allies employed a devastating strategy of pounding the pocket with aircraft and heavy artillery, leading the German high command to decide, on August 13, that it had indeed made a terrible mistake. Thereafter, the German focus centered on getting as many men out of the pocket as possible before the Allies closed the gap, which they began to do, as planned, around August 14. By August 18, the Allies had narrowed the gap to just three miles.

The failed Mortain offensive and the battles to close the Falaise pocket decimated the German Army in the west. An estimated 10,000 Germans died and another 50,000 became prisoners of war by the time the pocket finally closed on August 19. Eisenhower described Falaise as "unquestionably one of the greatest killing grounds of the war," and Montgomery called the carnage "almost unbelievable." In Eisenhower's chilling recollection, "forty-eight hours after the closing of the gap I was conducted through it on foot, to encounter scenes that could be described only by Dante. It was literally possible to walk for hundreds of yards at a time, stepping on nothing but dead and decaying flesh." Since June 6 the German Army in France had lost 158,930 men and received only 30,069 replacements. The German position in France, weak to begin with, was coming close to collapsing, even if thousands of German soldiers had managed to escape the Falaise gap's final closing.[16]

The failure of the Mortain counteroffensive convinced even many of the most ardent Nazis that the German Army's days in France were numbered. Hitler's headquarters continued to dream of a German thrust to the English Channel coast as late as August 13. Knowing full well that such visions were completely without a basis in reality, German commanders in the west sought by mid-August to find ways to get as many men out of France as possible. They knew that the Allies would try to exploit the massive defeat they had just inflicted and that the dominance of Allied air power made the movement of men and supplies almost impossible except at night, when they could move under the cover of darkness. Only the Allies' own supply problems, most notably the desperate shortage of gasoline, could stop them from crossing the Seine and cutting off German avenues of retreat.[17]

Those supply problems, plus the continued presence of thousands of German soldiers from the Falaise pocket, continued to prevent Allied commanders from making plans for Paris. At the same time, events in other parts of France also occupied Allied attention in mid-August. On August 15, just one week after the Germans' Mortain counteroffensive began, the Allies landed in southern France as part of Operation Dragoon. The landings put 94,000 men and 11,000 vehicles between Toulon and Cannes on the first day, opening up new supply routes for the Allied advance and sending thousands of German soldiers north in flight. The fighting was far less intense than in Normandy, giving the operation the nickname the Champagne Campaign, and it provided a tremendous boost to

French morale, especially since more than half of the forces for Dragoon were French. France was, at long last, taking an active role in its own liberation.

To move all of their retreating units and reestablish a fighting line in the east, the Germans desperately needed Paris and its transportation infrastructure intact. Although they sent no new infantry or armored units to the city (as a result of the disaster at Falaise, there were none to send), the Germans did deploy twenty additional 88 mm antiaircraft guns to the Paris region as part of an effort to protect the bridges they needed against attacks by Allied bombers. These deployments show that the Germans were not planning to hold Paris for longer than a few weeks. But they still needed to be able to use the city as a supply and transportation center for the German units streaming in disorder and disarray toward the Seine. To Choltitz, the chaos on the French front meant that Paris was even less defensible against an Allied attack than it had been just a few days earlier. On August 14, he informed Kluge that in his view, the Germans should not hold the city, for risk of being encircled and cut off. Nor did it make sense to plan for ultimately futile street fighting in an attempt to defend Paris.[18]

Better, Choltitz argued, for the Germans to hold the city long enough to enable an orderly withdraw to the east. To do so, the Paris garrison would need to maintain order in the city for as long as possible at any cost. German reports continued to suggest that the Allies were still preparing to move around the city rather than through it, meaning, for Choltitz, that internal security remained the most pressing problem. He would need to make sure that the residents of Paris would continue to obey his orders without question. Such exigencies led Choltitz to justify some of the harshest measures he ordered during the occupation, although his callousness would not, ultimately, stave off disorder.[19]

What to do with Paris once the Germans finally did have to give it up became a point of debate among leading German officials. Kluge and General Alfred Jodl, Hitler's closest military adviser, wanted the city's bridges and industrial sites rigged for demolition and then destroyed as soon as German forces had moved east. To accomplish this mission, Jodl had promised to make available the warheads of thousands of torpedoes destined for German U-boat pens in Brittany that now sat in Allied hands. Jodl also dispatched four German engineers with blueprints of key sites, such as the Palais du Luxembourg, the main railway stations, and the central telephone exchange. They were to advise the German high command on the best way to cause maximum destruction with the explosives available. In addition, Jodl wanted forty-five bridges, as well as aqueducts, gas works, and electric substations, to be demolished.

Choltitz pronounced the plan "perfectly sound" and told Kluge that he had no problem with it in theory. Even Taittinger noted that Choltitz was prepared "to destroy Paris as indifferently as if it were a crossroads village in the Ukraine." Choltitz did, however, want to delay the plan's implementation as long as Paris remained calm. Because the German Army still needed Paris, he saw no reason to provoke its residents unnecessarily. Kurt Hesse, commander of the St. Cloud garrison west of Paris, agreed with Choltitz, noting that no one in the Paris garrison in mid-August doubted the German ability to hold the city until the German Army had escaped to the east. Jodl thus consented to delay the plan's implementation, although he reminded Choltitz of Hitler's desire to see Paris demolished rather than for it to be handed over to the Allies intact.[20]

While Parisians sat anxiously monitoring German actions, some of their countrymen were beginning to get into the battle. To accomplish the remarkable feat at Falaise, the Allies had relied on units from the United States, Great Britain, Canada, Poland, and, crucially, France. As part of the drive to close the southern shoulder of the Falaise pocket, Bradley had ordered into action the Deuxième Division Blindée, the Free French Second Armored Division. Composed largely of men from the French Empire in Africa, the Deuxième Division Blindée had come over from England in the wake of the Normandy invasions under the command of the determined Major General

Philippe Leclerc. Born Philippe François Marie, comte de Haute-clocque, into an aristocratic family that had served France since the Crusades, he had attended the French military academy at St. Cyr and risen quickly through the ranks. Wounded in action in 1940, Leclerc had twice escaped from German prison camps before finding his way to join de Gaulle in London. He had changed his name to protect his family from Nazi reprisals.

At age forty-two and cutting an impressive military bearing, Leclerc projected energy and competence to a badly demoralized nation. In August 1940, de Gaulle sent him to French Equatorial Africa, where he took command of Free French forces in Cameroon and Congo and persuaded the administrations of both colonies to rally to de Gaulle's cause. Through sheer will and determination he built an army out of former Vichy French soldiers and Africans from France's empire, then led it 1,500 miles in thirty-nine days across the desert to link up with the British Eighth Army in Tunisia. Containing men of all political, ethnic, and national backgrounds, the Deuxième Division Blindée was a truly imperial unit with a high level of cohesion and morale. Leclerc, its leader, attained legendary status and de Gaulle's trust. He became the face of Free France's military efforts and, being a more sympathetic figure than de Gaulle, the frequent subject of Allied newsreels. Eisenhower quickly saw the value in having a formidable French unit take part in the Normandy campaign. He had the Deuxième Division Blindée fitted out with modern equipment and American uniforms, although they also wore distinctive red berets that identified them as French. The Deuxième Division Blindée became attached to the American Fifth Corps and Third Army in France, landing on Utah beach on August 1 to great fanfare.

Leclerc had long set his eyes on Paris, but, consistent with American strategy, he had received orders instead to head for the town of Alençon on the southern edge of the Falaise pocket. Leclerc was doubtful of American strategy and suspicious of the unwillingness of American leaders to let him drive toward Paris. He therefore went toward Alençon as ordered, but he disregarded the plan drawn up by his corps commander, an American general who had once been a student at Paris's École Militaire on the Champ de Mars just opposite the Eiffel Tower. Oddly enough, the American, Major General Wade Hampton, had fonder memories of Paris than Leclerc did. Leclerc did not particularly like Paris or big cities in general, but he understood the strategic importance of the capital and bristled at what he saw as American indifference to Paris's plight.

At Alençon, the Deuxième Division Blindée had fought well, gaining thirty miles and helping to begin the final encirclement of German forces in the Falaise pocket. Leclerc, however, had followed his own vision of the battle instead of the orders he received from Hampton, creating confusion along Allied lines of communication. He thought that the American orders contained mistakes resulting from American inexperience and overreliance on bureaucracy. He was also deeply offended when he received orders for the Deuxième Division Blindée to remain at Alençon while American units headed east toward the Seine in an effort to pressure German supply lines. Believing that his division had earned its stripes in battle and was thus entitled to an equal role in the push eastward, he went to see his army commander, George Patton, who spoke French and did not hold his French colleagues in the same contempt that characterized the attitudes of many senior American officers.

Their meeting, on August 14, did not go as Leclerc had hoped. Patton refused to change his orders. Leclerc threatened to resign if American forces were positioned closer to Paris than French forces. "I told him in my best French that he was a baby," Patton noted in his diary, "and said I had left him in the most dangerous place on the front. We parted friends." Patton's eyes remained fixed not on the Seine but the Rhine, which he saw as the last major barrier into Germany itself. Patton still hoped to cross it before the Germans did, if only he could get enough gasoline to drive his tanks there.[21]

Patton and Leclerc may have remained friends, but Leclerc's corps commander, Lieutenant General Leonard Gerow, an American, soon grew tired of "that miserable man" and his insubordination. More than personalities and national differences were at stake, however. As late as mid-August, the American and French leadership still had radically different views of the importance of Paris. To the American military leadership, Paris remained strategically insignificant. Nothing that happened around Falaise had changed the attitudes of senior American leaders toward the city and its liberation. The Americans therefore refused pleas from de Gaulle and Leclerc to allow elements of the Deuxième Division Blindée to leave its designated position and move toward Paris. Nor did they believe that the FFI inside Paris was in a position to make a significant contribution to its liberation, in part because the Allies still refused to air-drop supplies into the city out of fear of giving the communists weapons. A furious Leclerc, and only slightly less furious de Gaulle, could do little to change the situation, given that the Americans controlled access to gasoline, the most vital of all resources for a mechanized military. Reports (which were correct) that Leclerc had ordered his commanders to begin hoarding gasoline without telling the Americans only increased the mistrust that was beginning to build inside the alliance over the subject of Paris.[22]

Inside the city, there were some signs that the German hold was at long last starting to crack. The Germans began to withdraw thousands of noncombat personnel from Paris in mid-August. Francophile staff officers such as Gerhard Heller and Ernst Jünger left along with men like Luftwaffe officer Karl Kitzinger, who had good relationships with many of the city's most important leaders. Such cultural liaisons had helped to provide a crucial buffer between Parisians and some of the most vicious elements of the German and Vichy system. Now they were gone, leaving mostly combat officers with no ties to the city and few sympathies for its residents. Some Germans who had signed leases through the end of the year told their landlords to keep the apartments unoccupied, as they would soon return, once Germany's fortunes turned around. Whether such talk amounted to optimism or bravado, Parisians watched with glee as their occupiers started to depart, even if they took with them everything they could carry. Artworks, furniture, and, most importantly, food, left with the Germans on any vehicle they could find.[23]

Among those Germans leaving the city were the especially despised Wehrmacht female auxiliaries, known around Paris as the Little Gray Mice because of the color of their uniforms and their constant smiles. Well fed, well paid, and doted upon by German officers, they were the very symbols of German extravagance at France's expense. Parisian men may have also despised them because they were sexually inaccessible, whereas German men had wide access to French women. Many of the Little Gray Mice left Paris, where they had lived well, in tears. They were headed back, one Parisian noted, "to ruin, defeat, and death. I imagine that there has never been so awful a fate as to leave the beauty of France for the harshness of Germany." Beautiful France may still have been, but Paris was in a dire condition. Food remained more scarce than ever, the Métro had stopped working almost entirely, and some parts of the city received less than an hour of electricity a day. Terrible rumors, based upon German behavior at Oradur, Tulle, and elsewhere, were also flying around the city that the Germans were planning to use poison gas or special SS units to kill as many people as possible before they left.[24]

Anxiety led to action. On August 10, three days after the beginning of the Germans' Mortain counteroffensive, a new wave of strikes began that were aimed at disrupting German industrial production in Paris factories. Posters of de Gaulle and small tricolor flags also began to appear in the city as residents began to feel more comfortable expressing their hopes for liberation publicly. One Parisian took heart from the sight of a World War I veteran teaching a group of neighborhood kids to sing "(It's a Long Way to) Tipperary," a popular British soldier's song from that war, so they could properly welcome their liberators. From BBC Radio, meanwhile, Parisians learned that Leclerc's Deuxième Division Blindée was less than 150 miles away in Alençon. Perhaps most importantly, by August 14 the Paris police had all but disappeared from the city's streets. Charles Braibant wondered if the Germans had arrested the entire police force. "This is serious," he wrote. "No more screen between the brutes in the German military police and the population of Paris." In fact, thousands of policemen had decided not to work for the Germans any longer—a decision that would soon have crucial repercussions for the fate of the city, though not the ones that Braibant feared.[25]

Still unsure of when, if ever, the Allies would move toward Paris, Rol decided to take action. Knowing that the Germans were less in evidence on the streets of Paris, and that the police force was unlikely to stop FFI agents from carrying out attacks, Rol decided to become more aggressive. He was also aware of the massive German defeat at Falaise. He therefore issued new instructions to the FFI that began with the sentence, "The German debacle has begun." First, he ordered attacks on the "gangsters who abused their situations to serve themselves" at the expense of the people of Paris, a clear mandate to target collaborators and black marketeers. He also began planning for FFI takeovers of public buildings. He hoped to launch a general insurrection in Paris no later than August 18. Finally, he increased his contacts with the police, working to unite the four separate Resistance groups inside the force. He distributed an appeal from the FFI to the Paris police that read: "The hour of liberation has sounded. Many among you have already participated in the struggle against the invader. You should no longer participate in any activity that helps the enemy maintain order. Refuse to participate in the arrest of patriots, the searches of houses, the creation of checkpoints, identity checks, or prison guarding."[26]

Rol's message to the police was intended to limit their effectiveness as agents of the regime, but he also knew that the leaders of the Paris police Resistance groups were meeting to discuss a general strike in response to rumors that the Germans would react to their inactivity by ordering them to turn in their weapons. One way or another, he hoped, the police would tacitly, if not actively, aid the résistants.

But despite Rol's efforts to unite Parisians, the battle lines inside the Paris Resistance groups remained the same. Rol and the FFI leadership urged that an uprising was the only possible response to recent events, even if they had to act without help from the Allies. The possibility that the FFI might suffer terrible reprisals did not deter them. An uprising, Rol argued, would force the issue in the city and give Paris an opportunity to fight against its oppressors. The strikes and demonstrations of the past month had proven to Rol that the mass of the population would rally to the cause once an insurrection began. The approach of Allied armies and the obvious disorganization of German forces in the city made Rol think that the time had come. On August 14, he issued instructions to his men on the best ways to disable German tanks; his prewar training as an antitank gunner came in handy, if four years later than intended. His General Order #8 said: "The Paris region, a concentration point for enemy transportation, must multiply and intensify its efforts to render these assets unusable. Our operations must not only be considered as harassing or delaying actions destined to help the Allies to the west; they must equally be the first phase of the conquest of French territory by the FFI. . . . In this case, operations directed against the enemy's movements, transports, and communications must lead to his complete paralysis."[27] Rol thus showed that he intended the liberation of the city to be a means, not an end. French control of the capital was designed not just to evict the occupiers, but to deal them a military blow in the west from which they could not recover.

De Gaulle's representatives in Paris disagreed with Rol's calls for an uprising and sought to delay an insurrection until the Allies could arrive in force. Both Chaban, de Gaulle's military representative, and Alexandre Parodi, his political representative, argued with Rol that an insurrection was premature. If he waited, Allied forces could offer the FFI some protection against possible German retribution. Chaban had, in fact, just returned from a dangerous trip to London where he had urged de Gaulle to convince the Americans to drive on Paris. Failure to do so, he feared, would lead to a premature uprising in Paris that the Germans could easily destroy, with thousands of Parisians, both FFI members and innocent bystanders, at risk of being killed. De Gaulle, in no position to change the strategic thinking at Allied headquarters, urged Chaban to return to Paris and delay the insurrection as long as he could. The British also remained disinclined to support an uprising, ordering their few agents in the city not to assist any French Resistance attempts to rise against the Germans.[28]

De Gaulle, Chaban, and Parodi were afraid of what the Germans might do to Parisians who took up arms in an insurrection, but they were equally afraid of what might happen if the FFI members actually gained control of the city. If they did, they would undermine de Gaulle's claims to speak for France and possibly even resist the efforts of the provisional government to assume power once the Germans left. As one of de Gaulle's advisers warned him, "at the very minute the Germans leave, the communists will go back to their old tricks; they will try to take the levers of power for themselves." De Gaulle wrote: "[If the communists] establish a base of power in Paris, they will have an easy time establishing a government. . . . They can present themselves as the leaders of an insurrection and [form] a kind of commune. That such an insurrection in the capital would, for certain, lead to a power dominated by the Third International I have known for a long time."[29] Once again, the deadly specter of a civil war—like the one in 1871—raised its ugly head. The only way to prevent it, de Gaulle believed, was to get regular military forces into the city as quickly as possible.

The thought of the communists taking over as the Germans left terrified not just de Gaulle but many of the city's residents as well, especially those in the middle class and those who had collaborated with the German occupiers. As late as August 15, Parisian Jean Galtier-Boissière noted a desire among some middle-class residents for a return of Pétain to the city to keep power out of the hands of the FFI. Pétain, they hoped, might ensure a legal transfer of power from Vichy to the government that would follow, thus preventing the FFI from installing a commune by force of arms. A British war correspondent captured the same sentiment and later wrote that most Parisians whom she met "would have preferred to see the Germans marching out by an eastern gate while the Allies marched in through the Bois de Boulogne, without any interlude in which disheveled youths from the [working-class] St. Antoine quarter roamed the placid streets of [middle-class] Passy, with FFI brassards on their arms and no safety catches on their rifles."[30]

The collaborationist and anti-Semitic writer Paul Léautaud called the FFI "a gang of Apaches," a reference to the groups of loosely organized street criminals that had plagued Paris in the prewar years. These new Apaches, he feared, were not interested in selling drugs or petty larceny, but in leading a "bloody hunting party" for collaborationists like him. He was right to worry, as his name was indeed on an FFI list of people to be arrested.[31]

Fear of open hostilities with the Germans thus competed in Paris in the middle of August with fears of an imminent civil war. The collaborationist Clara Longworth de Chambrun thought (incorrectly) that the Paris police were intimidated by the FFI into staying off the streets in order to pave the way for what she called "mob rule" once the Germans had left. An FFI takeover would then lead, she feared, to circumstances that would make the Reign of Terror during the French Revolution look like "an inconsiderable disturbance." Like many collaborationists, she was still willing to support Vichy out of her fear that the FFI was planning "a veritable orgy of violence, disorder, and rapine" against collaborators and members of the middle class like herself. Only the intervention of Pétain or the arrival of an Allied army into the city, she thought, could prevent the calamity of a communist takeover.[32]

The end, however, was clearly coming for Pétain and his collaborationist regime. Starting on August 6, the collaborationist and anti-Semitic writer Marcel Jouhandeau began receiving threatening phone calls daily. They were all from the same man, who said, "The day of your execution is close." The calls continued for two weeks until finally the man told him, "The day of your execution is here." Jouhandeau then hid at a friend's house rather than risk leaving the city. Three days later, the phone rang at the friend's house and the same voice said, "We know exactly where you are hiding." Another friend of Jouhandeau's, a collaborationist factory owner, gave his chauffeur a pistol with orders to shoot him rather than let him fall into the hands of the FFI.[33]

Anxious and even terrified though many people were behind closed doors, on the streets the atmosphere of the city remained surprisingly tranquil. The famous French writers Simone de Beauvoir and Jean-Paul Sartre, who had links to the Resistance, had been hiding outside the city. On August 11 they decided to sneak back into Paris in order not to miss the momentous events they expected to unfold in the coming days. They had heard that advance elements of the Allied armies were less than seventy miles away at Chartres, and thus they expected to find a markedly different Paris from the one they had left a few weeks earlier. Yet despite the "discreet departures of some German officers," they found the city calm and little changed almost everywhere they went.[34]

Part of that calm might have been due to fear. Most residents assumed that the Resistance could do little to liberate the city until the Allies made a show of force near Paris. The question "Où sont-ils?" ("Where are they?") was on everyone's lips. Unlike Beauvoir and Sartre, Parisian resident Louis Chavet had no idea where those Allied armies were. He did know that even commodities that were once common, such as candles, were getting hard to find on the black market. On August 14, the Germans cut the bread ration again, from 300 grams to just 100 grams. They also closed the Métro altogether. Alexandre Arnoux, another Parisian with no knowledge of the location of the Allies, was thrilled to see a poster in the city carrying de Gaulle's signature and bearing the "uplifting and surprising" words, "Gouvernement Provisoire de la République Française." Still, he recorded in his journal that night: "Where are the Allies? Are they going to move around Paris? Will they leave us here to die?"[35]

Food and the potential of famine haunted the residents. If the Allies decided to encircle and besiege the city, thousands would die of starvation. The Germans were already taking as much food out of the city as they could, and supplies from the countryside had all but stopped. A prolonged battle or siege would create a humanitarian crisis on a massive scale. Once again, memories of 1871, when the city's residents had sometimes been reduced to eating rats, came back to haunt Parisians.

Contributing even more to the fear of Parisians was their knowledge of the awful fate of Warsaw, another European capital that had tried to liberate itself around the same time. The journals and diaries of Parisians show that they were fully aware of what was happening in Warsaw, and the events in Poland terrified them. Parisians first learned of the uprising in Warsaw in August, as Russian troops approached the Polish capital. Rather than enter the city, the Russians had halted, leaving the residents of Warsaw dangerously exposed to savage German reprisals from both the regular army and the SS. The battle for Warsaw lasted for sixty-three days. By the time it was over, one-quarter of Warsaw's buildings had been destroyed, and as many as 200,000 civilians had been killed, most by German execution. The Soviets, reluctant to help the anticommunist leadership of the Polish Home Army, had been willing to see the Poles massacred.

The omens for Paris, which also had an Allied army just outside city lines, were chilling. In this case, the political situation was reversed, with the Resistance inside the city being led largely by communists and the outside army being noncommunist, but the danger was largely the same. If the FFI ordered an uprising and the Allies refused to help Paris, just as the Russians had refused to help Warsaw, the results would be calamitous, especially given what Parisians knew about German reprisals in Oradur, Tulle, Vercors, and elsewhere. Throughout June and July, Parisians had held out the hope that they might share the fate of Rome, which had been evacuated by the Germans and taken by the Allies with little bloodshed. The charnel house that Warsaw had become, however, presented another, far more horrifying, possible future for Paris.

Warsaw's fate was an especially terrible omen to Andrzej Bobkowski, a native Pole who had been in Paris since 1939, when the outbreak of war had interrupted his plans to work and study in South America. Thereafter he and his wife had been cut off from his homeland in a Paris dominated by two ideologies that he detested, Vichy France's fascism and the communism prevalent in elements of the French working class. Observing events in Poland through the BBC and clandestine newspapers, he perceptively saw that the Warsaw Rising had been a strategically meaningless event. It had done little except kill the future leaders of Poland, paving the way for the Soviets to run his homeland after the war. "Warsaw is a hell," he recorded in his journal on August 7. "Everyone is fighting and the Russians are just watching it all happen. After the Germans have massacred the entire Polish population, the Russians can occupy the city." Warsaw, he noted with sadness, was a victim of "too much heroism."[36]

Bobkowski's conclusions were widespread. Most Parisians saw the "Warsaw Rising" as brave but ultimately pointless. While almost all Parisians admired the courage of the Warsaw Home Army, few wanted the French Resistance to imitate it. The thought of Paris turning into Warsaw or Stalingrad was too much for most residents to contemplate, and yet the possibility of such an outcome was terrifyingly close. Chaban had warned the British on his daring trip to London that "if you want Paris to become another Warsaw you have only to continue your policy." Just outside the city, a young officer in the Deuxième Division Blindée who had lived in Germany before the war—and had seen the Nazi danger firsthand—thought that events in Warsaw were reason enough for the Allies to change their plans and drive onto Paris as quickly as possible. Captain Raymond Dronne, whose role in the liberation of the city later vaulted him to a seat in the French Senate, thought that "if they [the Germans] were reserving for Paris the fate that they were imposing on Warsaw," then the soldiers of the Deuxième Division Blindée had a moral obligation to liberate the city, with or without the Americans by their side. Not for nothing was Leclerc hoarding gasoline for his tanks and trucks.[37]

Although most Parisians drew the same conclusions from Warsaw's terrible precedent, they had differing interpretations. For collaborationists and Paris city officials, Warsaw was a grim specter of what happened when civilians took up armed struggle. Pierre Taittinger later justified his close working relationship with Choltitz by saying that the two had to work together so that Paris "might, above all, avoid the fate of Warsaw." But if Warsaw held out the terrifying possibility that Paris might be destroyed in the very act of its liberation, the thought did not intimidate everyone. Alexandre Parodi, de Gaulle's political representative in Paris, later wrote that "the fate of Warsaw has, since [1944] shown us how much this might have cost." Still, he noted, "the risk was known and taken."[38]

Like the residents of Warsaw, the members of the FFI and countless thousands of other Parisians were unwilling to stand by any longer. As Léo Hamon, editor of the clandestine communist newspaper *Combat* and one of the bravest Resistance fighters in the city, noted, "Parisians cannot sit like passive spectators at their own deliverance." The Allies were approaching, but no one knew whether they planned to fight for the city, bypass it, or besiege it. As Parisians went to sleep on August 14, their deliverance was anything but certain. Nor did anyone know where that liberation might lead or how much it might cost in blood. But Parisians were increasingly steeling themselves to try to regain their freedom and their city with or without the help of the Allies. The city was approaching an insurrection. All that was missing was a spark.[39]

5

THE GUNS GO OFF, AUGUST 15–18

WRITING OF ANOTHER LANDMARK PERIOD IN PARISIAN history, Victor Hugo had once observed that "the great city is like a piece of artillery. When it is loaded, a spark need only fall and the gun goes off." The angst and anger of Paris's residents had been developing for years, as it had been in the buildup to the 1832 revolution that Hugo described in his novel *Les Misérables*. But without a catalyst, the city's explosive tensions had stayed pent up even as the pressure mounted.

The spark that lit the guns of insurrection in Paris during the hot days of mid-August 1944 came from a surprising and unlikely source: the Paris police. Reviled by many of the city's residents for the dirty work they had done assisting the Germans and Vichy officials, the police were soon to rescue their reputation. That reputation had been badly tarnished by years of collaboration. In 1940, the police had moved seamlessly from serving the French Republic to serving the German occupiers, doing some of the regime's dirtiest work, most notoriously during the roundups that led to the virtual disappearance of Paris's Jewish community. The police had also been instrumental in the arrests of anti-Vichy political activists and in forcing compliance with the labor conscription system. Enforcing the laws of the occupiers did not endear the police to the population of Paris. Like most Parisians, however, the city's police officers saw little choice but to accept the authority of the new regime, especially once Vichy assumed the legal mantle of the French state.[1]

But there was another, if much less obvious, side to the Paris police. As their fellow countrymen became increasingly disillusioned with Vichy after 1942, so, too, did many members of the police force. By spring 1944, perhaps as many as one in ten members of the police force belonged to one of three major police Resistance groups. These groups, of course, operated under the strictest silence. They were further hampered in their activities by internal divisions. Recruitment was furtive, with police officers carefully approaching comrades who might share their political views. They had good reason to be secretive: The constant presence of unsympathetic officers and the looming shadows of the Gestapo made the organization of Resistance activities within the police force extremely dangerous.

Nevertheless, some police officers were willing to take the risks. As events later showed, even if only one in ten members was an active member of a Resistance group, there was a large reservoir of support inside the force for their activities. Like the Resistance more generally, the three police Resistance groups were based around political affiliations. The Gaullist Honneur de la Police, with around 400 members, was the first group formed and was the best organized. It contained most of the high-ranking police Resistance leaders, a factor that proved to be critically important in the crucial days of August. The socialist Police et Patrie, which represented 250 police officers and 400 nonuniformed police employees, had been the most active group, specializing in providing identity cards and passports to résistants and escaped prisoners. These documents carried false names but were in every other way genuine, coming as they did from the police themselves. As such, they were critically important to the Resistance movement. The largest of the groups was the communist-influenced Front National de la Police, with almost 800 active members and many more sympathizers within the force. It was part of a much larger movement inside Paris directed and led by the French Communist Party. Its close links to the communists made it suspect in the eyes of the other two groups, some of whose members feared it might be the armed vanguard of a future communist coup d'état.

Although they shared many common goals, political differences led to much mutual suspicion between the police Resistance groups in the tense and murky world of occupied Paris. All of the police groups, moreover, ran the risk of being infiltrated by the Gestapo or by French fascist groups like the paramilitary Milice. Each group also feared infiltration and double-crossing by one of the others. Still, each brought its own strengths to the movement to oust the Germans and the Vichy-led administration of Paris. As a result of these fears and the natural secrecy that surrounded the Resistance movement, the three police groups had worked carefully behind the scenes, but had not fused together.

Mutual suspicions and fears notwithstanding, there were a few linkages between the police and the leadership of the Resistance more generally. Over the years of the occupation, the leaders of the French Resistance had urged policemen who opposed the occupiers to remain on the job. The Resistance saw the obvious value of having some police officers working clandestinely on the side of the people of Paris, even if those same policemen had to simultaneously carry out some of the more odious orders they received from the Germans and Vichy. As a result, the leaders of the French Resistance advised the police to "disobey orders intelligently," meaning that they were to act with all due caution and even to look the other way when French patriots committed acts of resistance, but were to do nothing that would attract suspicion or reveal their true political leanings. To do so might bring interrogation and the end of the clandestine police networks the Resistance was then trying to establish. These efforts seemed to pay important dividends. As early as August 1943, the Germans had begun to acknowledge that the Paris police were no longer fully reliable.[2]

The untrustworthiness of the Paris police to its German and Vichy masters grew throughout 1944. The behavior of the police during the strikes of July 14, inspiring calls from the crowd of "La police avec nous!" ("The police are with us!"), had not been an isolated incident, as the police had virtually stopped monitoring the activities of Resistance groups. They had also looked the other way when Resistance figures in the city committed nonviolent acts of opposition, such as posting notices and organizing demonstrations. In some working-class neighborhoods, it was even possible by spring 1944 for Resistance members to meet in cafés that the police were known to intentionally avoid.

Some police officers did more than take a passive attitude toward the Resistance. Many members of the police Resistance groups had begun monitoring Gestapo activity and taking careful note of the German Army's defensive positions. The police were the only Frenchmen allowed on the streets at night, giving them a rare and strategically important opportunity to observe the Germans. As a result, the police became a critical source of badly needed intelligence on the comings and goings of the Germans and of Vichy officials.

Still, on the surface the police continued to work with the Germans and Vichy, mainly out of fear of being arrested or disarmed. Most police officers still took their orders from the occupiers; they played the enabling role in the deportation of hundreds of Jews (including many children) to Drancy on July 31, 1942, following the horrific Vel d'Hiv roundup of July 16 and 17. The clandestine communist newspaper *L'Humanité* was concerned enough about the role of the police in supporting the regime to note, in late June, that "if, by lack of courage or lack of patriotic conscience[,] the police remain in the service of (Joseph) Darnard [the widely despised leader of the Milice] they will be committing a crime against the Fatherland for which there will be a settling of scores." Nevertheless, it is clear that a change of heart had begun to occur among many police officers who, as one of them noted, "were against the Germans and only waited for the chance to settle some scores." Others stayed on the job out of a sense of duty (the Paris police had never in its history gone on strike) or out of a belief that they served as a shield between the people of Paris and the German and Vichy security forces. Some police therefore followed the thinking of the Vichy prefect of police, Amédée Bussières, who told his officers, with typical collaborationist logic, "Imagine what will happen if the Gestapo or the Milice takes your place." Or, as another police officer noted, "to resist by night, we had to collaborate by day."[3]

All three police Resistance groups had ties of varying kinds to Charles de Gaulle's political allies in Algiers and London. De Gaulle and his advisers had known of the resistance sentiments inside the police and had counted them as a political asset since at least the middle of 1943. De Gaulle expected the Paris police to provide most of the security for the city after the German departure, thus avoiding the need for a postliberation government to rely upon FFI agents, who were not government employees, for policing. If de Gaulle did not want the untrained and politically unreliable FFI in control of the city's security, he also did not want the Allied armies to assume responsibility for policing Paris. Neither owed any loyalty to his provisional government, meaning that they could not form a critical foundation for the security of a future French state. Nor would either necessarily respond to his leadership. He preferred to keep the Paris police on the job, but he knew that for the police to have any legitimacy after the war they would need to gain at least some modicum of trust from the people of Paris.

How the police responded to the coming crisis would therefore determine much of the future of the liberation. The Resistance leaders who favored a general uprising hoped to convince the police to join their efforts, or at the very least not interrupt them. Rol addressed a meeting of about a dozen police Resistance leaders on August 14 in response to a German decision to disarm the police in two Paris suburbs, St. Denis and Asnières, because of the refusal of the police to put down strikes. Police officers in both places pledged to go on strike themselves unless the Germans reversed the disarmament order.

Events in the suburbs foreshadowed a possible confrontation between the police and the Germans in Paris itself. For more than a month, Rol, the police, and Roland Pré, a senior Gaullist agent living in Paris, had envisioned just such a scenario. They knew that if the Germans threatened to disarm the Paris police, the situation in the capital, where France's largest police force resided, would be much more serious than that in two relatively unimportant suburbs. Now the events in St. Denis and Asnières, combined with the widespread disappearance of Paris policemen from the city's streets, had made the disarmament of the Paris police a distinct possibility, leading Rol to arrange a meeting of the representatives of the police Resistance groups.

The debates inside the police Resistance groups mirrored those inside the Resistance more generally. Rol and the Front National de la Police leadership argued passionately that the police could not allow themselves to be disarmed, even at the risk of a direct confrontation with the Germans. They must, Rol contended, go on strike instead, both to ensure that they did not find themselves without weapons at the crucial moment and to inspire the population of Paris. A police strike would show the entire city that the police, at long last, were actively and unquestionably on their side. Most importantly, the lack of a police presence on the streets would signal to the FFI that they could step up their efforts against the occupiers without police interference. The most radical members of the police Resistance threw their full weight behind Rol's plan; the Front National leaders went as far as to urge that any police officer who did not honor the strike be tarred as a traitor.

Both the idea of a general strike and the harsh tone of the Front National scared the members of Honneur de la Police, the much more moderate Gaullist group. They argued that the Front National's overheated rhetoric threatened to split the police Resistance movement in two at the very moment that it most needed unity. More importantly, they, like Parodi and Chaban, thought a general strike premature unless and until Allied armies could provide direct assistance. Otherwise, they feared that the Germans still had enough combat power in the city to arrest or kill them in large numbers. The leaders of the socialist Police et Patrie also urged caution, arguing that they could not be responsible for starting a strike that might lead to Paris becoming another Warsaw.[4]

Rol broke the logjam, arguing that the other groups would be left behind if they did not follow the lead of the Front National. Implied in Rol's argument was the notion that the Front National, and the Communist Party to which it was closely connected, would get the credit for leading the people of Paris out of their misery while the other groups, and the police more generally, remained blackened by their direct association with the Germans and Vichy. After some heated debate, the three groups agreed to distribute leaflets with printing on both sides: on one side, an appeal by the FFI for a strike, and on the other, a similar appeal by the Paris police Resistance groups. The objective was to show the unity of the Resistance generally and the police in this critical hour. Although there had been debate about the exact wording of the leaflets, the FFI appeal did in the end include strong language warning any police officers who failed to honor the strike that they would be seen as traitors and treated as such. The leaflets soon took their place among others calling for resistance on the city's many kiosks as well as on walls and park benches. "For the final combat," they read, "everyone must go forward with the people of Paris." That night, messages appeared at every Parisian police station that read, "No police officer shall allow himself to be disarmed or become the target of any coercive measure whatsoever."[5]

Bussières, the prefect of police, urged his policemen to ignore the telegrams and stay on the job. "Will you abandon your responsibilities to the people of Paris at the hour when our hopes may soon be realized?" he asked his men in a message sent to all police stations in the city. "Will you fail to be there at the moment that the Anglo-American armies arrive at the gates of Paris?" Even though the last part of the message seemed to point toward a time when the police would no longer need to obey the Germans or Vichy, it was clear from the behavior of the police that Bussières had lost the confidence and faith of his force.

The rapidly spreading police strike sent the immediate message to other Resistance groups that they could now operate more freely throughout the city. Among their sympathizers were the city's printers, members of one of the most pro-Resistance of professions. Having worked carefully and quietly behind the scenes for years to print clandestine newspapers, the printers could now begin to flood the city with newspapers and leaflets designed to extend the police strike throughout the entire city. Cooperating police officers sped around Paris through the night to post leaflets on the walls of neighborhood police stations, known as *commissariats*. Word also spread like wildfire by word of mouth. The printers then stopped publishing collaborationist newspapers, which disappeared immediately, sending another clear message that the days of Vichy were numbered.

The next morning, August 15, Parisians awoke to a strange, unprecedented sight: The streets were empty of policemen. All but a small handful of the city's 15,000 police officers had obeyed the call to strike, an indication of the depth of anti-German feeling that the police had harbored despite their history of collaboration. The strike had been flawlessly executed, with police officers taking the time to remove and hide weapons stored inside their commissariats in order to keep them out of German hands. While some policemen began to picket outside their commissariats in civilian clothes, others worked to encourage their fellow public-sector employees inside the city to join the general strike. Meanwhile, the FFI took advantage of the situation to begin moving around the city openly, often sporting armbands with the widely recognizable Cross of Lorraine, the symbol of Free France.

The German reaction to these developments was surprisingly tame and slow. Part of the reason may be that Choltitz had been away from the city on August 15, attending a conference at Seventh Army headquarters. At that conference, he and his commanding officer, Guenther von Kluge, agreed that the Germans could not hold the city for much longer. They were thinking in terms of external, not internal, threats. Choltitz did, however, present an intelligence estimate suggesting that the FFI would likely begin an uprising as soon as Allied forces arrived near the city. He argued that he had far too few resources to deal with simultaneous external and internal threats to Paris.

Choltitz's immediate response to the police strike reflected these limitations. Knowing how thin his forces were, he opted for purely symbolic measures to counteract the strike, including the parading of German units through the city on their way to and from the front. He wanted to show the residents of Paris "the number of troops that were still available at this late hour," even if most of them did not remain in the city for long. On the day the strikes began, Choltitz also issued an order for three thousand political prisoners to be assembled at the Pantin train station, located near the slaughterhouses of the La Villette neighborhood and known to Parisians as the animal platform. From there, the Germans dispatched the prisoners to the Buchenwald and Ravensbrück concentration camps in cattle wagons; half of the deportees died within a year. Choltitz hoped that this show of force, combined with new defensive measures for German strongpoints, would suffice to keep order in the city for a few more weeks, by which time the Germans would have either abandoned the city or seen some dramatic reversal of their fortunes.[6]

Choltitz also ordered that more repressive measures be taken inside Paris. Although he and Kluge had discounted the military utility of damaging the city's infrastructure, there were still ways that the Germans could make life even more unpleasant than it already was for its residents. Parisians were by now living largely without bread and had just a few minutes of electricity per day. On the night of August 15, German authorities announced that they could not assure the city of even its current levels of food, water, gas, or electricity in the event of an uprising. "It is the innocents who will pay for the crimes of the guilty," the announcement read. Choltitz also ordered the city's curfew moved up one hour and established more roadblocks and identity checkpoints. But despite these threats and new restrictions on Parisians' mobility, there is no evidence that he saw the strike by the Paris police as a serious crisis or the start of an actual uprising. Choltitz's description of the Paris police at an August 15 staff meeting as "weak" may indicate that he saw the police as unreliable and ineffective but not necessarily a threat to German interests.[7]

More importantly to Choltitz, on the same day that the Paris police strike began, the police strikes in St. Denis and Asnières ended peacefully. Vichy authorities had worked behind the scenes to keep the police in these industrial suburbs on the streets, pressuring the police to return to work while also convincing the Germans that a police presence on the streets of St. Denis and Asnières served everyone's interests. They then issued a statement saying that the strikes had been the result of a miscommunication in orders between the police and the German Army. Although the statement fooled no one, it allowed all sides to save face. The Germans undoubtedly hoped to find a similar solution to the much more important strike of the Paris police. They were correct to think that the police might go back to work, for even as they began to strike many members of the Paris police had reservations about exposing themselves and the people of Paris to the Milice and the Gestapo. Even Rol feared that the police might end their strike if the Germans offered to negotiate.[8]

But a solution for Paris along the lines of the one in St. Denis and Asnières was not possible. Paris was not the suburbs, and the police strike inside the city had much deeper symbolism and more significant political ramifications than the strikes outside the city. Once begun, moreover, the Paris police strike had too much momentum for it to end by negotiation. Raoul Nordling, the Swedish consul, noted that "the situation inside Paris was entirely transformed in the space of a few hours" by the strike. A strike meant that final battle lines were being drawn. Like so many Parisians, Nordling wondered if the strike presaged even more momentous events or if it would provoke a savage German reaction. "We knew that somewhere in the shadows great events were transpiring that could perhaps unleash rivers of blood," he wrote. The possibility that one or both sides might see in the police strike a cause for a final showdown of arms scared Parisians even as they understood that the strike might help to speed up their liberation.[9]

Without a working police force, Paris was a nervous and anxious place. Even those groups that had traditionally had tense relations with the police saw their sudden absence from the streets as a sign that anarchy, revolution, or disorder might not be far behind. Furthermore, the police had given little indication as to whether they saw their strike as the start of an insurrection, as Rol hoped, or merely as a temporary statement of opposition to plans to disarm them, as the Germans hoped. Gilles Perrault, a teenager not well disposed toward the police, was among those who were confused by the turn of events. In his eyes, he wrote later, the police were "precisely those who had been for so long the docile henchmen of the enemy, the Jew hunters, and Resistance trackers." He wondered what was truly motivating them: "Opportunism? [A] last minute *volte-face*?" He would not have to wait much longer to find out.[10]

Neither would the collaborationists have long to wait. They understood clearly that the lack of an effective police force put them at even greater risk in the event of an uprising inside the city. Jean Galtier-Boissière noted in his journal on August 15 that the collaborationists were "starting to get scared" as the FFI became more visible and more assertive. If the FFI's tricolored brassards with the Cross of Lorraine inspired some Parisians, they terrified others, who saw in them an armed mob waiting to exact their revenge. If the Paris police could not maintain order, the collaborationists would need to find a new protector.

The absence of a police presence gave the Resistance new opportunities. It also changed the dynamic on the streets, as the Germans lost a critical source of information and muscle. In the words of Maurice Kriegel-Valrimont, "fear changed sides." Without a pliant or complicit police force on their side, Kriegel-Valrimont reflected, the Germans were stuck in a "trap that they could not escape." Neither could they move around safely, choosing instead to hunker down at their thirty-six strongpoints across the city. The initiative was rapidly passing from the Germans to the FFI, seemingly without Choltitz and his staff taking notice of it.[11]

The changes were evident almost immediately. The city's printers, working full-time for the Resistance since the start of the strike, began to mass-produce leaflets written by Rol and his FFI agents. They urged Parisians to take advantage of the absence of police on the streets by demonstrating and striking. In this way, Rol hoped, the police strike might lead to a more general uprising. The leaflets appeared in cafés, in offices, and on the walls of buildings. For most Parisians it was their first exposure to the name Rol. "People stop themselves and read these seditious writings in the streets," Galtier-Boissière noted with some surprise. For the first time in four years, no police officer or German was there to watch them as they did so. Conversations in cafés also grew more daring and more open. Resistance cells all across the city now held their meetings in public places instead of in cramped apartments with the shutters tightly drawn and voices held to a low whisper.[12]

The FFI's most pressing problem remained a lack of weapons. Although numbers are nearly impossible to assess with certainty, it appears that the FFI had around 165 light machine guns and submachine guns, 550 rifles, 825 pistols, and 200 grenades. The rifles and pistols, gathered from a wide variety of sources, fired a dizzying number of calibers, presenting a supply problem that would have challenged any regular army. Many of these weapons, moreover, were in poor condition, and no one had enough ammunition. Without weapons, the FFI had little hope of fighting against German soldiers, who were well protected in their strongpoints and supported by armored cars and tanks. The Allies, moreover, continued to show little interest in the fate of Paris. There were still no arms drops into the city, and the actions of the Allied armies from the August 15 to 18 continued to suggest that they would bypass the city to the north and south. An announcement on BBC Radio that the liberation of Paris was near struck most residents as scant compensation for the continued lack of material help.[13]

The police strike therefore represented more than a symbolic change to the delicate balance of power within Paris. As the Germans well knew, the police had access to vital intelligence. They were the only group in Paris that could effectively control the city in the absence of either the Germans or the Allies. They also had access to weapons, including rifles, pistols, and ammunition. Each commissariat contained small arms caches, but the main armory sat inside the imposing prefecture on the Île de la Cité. The strike kept those weapons out of the hands of the Germans, who likely didn't need them in any case, but few police officers were willing to transfer weapons to the FFI yet, despite pleas from Rol and others. The German decision not to try to force the issue with the Paris police may have been motivated by a belief that it was far better to have the police on strike, but still politically neutral, than to risk pushing them over to the side of the Resistance.[14]

By the morning of August 16, virtually the entire Paris police force was on strike, preparing to defend their commissariats in civilian clothes. Their behavior remained hard for the Germans to read. Although they refused to go to work, they were also careful not to show an outwardly anti-German attitude, as long as the Germans did not try to use force against them. There remained little indication that the strike was going to be the start of a general insurrection. Parisians who recorded their impressions of the police remained rather cynical, seeing in the police behavior an attempt to clear their names and save their skins before the departure of the Germans left them exposed to retribution and punishment from the people whom they had so recently oppressed.[15]

The police strike inspired strikes in other public sectors, however, indicating that at least some Parisians saw more lofty motivations for the police. On August 16, workers for the telephone and telegraph company, the Métro, and the French railway company all went on strike as well. These strikes had less direct impact on Parisians than they did on the Germans, as the Métro, owing to power shortages, had largely ceased operating anyway. Few French people had been able to ride on trains anymore in any case because the Germans had almost completely taken over the Paris railway network. These strikes were therefore mostly political in nature, aimed as they were at paralyzing the German military presence in Paris. The strike wave soon spread, eventually resulting in as many as 60 percent of Paris's workers refusing to go to work.[16]

The strikes of August 15 and 16 gave new impetus and momentum to those in the FFI, who urged their fellow résistants to be bolder. Although Resistance members had taken to meeting and displaying their sympathies in public, they had yet to mount a direct challenge to the Germans. Rol and the FFI leadership met on the night of August 16 with Chaban and Parodi to announce plans for seizure of public buildings and the beginning of a general insurrection on August 18 or 19. But Chaban urged the FFI to wait, warning Rol that the Allies might not arrive in Paris for several weeks. He wanted the FFI to postpone its uprising until he could make one more effort to convince de Gaulle to lean on the Americans to change their minds and drive on Paris. Otherwise, Paris could become a battleground like Warsaw if the Germans decided to fight. The contentious meeting ended without a final decision but with Rol stating clearly that he was willing to risk a major uprising with or without help from the Allies.[17]

The German response to the strike and the new mood in the city remained curiously muted, showing a clear lack of initiative from Choltitz and his headquarters. Once again, a shakeup at the highest levels of the German Army in France played a critical role in the city's fate. On August 17, Walter Model, a devoted Nazi and one of Germany's best defensive generals, replaced Kluge as head of German forces in France. A favorite of Hitler's, Model had stabilized the situation on the eastern front following the Russian breakthrough in June. He arrived in France just as the situation in the Falaise pocket was approaching its bloody dénouement. At first he hoped to turn the defeat at Falaise into a victory, but he quickly realized that he had no choice but to use his connections to Hitler to convince the German high command that an evacuation of German forces out of the pocket was the only logical course of action.[18]

Like his Allied counterparts, Model gave little thought to Paris, which struck him as far less important than the ongoing calamity at Falaise. He accordingly devoted most of his attention to trying to rescue as many men as he could before the Allies sealed the gap. Paris received only a small part of his attention. Model argued that he needed 200,000 men and several tank divisions to have any hope of holding Paris against a determined attack, resources that he knew were not available. His demands might have been his way to communicate to Hitler how unrealistic it was for the German high command to hold on to the hope of keeping Paris. He also told Choltitz that although he still envisioned demolishing large parts of Paris rather than leave the city intact for the British and Americans, he wanted him to suspend all demolition work until he had evaluated the situation. The order came as a relief to Choltitz, who knew that he did not have the resources on hand for the kind of widespread demolitions that Model envisioned and Hitler demanded. It also freed him from the awkward possibility of having to destroy the city while he still thought such a measure to be unnecessary. Choltitz could now respond to critics of his lack of action in Paris that he was only following orders. Given Model's preoccupation with Falaise, any further orders might be a long time in coming, permitting Choltitz wide latitude inside the city.[19]

But if the Germans were moving slowly, others were moving quickly. Foremost among them was the most widely respected diplomat in the city, the Swedish consul Raoul Nordling. Sixty-three years old, but looking worn and tired because of heart problems, Nordling had spent virtually his entire life in Paris and thought of the city as home. He had been born there, and his father had run a successful paper company in the city. Returning to Sweden only for short visits and to complete his mandatory military service, Nordling spoke better French than Swedish and had married a Parisian woman. By 1905 he had been living full-time in Paris, helping to run his father's company and serving as Swedish vice-consul. Twelve years later, in the midst of another war between Germany and France, he was promoted to consul, completing a meteoric rise in the diplomatic arena.

Like most other diplomats from neutral countries, Nordling had spent the early years of the occupation trying to secure contracts for his country's firms, including his family's own impressive industrial holdings. By summer 1944, however, he had reached the conclusion that Germany would soon lose the war and that the German deportation of French political prisoners would result in the future leadership of France dying needlessly in concentration camps. On August 6, he had gone to the prison at Fresnes to try to help a friend who was about to be deported. The sight of so many young Frenchmen imprisoned and perhaps about to be murdered merely for their political beliefs convinced Nordling that he, and perhaps he alone, could save thousands of people from a pointless death.[20]

Nordling at first sought the intervention of Otto Abetz, the German chief diplomat in France. Like Nordling, Abetz had long-standing ties to France, including an aristocratic French wife. Abetz's close association to France dated back to the 1920s, when he had helped to form a Franco-German social group dedicated to repairing links between the two nations after World War I. He had initially cut his teeth in left-leaning politics in France and Germany, but like many other ambitious Germans in the early 1930s, he saw the benefits of moving into Nazi circles. He also made important contacts with some of France's leading fascists, many of whom later became collaborators. He had been expelled from France shortly after the Munich Conference (where he had served as a German adviser on France) on the charge of bribing French newspapers to write positive stories about Germany, but he had returned after the German conquest in 1940. His first assignment was to catalog and seize artistic treasures in Paris coveted by the German Foreign Office, but he soon moved on to more sinister roles. He was, for example, instrumental in the implementation of anti-Semitic policies in the occupied zone.

Tall, well-dressed, and affable on the surface, Abetz was, like many other Nazis, able to cover the brutality of his views with a veneer of gentility that fooled those who were willing to buy into his lies. He and his wife, whom the French executed in 1946 (after Abetz himself had returned to Germany), helped to direct the rather lenient occupation policies of the first years of the war. By 1944, however, Abetz had become enraged at the FFI and the Resistance; he believed that France should have been grateful to him, and to the collaborationists with whom he worked, for sparing France the fate of the conquered countries of the east. He saw all Resistance members as terrorists and at one point recommended burning down the École Normale (which trained teachers and had produced a number of résistants) because he saw it as a "school of assassins." By August, his genteel veneer had largely faded, revealing only the baleful soul of a man willing to kill thousands for a lost cause.[21]

Nordling had hoped that, by appealing to Abetz's love for France, he could convince him to authorize the release of some of the prisoners at Fresnes and elsewhere, but he found little in Abetz's demeanor to encourage him. Abetz told Nordling that because of the German Army's transportation difficulties, he could not move the prisoners out of Paris. Nordling then asked Abetz to release the prisoners from their squalid jails, but Abetz chillingly turned him down. "There is nothing left to do but kill them all," he said. Abetz did finally propose to Nordling that he might be willing to exchange French prisoners for German POWs in Allied hands at a ratio of one to five, but Nordling had no authority to make such a deal and no way to implement it even if he could get an agreement from all parties. Under the circumstances, Abetz must have known that no diplomat could have arranged such a deal.[22]

Having failed with Abetz, Nordling then went to see Choltitz, who proved to be far more accommodating. Although Choltitz shared

Abetz's view of the FFI and the Resistance as terrorists, he seems to have recognized that many of the prisoners Nordling sought to free were in jail simply for their beliefs, not for any overt or violent act committed against Germans. Choltitz also undoubtedly saw the value in making a positive gesture toward the people of Paris. He therefore agreed to release three thousand prisoners on two conditions: that none of them were members of the FFI and that Nordling would assume responsibility for their behavior. Nordling agreed, likely saving their lives (for, despite Abetz's claims about transportation difficulties, deportations to the death camps did continue). Perhaps more importantly, Nordling and Choltitz had begun to build a professional relationship that would soon have dramatic impacts on Paris.

Abetz left Paris soon after his meeting with Nordling, joining a growing eastward tide. Seeing the writing on the wall for the Vichy regime and understanding that the departure of the Germans would expose collaborationists to vicious reprisals by the FFI, the rats began to flee the sinking ship. Among the most notorious was Pierre Laval, the Vichy state's prime minister. Hoping to save his own skin and the Vichy regime he had helped to lead, Laval came to Paris on August 17 on the pretense of holding a meeting of cabinet officials based in the city. In reality, he was trying to hatch a frantic scheme under which he could transfer power to a new French figurehead who would then negotiate with the Americans as a new Italian government had done the previous year. Laval saw himself in the role of Marshal Pietro Badoglio, the Italian soldier whose deal with the Allies had allowed him to keep power for nine months after the fall of Mussolini. The Vichy leader hoped both to keep de Gaulle out of power and to protect himself from retribution.

Laval, who had no political clout with the Allies, knew that he needed a nonfascist figurehead to lead the negotiating on his behalf. The man he chose to lead this desperate gambit was Edouard Herriot, a three-time prewar prime minister of France who had been serving as mayor of Lyon when the Germans invaded in 1940. After the invasion, the Vichy authorities put him under virtual house arrest, then formally imprisoned him. Laval ordered Herriot, whose distrust of de Gaulle was well known, to be released from his jail cell and brought to Paris. When the two men met on August 17, Laval explained his scheme. Herriot exploded at Laval in an understandable fit of anger. He was being asked to rescue the same regime that had kept him imprisoned for four years.

Pétain, like Laval, tried to save himself, working from Vichy to contact de Gaulle through intermediaries in the hopes of making an arrangement to transfer power through the legal mechanism of Vichy. De Gaulle, who never saw the Vichy regime as legitimate, rejected all notions of negotiation. Given his links to the powerful Allied armies, it was a position he could take with confidence.

All of these self-serving plans by Vichy leaders came quickly to naught, only serving to reinforce German fears that their erstwhile French allies were trying to sell them out or trick them. The Germans arrested Laval on the evening of August 17, shortly after his failed meeting with Herriot, and sent him to Germany, ostensibly for his own protection. Pétain, "invited" to leave France by his German masters, soon joined Laval in a golden cage at Sigmaringen castle in southern Germany, where they spent the rest of the war. Just for good measure, the Germans rearrested Herriot, who spent the remainder of the war in far less comfortable conditions than Laval and Pétain.[23]

The departures of Laval and Pétain dashed the hopes of collaborators seeking an easy political solution to the building crisis in Paris. Indeed, the Germans hustled their former puppets out of France in large part to keep them from opening any negotiations that might further complicate Germany's already tenuous hold on France. It is doubtful that the Americans would have negotiated with Pétain, much less the widely detested Laval, but French Resistance officials and de Gaulle himself had reason to fear: They had seen the Americans work with Vichy officials in North Africa and in Normandy. Now, with Pétain and Laval out of the country and out of communication, the Vichy period could finally close. What, exactly, might replace it remained an open question, but it was clear that the key actors in this rapidly developing drama no longer owed any allegiance to Vichy.[24]

Pétain and Laval were not the only ones leaving France. German and senior Vichy officials all over Paris were burning their papers and getting out of the city as quickly as they could. Foremost among them were the officers of the Abwehr, the German Army's intelligence service. With the front obviously about to move to the city's east, it would have been pointless for them to remain in Paris. The flight of these officers and other high-level agents of the occupation created an environment that struck Charles Braibant as "June 1940 in reverse," an image also used by Jacques Bardoux in his journal. Braibant, however, was careful to note that thousands of beleaguered and battle-fatigued German soldiers from Falaise were likely to pass through the city, and no one could guess what they might do. Bardoux similarly repeated a fearful rumor he had heard that among those troops headed to Paris were two SS divisions like the ones that had committed atrocities elsewhere in France. He also noted that the Allied failure to close the Falaise gap had kept the battle of Normandy from being a German Waterloo. Germany, he knew, still retained significant combat power.[25]

Even though the evacuations did not mean the Germans had been defeated outright, they did change the tenor of the occupation. Some of the city's most visible collaborationist institutions and their leaders disappeared without warning. On August 17, Radio Paris, which for four years had faithfully served the German occupiers, announced in its regular news programming that the German Army had defeated the Allied landings in southern France. Then it simply stopped broadcasting and its directors left the city. The most important of the pro-German media outlets had closed its doors and quietly left, leaving the airwaves blissfully free of anti-Allied and anti-Semitic propaganda. Pro-German and pro-Vichy newspapers also stopped appearing as the printers refused to work with them. The Germans continued to evacuate noncombat personnel from the city. Powerless to prevent all collaborationists from leaving, FFI leaders spoke about the national purging that would come when the collaborationists lost the protection of the Germans and had to face the vengeance and fury of the French people, whom they had wronged.

The Gare de l'Est, the train station that handled eastbound rail traffic, was jammed with Germans, military and civilian alike, who were fleeing the city. "All over Paris," noted the young Gilles Perrault, "the enemy were packing their bags, burning their files . . . [and] piling away their most treasured spoils." Even on the infamous Rue des Saussaies the Germans were packing up and preparing to leave. Yves Cazaux watched Gestapo officers take everything, including the furniture, out of their offices and torture chambers. This time, however, when the trucks left, they did not come back.[26]

Abetz's departure on August 17 may have been a welcome sign that the German presence in the city was ending, but with diplomats like him fleeing the city, the evacuations left the Germans with no official diplomatic representatives with whom to negotiate. The future of Paris would now be decided by force of arms, a thought that scared Nordling, even though he knew full well what Abetz was capable of. But in the midst of all the uncertainty, there was cause for hope. The disappearance of many members of the Milice, who followed their German masters out of town, was a joyous sign that Paris's fortunes were starting to turn for the better. Without the Milice or the Paris police, the Germans could not hope to maintain anywhere near the level of control over the city that they had had during the four years of the occupation.

On August 18, a Friday, Parisians awoke to much hotter temperatures, a symbolic indication that more than the mercury was rising. The momentum in favor of an uprising with or without Allied help was clearly building. For the first time in four years, French tricolor flags were beginning to appear sporadically across the city, including on a few public buildings. In some sections of the city—notably in the Latin Quarter, where university students were making their presence felt on the streets—tensions were rising high enough to produce violence. German soldiers had begun to fire on any large group of

French youths they encountered, killing twenty-five people (most of them students) in the St. Michel area.[27]

The rhetoric, too, was heating up as Parisians began to view a future without the Germans or Vichy. They also saw a chance to liberate the city themselves, an issue of pride that mattered greatly to them. On August 18, one of the Paris-based political leaders of the Resistance wrote, "It is not possible for us to stand by as spectators of the great victory. We have emerged from too great a trial, too grievous a betrayal for our hearts, too, not to be committed to performing our task at the hour appointed by History." In another pamphlet that appeared on the same day, the Resistance promised that "the [return of the] Republic will be proclaimed in the presence of the people of Paris," not as a result of the Allies liberating the city on their behalf.[28]

Remarkably, however, the Resistance leaders still need not have worried about the Allies coming to the city, because the events inside Paris had thus far made little impression on the Allies. Allied officers had no direct means of learning about the situation in the city, and the eyes of the generals remained focused on the still tense situation around Falaise. Consequently, Eisenhower and his staff gave no serious thought to Paris, despite the fact that on August 18 lead elements of the U.S. Army were preparing to encircle German forces west of the Seine River at Mantes la Jolie. This location was less than thirty miles to the northwest of the capital. American planners had a report indicating that FFI members were moving freely through the city, but they were reluctant to change their plans based on such thin intelligence. The official U.S. Army history noted that the Allies judged the situation in Paris on August 18 to be serious but "far from formidable." The main American axes of advance, therefore, remained toward the port cities of Le Havre and Rouen, not Paris; supply problems were still more important to the Allies than driving on the French capital.[29]

The Allies' indifference to their situation notwithstanding, Parisians were growing feverish as they waited for the dam to break. Adding to the growing momentum in favor of action was the arrival of another Gaullist agent, Charles Luizet. The forty-year-old Luizet was a graduate of the French military academy at St. Cyr, where he had been Philippe Leclerc's roommate and one of Charles de Gaulle's students. In 1940 he had been serving in North Africa when he heard about the appeal of June 18 from his former professor. Luizet immediately offered his services to de Gaulle, who made him head of intelligence for Free France in North Africa, a position he secretly held while also serving in the Vichy administration. This made him a particularly valuable agent. After the Allied liberation of North Africa, he took a senior position in the Free French administration in Algiers, quickly becoming one of de Gaulle's most important confidants.[30]

Luizet had learned the politics associated with war and resistance so well that de Gaulle wanted him back in France as quickly as possible. He nominated Luizet to become the prefect of Corsica in September 1943. The post was important and symbolic, as Corsica was the first part of metropolitan France to be liberated. Fiercely loyal to de Gaulle, Luizet worked quickly to ensure that the new administration in Corsica was filled with Gaullist supporters, although he also proved capable of working with the island's nationalists and communists. In late July 1944, de Gaulle called Luizet to London to offer him a new assignment. He wanted Luizet to go to Paris and take control of the Paris police force, so that it would be in the hands of the provisional government even before the Allies arrived. Luizet's mission was to ensure the loyalty of the police to de Gaulle and to make certain that at least one of the two Paris prefect positions was in Gaullist hands. To this end, de Gaulle provided him with a written directive naming Luizet the rightful prefect of the Paris police, a position that would both allow him to hold sway over the Paris police and deliver one of the two prefect seats to de Gaulle.

Luizet immediately accepted his new assignment, and he left England on August 2. Owing to the difficulties of getting him into France without anyone (including the Americans) knowing his mission, he took a circuitous route from Croydon to Corsica to Algiers to Italy. From there he was flown to the southern French town of Apt on August 11, where he met Resistance agents who were ready to smuggle him into Paris. It took six days to move through a chaotic French countryside. Luizet finally arrived in the city on August 17 only to find, to his great surprise, that the police force he was supposed to lead was on strike.

Luizet met with other Gaullist officials in the city, most notably Parodi and Chaban, and found them opposed to the strike and the idea of an insurrection. But Luizet made a different assessment. In his mind, the strike of the Paris police showed clearly that a general insurrection was imminent; if the Gaullists in the city did not move to gain control of it, then Rol and his FFI would. In effect, he argued that if an insurrection was inevitable, there was nothing for him, Parodi, and Chaban to do but to try to assume key roles in its leadership. Luizet also knew that if they moved quickly, and if the police accepted his leadership, then the Gaullists would be able to take control of the police force. This would give them an enormous advantage not just over the Germans but over the FFI as well. But they would need to move quickly, lest Rol beat them to the punch.[31]

There is little evidence to suggest that Rol was thinking in terms of a struggle for power inside Paris. Instead, he seems to have remained focused on the fight against the Germans and their Vichy collaborators. Under his guidance, the FFI distributed intricately prepared orders to their agents on August 17 calling for the seizure of eighty strategic places throughout the city, including prisons, the gas and electrical works, banks, and telephone exchanges. Each site was either strategic to solidifying FFI control of the city or aimed at freeing those still in German hands. Posters went up all over the city urging Parisians to rise up and help the FFI in the struggle to come. Rol's General Order of August 18, announced to the general population in Paris, ordered additional attacks on German centers of communications in order to disrupt and confuse German defenses. It ended with the words "Chacun Son Boche" ("Everyone Kill His Hun"). An insurrection was about to begin in Paris, although where it might lead remained anyone's guess.[32]

6

"THE MOST BEAUTIFUL
DAYS OF OUR LIVES,"
AUGUST 19–20

CHARLES BRAIBANT AWOKE ON THE MORNING OF AUGUST 19, a warm and sunny Saturday, to the sounds of cannon fire far away in the distance. Before losing electricity the night before he had managed to catch a few minutes of the news on BBC Radio, which had announced that the German Army in France was in disarray and retreating all across the front. The artillery he was hearing suggested that the Allied armies were close to Paris. He and his fellow Parisians were elated at the idea that the Germans might finally leave their city after four long and tortuous years of occupation. Braibant noted that in the streets that morning Parisians were debating where the best places in the city might be to watch the liberating U.S. Army when it entered the city.

Although in his journal he described August 19 as being "without a doubt our golden day," Braibant was not quite as optimistic as most of his fellow Parisians. He had been able to divine from the BBC broadcasts that the Allied armies were advancing not toward

Paris but around it to the north. He also used the pages of his journal to express some of his deepest fears about the immediate future, including the possibility that an Allied advance might provoke a slaughter of civilians, or that the Germans might hold Paris hostage in an effort to protect Berlin from the vengeful wrath of the Soviet Red Army. Like most careful observers of the situation, Braibant swung between optimism at what he hoped was the imminent arrival of an army of liberation, on the one hand, and, on the other, despair at what might happen if the Germans, instead of retreating, opted for a reaction of violence and vengeance. There were still almost twenty thousand German soldiers in and around Paris armed with tanks, armored personnel carriers, and artillery, and they were supported by airplanes based at Le Bourget airfield north of the city. The Americans might be near, but the Germans seemed far from ready to surrender.[1]

Like Braibant, Dietrich von Choltitz and his staff still expected any serious challenges to German authority in Paris to come from the outside. The daily intelligence report that awaited Choltitz as he arrived at his desk that morning described the city itself as "perfectly calm." Choltitz approved the morning report and sent it along to the army group's headquarters as part of the day's routine paperwork. Even at this late date, the German high command in Paris discounted the possibility of a serious uprising; some of Choltitz's officers even left their headquarters that morning to help an elderly lady find her missing cat. Few of them thought that the Resistance was capable of a major uprising, and none of them read the police strike as the start of something more meaningful.[2]

Rol did not expect a day of revolutionary events either. Although he had written his impassioned "Chacun Son Boche" order the night before, and although his FFI agents were even then making final preparations to occupy eighty public buildings, he was still thinking that the popular uprising by the people of Paris might not begin for a few more days. That Saturday morning, Rol set off by bicycle, the only means of transportation available to most Parisians, to meet with the political leaders of the Resistance to discuss the exact timing of their plan as well as its primary targets, which included the remaining media outlets not yet under FFI control, the prisons at Drancy and Fresnes, and the *mairies*, the vitally important administrative centers that acted as district headquarters for Paris's twenty arrondissements. Rol was intent on planning for the dramatic days that he knew were ahead for Paris, but even he would be surprised at what this day would bring. As he pedaled his bicycle along the quays of the city's left (southern) bank, he began to sense that something had changed. The closer he got to the Préfecture de Police, the stronger the sensation became.

Across the Seine, in the Hôtel de Ville where he worked, Jacques Cazaux, too, began to sense that something important and dramatic was happening. Through his window, he wrote, he heard "a discordant *Marseillaise* more beautiful than any I had ever before heard in my life." People in and around the ornate Renaissance-style building on the site that had served as Paris's city hall since the fourteenth century were singing the French national anthem aloud for the first time in four years, but their throats were too choked up with emotion to form the notes properly. Cazaux ran outside to see what had inspired this incredible moment. He saw the same sight Rol saw at almost the same time from the other side of the river. Both men knew that what they were witnessing was about to change the history of Paris forever. Cazaux was so inspired that he ran into the basement of the Hôtel de Ville in search of the French flag that he had helped to hide there in 1940.[3]

But if Cazaux was inspired by what he was seeing, Rol was more circumspect. Like Cazaux, he knew it meant that the uprising he had desired for so long was now underway. But as he bicycled through the northern edge of the sixth arrondissement, he also worried that he was rapidly losing control of the unfolding events. Even more ominously, he realized that his Gaullist partners and rivals had stolen a step on him. The uprising he had hoped for was beginning, but he may have lost his chance to play a leading role in it.

The symbol that had inspired so much emotion on this Saturday morning was unmistakable and easy for thousands of Parisians to see: A French tricolor flag was flying above the prefecture for the first time since June 1940. At around 6:00 that morning, a courageous policeman had climbed on top of a car in the prefecture's courtyard and screamed, "In the name of General de Gaulle and the Provisional Government of the French Republic, I take possession of the Préfecture de Police!" Between 1,500 and 2,000 policemen then rushed into the courtyard to applaud and join him in singing the *Marseillaise*. It was all part of a carefully crafted and organized plan by the police to make a bold statement of their support for de Gaulle.[4]

The Paris police had decided to take their strike one level further and occupy the building, in the process arresting the prefect of police, Amédée Bussières, as he was eating his breakfast. Sympathizers and supporters rushed to the building to help prepare its defense, including the prefecture's female telephone operators, who would ensure communications with the outside world; the Abbé Robert Lepoutre, who rushed across the forecourt from Notre Dame to provide spiritual guidance, if needed; and Frédéric Joliot-Curie, the Nobel Prize–winning scientist and the son-in-law of Pierre and Marie Curie, who began to assemble Molotov cocktails to help the police defend themselves. He had brought the sulfuric acid and potassium chlorate with him; the champagne bottles were supplied by the police, who had sorrowfully emptied the champagne into drains in the prefecture's cellar. Another sympathizer was lawyer Emmanuel Blanc, who later that week wrote an account of the event that began, "If you read these lines, know that not all Frenchmen are Pierre Laval."[5]

Rol raced his bicycle to the prefecture as quickly as he could. Strapped to its frame was a bag that contained his carefully crafted plans for an uprising. Nowhere in those documents had Rol or anyone else called for the seizure of the prefecture, a massive and imposing structure that would be difficult for the Resistance to hold in the face of a determined German response. As Rol undoubtedly knew, the building's prominent location in the middle of the Île de la Cité made it a perfect target for German tanks and, if the Germans chose to use them, airplanes. Rol saw in the seizure of the prefecture an important symbol of liberation, but also a dangerous distraction. He worried that the Préfecture de Police could now become the scene of a massacre.[6]

Rol demanded entrance into the prefecture, but the policemen on guard did not know who he was and turned him away. Furious, he suspected he was being double-crossed (by whom he did not exactly know). He rode his bicycle as quickly as he could to a garage that also served as a Resistance safe house. There he tore off the bag attached to his bicycle and removed from it the Spanish Civil War uniform he had worn when he had fought the fascists as a member of the International Brigades. Perhaps, he thought, the uniform he had worn when defending Barcelona might give him the gravitas he needed to play a role in the liberation of Paris.

Rol was right that someone was trying to take control of the prefecture away from him. That man, wearing a crisp suit and large eyeglasses, was sitting calmly on the terrace of the famous café Les Deux Magots, reading a newspaper. He was doing his best to look like just any other Parisian trying to make the most out of a dreadful cup of ersatz coffee on a beautiful summer morning. His thin, gaunt appearance helped him blend in with malnourished Parisians, although he had not spent much time in the city. At around 11:00 a.m., soon after Rol had put his Spanish uniform on, a black car belonging to the prefecture pulled up at the sidewalk of the Boulevard Saint-Germain in front of the terrace of the Deux Magots, which sat just a fifteen-minute walk from the Île de la Cité. A policeman who had helped to organize the seizure of the prefecture leaped from the car and approached the man reading the newspaper. "Monsieur le Préfet," he said in a calm, measured voice, "the Préfecture is taken; it is now under your orders. Your car awaits."[7]

Charles Luizet, Charles de Gaulle's former student, who had sneaked back into the city just a few days earlier, put down his newspaper and left the café. He stepped into a second car that had just arrived and drove off to his new job as the prefect of the Paris police. The two cars turned left on the Rue du Dragon, going the wrong way down an empty one-way street, and met a third car that contained an armed escort for Luizet. His plan had worked to perfection. The Gaullists had taken control of the prefecture without firing a shot. They now had access to the weapons and other supplies inside the building as well as the right to claim that they had seized this important symbol of a free Paris. Even before the end of the week, Parisians would be referring to the courtyard of the prefecture as the "Courtyard of August 19."[8]

Whether Luizet and his allies could hold the prefecture against the Germans—or Rol—remained to be seen. Mollifying Rol would not be easy. Although stealing a march on him and his FFI was undoubtedly a wonderful side benefit of the police uprising, Luizet had not intentionally sought to shut Rol out or provoke a confrontation with the FFI. Rather, he was following de Gaulle's orders to ensure the loyalty and dependability of the police. Nevertheless, Luizet's lightning *coup de main* had put Rol on the defensive and created an atmosphere of mistrust at a moment when the Resistance would most need unity of effort. Rol steeled himself for the scheduled 1:00 p.m. meeting with the leaders of the Resistance to discuss the uprising that had broken out without any of them having given the order. Now, rather than planning an uprising, they would have to decide how to react to the one in progress.

Neither Rol nor any of the other leaders of the Resistance could have missed the obvious point that the seizure of the prefecture had energized the people of Paris. Claude Roy, an FFI leader who spent part of the day in the building, observed that "the metamorphosis of the Paris police, from the hated symbol of authority to the beloved champion of the populace," was confusing and inspiring at the same time. The Polish exile Andrzej Bobkowski noted the "crazy world" that Paris became on that day as liberation increasingly appeared to Parisians as a real possibility rather than a distant mirage. Raoul Nordling, the Swedish consul, noted that, for him, the sight of the tricolor flag over the prefecture had two layers of significance. It meant not only that the situation had grown much more serious but also that a showdown between the Gaullists, whom he knew had now "taken in hand the leadership of the affair," and the left-leaning FFI was now possible. Sporadic shooting had begun in the morning and increased throughout the day, although it remained hard for people in the city to figure out who was shooting at whom. One resident noted that his neighborhood had "the atmosphere of a city on the front lines" and worried about possible German responses.[9]

He was right to worry. A little over a mile away, at the luxurious Hôtel Meurice across the Rue de Rivoli from the Tuileries Gardens, Choltitz, already in his office, received reports of the seizure of the prefecture and the sporadic shooting. His officers could easily see the flag flying over the prefecture as they came into work. Tricolor flags soon went up on both towers of Notre Dame as well. Choltitz, according to his own memoirs, saw "no reason at all to worry about the military plan" he had in place to defend the city. Nevertheless, his instinctive professional bias against irregulars and civilians in arms led him to order preventive measures, including the authorization for German units to destroy any building from which a shot was fired at a German soldier. He also approved collective reprisals for any act of violence committed against German soldiers and ordered tanks to prepare to advance on the prefecture.[10]

Although quickly informed of the events in Paris, Hitler's headquarters shared Choltitz's lack of concern. The high command persisted in viewing the city in terms of its importance to German operational plans on the western front, and the seizure of one building seemed unlikely to significantly affect that role. Hitler's headquarters thus ordered Choltitz to keep the bridges of Paris intact. The city's transportation network might still be necessary in order to assure the safe withdrawal of German armies. German headquarters promised to dispatch more antiaircraft guns to protect the bridges from Allied air attacks, but the German high command offered little else, an indication that the events in Paris itself had made little impact on the thinking of those at the top decision-making levels. These responses revealed both how little the German headquarters understood about Paris and how low the city was on their order of priorities. Even General Walter Model, the commander in chief of German forces in France, thought that the Seine basin's river crossings were more important than Paris itself.[11]

While the Germans slowly deliberated, the leaders of the Resistance met in an apartment on the Rue de Bellechasse, just a short walk from Les Deux Magots café. They had hurriedly called the meeting to discuss the pros and cons of launching an insurrection, but the sounds of gunfire outside their windows and the revolutionary air in the streets showed conclusively that the people of Paris had already made that decision for them. Alexandre Parodi, de Gaulle's senior representative in the city, accused the communists of having launched an insurrection prematurely in a bid for power, a charge that infuriated the communist representative André Tollet, who shot back that if an insurrection had begun prematurely, it was because of the Gaullist seizure of the prefecture.

The meeting was fraught with tension, recrimination, and fear for the safety of the city and its residents. All representatives present expressed their concern about possible German reprisals against the people of Paris. Rol, Tollet, and others also argued that from a military perspective, the concentration of the police inside the prefecture posed a grave risk. Rather than dispersing their strength through the city and fighting a guerrilla campaign, the police had put themselves in a terrible position. They could neither give up the prefecture, which was now too important a symbol even to consider yielding, nor defend themselves inside the building against German tanks. If the Germans mounted a major assault on the prefecture, where two thousand policemen shared just five hundred weapons, the result would be a bloodbath and a major setback to the Resistance, which was still starved for men and weapons. Somehow, they would have to get help to the prefecture.

Mutual anger and suspicion notwithstanding, cooler heads prevailed, and all sides recognized the need to come together at this critical time. Parodi realized that failing to support an insurrection brought with it the risk of losing all moral and political authority in the city, so widespread was the desire to fight. Parodi thus did what he could, given the obvious fact that the situation threatened to get away from him. Using the authority he had been given by de Gaulle and Koenig, Parodi ordered the mobilization of all Resistance members in the city eighteen to fifty years old. The orders were issued on letterhead that read "République Française" and ended with the words "Vive de Gaulle. Vive la France." Then, probably to atone for the Gaullist seizure of the prefecture without informing Rol, Parodi offered to place all Resistance forces in the city under the FFI and therefore under Rol's orders. The decision made tactical sense, because only Rol had the necessary command and control structure in place to manage a battle across the city. It also underscored the willingness of both sides to put their differences aside in the fight to save Paris.[12]

Parodi concluded that he and Luizet had no choice but to make common cause with the communists and support a general uprising as part of a united Resistance front. In doing so, he knew he was acting against de Gaulle's express wishes to delay any uprising until the Allies could move regular forces into the city. Nevertheless, even more than he disliked the idea of disobeying de Gaulle, Parodi feared that the communists would take control of the insurrection, which he knew he could no longer prevent in any case. Therefore, despite the many risks he knew he was running for himself and the people of Paris, he threw his entire support behind the insurrection. "If I have made a mistake," he said, "I shall have a lifetime to regret it in the ruins of Paris."[13]

By the time the meeting ended, the Germans were taking their first concrete steps to evict the police from the prefecture. Armored personnel carriers arrived on the Île de la Cité just before 3 p.m. carrying around fifty German soldiers. They moved down the Boulevard du Palais on the prefecture's west side, turning the street into a shooting gallery as they fired into windows. German soldiers also set up a security perimeter on the forecourt between the prefecture and Notre Dame to cover the arrival of three German tanks, one of which was a powerful 55-ton Tiger I that carried an 88 mm cannon capable of inflicting tremendous damage. It fired two shells at the main entrance, knocking out the left door on the prefecture's massive double doors and sending up a cloud of smoke. Then, as quickly as they came, the vehicles drove away.[14]

Exactly why the tanks did not continue to fire on the prefecture until they compelled its surrender remains a mystery. The tankers may have been afraid to leave their slow and plodding machines vulnerable to cross-fires and Molotov cocktails; as events soon showed, they had good reason to fear both. Choltitz himself, a veteran of many urban battles, was reluctant to use tanks in city combat, believing that they were too exposed in closed spaces. The Germans may have been trying to force the police into a negotiation on Choltitz's terms without sparking a confrontation that could lead to a city-wide battle. Whatever their motivation, the decision to fire into the prefecture did not have its desired effect. Léo Hamon, a socialist Resistance leader inside the prefecture, helped to maintain calm by rallying the police with an appeal to their new role: "The people of Paris have often struggled against you. Today, you are on the same side. They will never forget it. This will become a lasting bond." His rallying cry helped to calm the nerves of the policemen inside the building and enabled them to focus on how to repulse the next German attack.[15]

That attack was not long in coming. At 3:30 p.m., three German armored vehicles, including two Panther tanks, tried to move across the Île de la Cité on the other side of the prefecture from Notre Dame, once again along the Boulevard du Palais. The tanks fired more rounds into the iron doors of the building, blowing them off their hinges and sending policemen in the interior courtyard scurrying behind sandbags for cover. But other policemen were ready for the slow-moving tanks and counterattacked from two directions. Using the Molotov cocktails fashioned by Joliot-Curie, they disabled all three vehicles, one of which turned out to be carrying arms; another was carrying gasoline. The arms were badly needed, as the defenders of the prefecture lacked almost all critical supplies, most notably ammunition and medical supplies for their wounded. The gasoline proved critical to replenishing the supplies of Molotov cocktails. The capture of German prisoners, most of whom expected to be shot on sight, gave the police a bargaining chip, but it also led to fears that the Germans might retaliate by seizing or killing French civilians.

The police seizure of the building may have served as inspiration to the people of the city, but the police were ill-prepared to hold their ground for long. They knew that the lack of supplies and the difficulty of countering German armor could prove fatal. The police did, however, have two crucial advantages. Because the FFI had taken control of much of the city's telephone network, its agents could warn the police inside the prefecture of German movements; they could also use the now empty passageways of the Métro to supply the prefecture through the nearby Cité station. In addition, there was an underground Métro passageway that directly connected the prefecture with the Left Bank.

The second advantage derived from the near-total control of the St. Michel and Latin Quarter neighborhoods by the FFI. German tanks coming from their bases in the Jardin du Luxembourg region needed to pass through these areas to reach the Île de la Cité. German tankers were reluctant to run an urban gauntlet, especially given the heavy fire and attacks by Molotov cocktails that soon became a feature of the area. Their tanks could not move quickly through the streets and were sitting ducks for the Molotov cocktail attacks from the numerous windows of packed Parisian apartment buildings. Except for the broad Boulevard St. Michel, most of the roads in the neighborhoods near the Île de la Cité were narrow and winding—death traps for cumbersome armored vehicles. German tankers had good reason to fear being burned alive in their own vehicles.

Pierre Maudru, an FFI section leader, described in graphic detail the impact of one Molotov cocktail attack against a German armored vehicle. The driver, he said, "had been so badly burned that his skin was swollen and wrinkled like that of a chicken or a grilled lamb. His hands and face had doubled in volume. He had no hair left and his eyes were bulging. In place of his hair he had nothing on his head except a kind of black lump that continued to crackle."[16]

Few Frenchmen took much pity on the Germans, however they died. FFI members kept fighting with as much ardor as they could. They quickly scored two major successes, disabling one tank on the Place St. Michel directly across the bridge from the prefecture and disabling another right in front of Notre Dame. In all, the FFI destroyed or captured twenty German vehicles and took six hundred German prisoners that day. One policeman noted, from his station in the nearby commissariat of the sixth arrondissement, that "the Place St. Michel became a cemetery for all German vehicles that tried to enter it." He may have exaggerated a bit for effect, but the losses they inflicted made it clear that the FFI was able to restrict German movements enough to relieve some of the pressure at the prefecture.[17]

Nevertheless, the police inside the prefecture knew that they could not hope to stop the German attacks for much longer without significant help. German tanks would eventually find their way through. The police also knew, as did the leaders of the Resistance, that the Germans would not recognize them as soldiers; they would instead see them as terrorists and treat them brutally if they surrendered. Parodi and Chaban designed a scheme to evacuate the prefecture using sewer and Métro tunnels. Both men had determined that the seizure of the building had been "premature and vain, [the police's] sacrifices useless and the enemy's reprisals violent." But evacuation was impossible given the symbolism the prefecture had already assumed. The situation became more serious by the hour. Several policemen inside the prefecture used the building's telephone exchange to call loved ones and tell them goodbye. One of them called his wife and told her, "This is all going badly. We will probably never see each other again." In all, 193 Paris policemen died during the liberation, most of them on August 19 and 20.[18]

Seeking to extend the uprising beyond the prefecture, some FFI commanders argued for a strategy of holding and occupying strongpoints like *mairies*, the administrative centers of the arrondissements; city utilities; and key communication nodes. But Rol advocated a strategy of guerrilla warfare, striking German positions with quick, well-organized attacks to keep the Germans off balance. The guerrilla approach also had the advantage of not concentrating FFI forces in locations where the Germans could bring their superior firepower to bear. The FFI's seizure of the mairie of the Parisian suburb of Neuilly was a case in point. It had only taken the Germans a few minutes to move a Panther tank into the area, fire a shell into the roof, and retake the building, sending the FFI fighters scrambling into a sewer tunnel for safety.

FFI operations were too far flung for any one man to control, although Rol tried to implement some semblance of command. Following Rol's vision, members of the FFI were active all across the city and suburbs, forcing the Germans to pay attention to areas other than the prefecture. His goals for the day were to mobilize Resistance fighters, seize weapons from the Germans, and capture the eighty lightly defended targets of opportunity on his list. Many of these targets had been defended by the police before the strike but were now ripe for the taking. Among the FFI's most successful operations were raids on the prisons of Drancy and Fresnes, leading to the freedom from Nazi clutches of more than three thousand Jews and political prisoners. Their lives were now saved from deportation and incineration in a Nazi death camp.[19]

Still, the prefecture remained endangered. The Swedish diplomat Raoul Nordling feared the possibility of a massacre of the men inside the building, just as he had earlier feared what would happen to the political prisoners at Fresnes and elsewhere. As he had done in that case, he decided to try his hand, as a somewhat neutral arbiter, to defuse the tensions and find a peaceful solution. Despite the active combat in and around the Île de la Cité, Nordling went to the prefecture and asked to speak with the prefect. "The new one or the old one?"

was the response of the policeman to whom he spoke. Eventually Nordling spoke with Luizet and saw firsthand how dire the situation at the prefecture had become. He and Luizet had a dedicated telephone line established so that the prefecture could communicate directly with the Swedish consulate. Then Nordling agreed to find Choltitz and serve as an intermediary, although he had no idea what he might be able to negotiate.[20]

By the time Nordling and Choltitz met late that afternoon, approximately fifty Germans had been killed and more than one hundred wounded during the day's fighting. Choltitz was not in a forgiving mood. He raged at Nordling, telling the Swede that he intended to destroy the prefecture with a dawn air raid followed by an attack by the best soldiers he had at his disposal. Nordling warned Choltitz that there would be no way to protect the treasures of Paris that sat nearby, most notably Notre Dame and La Sainte-Chapelle. Destroying Paris, Nordling said, would be an unforgivable crime. "I am a soldier," Choltitz replied. "I get orders. I execute them."[21]

There were, however, three elements of Choltitz's thinking that provided an opening for Nordling as they continued their discussions. The first was Choltitz's belief that the uprising was the work of a small number of extremists whom he labeled terrorists. He believed that the FFI were making life difficult not only for the Germans in the city but also for Parisians, the vast majority of whom he believed did not support the FFI. Choltitz therefore saw himself and his army not as oppressing Paris but as protecting it from the gang of violent thugs he believed the Resistance to be. As he was talking to Nordling, Choltitz looked out the window of his office and noticed a pretty young Parisienne riding down the Rue de Rivoli on her bicycle. The sight seemed to make him think of the charms of Paris. Nordling recalled him turning from the window and saying, "Paris seems to me a magnificent city, its population seems calm and pleasant." Then his voice rose as he turned his attention to what he saw as Paris's less charming side. "Now I have just heard that some of my soldiers have been attacked and I must take energetic action! It makes me think that these measures must be severe, according to the orders I have received [to maintain calm]."[22]

One should not take the first part of Choltitz's statement too seriously as a testimony of his love for Paris, a city he had only known for a short time and was willing to reduce to rubble under the right circumstances. More representative of his thinking was the second element of his reasoning, that the violence in the city was mostly a result of internal French political struggles. Choltitz neither understood the nuances of French politics nor cared about them. He had already grown frustrated with all French politicians except the mayor, Pierre Taittinger, with whom he had developed a relationship based on mutual fear and hatred of the FFI. Nordling tried to exploit Choltitz's incomprehension by telling him that the combats across the city were between FFI and Vichy French followers and that his men were merely finding themselves trapped in the middle. Choltitz agreed with Nordling's assessment, because it absolved the Germans of responsibility for the outbreak of the violence. But he screamed at the Swede, "It is against my men that they shoot!"[23]

The third and final opening that Nordling detected was perhaps the most critical: Choltitz did not want to see events devolve to the point where he would have to fight a battle inside the city. He told Nordling that he had no interest in seeing Paris turn into another Stalingrad, the murderous urban battle that Choltitz had personally experienced. This sentiment had less to do with his admiration for Paris and its pretty girls than with his awareness that his forces were ill-equipped to fight an urban battle against guerrillas. Nor would destroying Paris serve any larger strategic or operational goals for the German Army. Choltitz said that he had no qualms about fighting for or in Paris, but he was reluctant to do so without a larger purpose that would justify the effort and, perhaps more importantly, without the necessary resources to ensure his men a chance to succeed in battle. He did not mention to Nordling one other reason for

his hesitation. Choltitz had already concluded that any further combat in and around the city was futile because the German Army's
days in France were clearly numbered.

Nordling began to suspect that what Choltitz really wanted was a
French or Allied command structure with which to negotiate. Choltitz
could not negotiate with the FFI or any other Resistance group because
in his eyes they were neither soldiers nor legitimate representatives of
the French government, which, as far as the Germans were concerned,
was still legally based in Vichy. To negotiate with men he characterized as terrorists would not only bring dishonor to himself as a soldier
but also expose his men to violent retribution in the event of a German surrender. His men were not required to recognize the FFI fighters as soldiers—a factor that accounted for the summary executions
of hundreds of résistants across Paris during the liberation—and he
feared that the FFI would not respect the laws of warfare if a surrender became necessary. If Choltitz could talk with someone he viewed
as a legitimate negotiator, perhaps he would feel he could surrender
the city with honor, particularly if he could receive a guarantee that
his men would go to prisoner of war camps instead of being left to
face the vengeful mobs for which Paris's history was justifiably famous. Nordling's instincts were correct. The situation would be different, Choltitz told him, if he knew that he was dealing with gentlemen,
not terrorists. What he really wanted was to negotiate with a new
authority who could speak for Paris. That statement was an implicit
recognition that the days of Pétain and Laval were truly over.[24]

Nordling left Choltitz optimistic that room existed for discussions
that might lead to the end of the bloodshed in and around the prefecture. He knew that Choltitz would fight for the city if he had to, but
that he might also accept another outcome if it met his needs. Most
of the discussions that followed that day occurred by telephone as
Nordling tried to stay in touch with both Choltitz and the prefecture.
By early evening, moreover, it had become too dangerous to move
around the city's streets.

Nordling soon developed the idea of a truce or ceasefire that would buy time and cool the passions that the uprising was unleashing. The time bought might allow for the police to give up the prefecture peacefully as part of a more permanent arrangement. More importantly, it might buy time for the Allies to get large regular formations into Paris. Choltitz could then surrender the city without violating his honor as a soldier. The truce would also stop the violence, which Choltitz continued to believe was not representative of the people of Paris. A few days of calm could help Choltitz achieve the mission of ensuring that the remaining German units could use Paris to retreat in good order to the east. Maybe by then the reinforcements that Berlin was constantly promising him might actually arrive, but even if they didn't, he would have a decent way out of the trap Paris was rapidly becoming.

Like the seasoned diplomat that he was, Nordling worked the telephones, talking both to the courageous but endangered policemen inside the prefecture and the calm, professional officers in the Hôtel Meurice. By 8:40 p.m. on August 19, he had worked out the general outline of the terms of a truce. The critical concession came from Choltitz, who agreed to recognize the FFI as regular combatants, thus protecting them from summary German reprisals. Nordling saw this concession as his great victory. It not only offered a way to end the violence, but also opened up the possibility that Choltitz might recognize the FFI leaders as legal representatives of the French government. If he did, then a long-lasting solution to the political and military problems of Paris might be reached without the Allies, whose intentions and plans regarding the city were still unclear to those inside. The Germans agreed not to fire on any buildings then occupied by the French Resistance or the police, thus saving the prefecture from another attack by German tanks or airplanes. In return, the French agreed not to fire on any German strongpoints or to disturb the movement of German troops in the city, thus giving Choltitz the calm and order he sought.[25]

The truce was a tremendous diplomatic achievement for Nordling, especially given the difficult circumstances under which he was working. It probably saved the lives of hundreds of policemen in the prefecture who would have been killed by the aerial and ground assault that Choltitz's staff had been designing for execution on the following morning. It also spared the buildings and irreplaceable architectural treasures of the city center. Perhaps most impressively, Nordling had gotten a German general to recognize part of the Resistance movement as a legitimate negotiating partner, even if Choltitz was not yet willing to recognize FFI agents as representatives of the French government.

But negotiating a truce is a far different enterprise from enforcing one. Choltitz refused to allow the terms of the truce to be broadcast over loudspeakers or on the radio, meaning that some parts of the city did not hear about it for hours, and even then, many people lacked any firm evidence that all the parties had agreed to it. Nordling suspected, correctly, that Choltitz wanted to keep the truce as quiet as possible for as long as possible. Once Model and Hitler learned about it, he would have some uncomfortable questions to answer. He might be replaced or arrested for negotiating without approval from the proper higher authority. Given the tense atmosphere inside the German high command after the assassination attempt, Choltitz's family might even suffer because of his actions. Better, Choltitz concluded, if Berlin did not find out about the truce for a few hours or even a few days. As a result, the news of the truce passed by word of mouth and through notices scrawled onto Paris's ubiquitous restaurant chalkboards.[26]

Although the shooting stopped around the prefecture, in other parts of Paris neither the FFI nor the Germans respected the truce. SS troops, in particular, ignored the ceasefire. They continued to fire into buildings and crowds of people, and they continued to execute any Frenchmen found to be carrying weapons. Each side accused the other of not respecting the truce and dealing in bad faith to improve its military position. The French accused the Germans of using the truce to move men and weapons into the Métro tunnels under the prefecture. Choltitz coldly rejected this charge, saying that if he wanted to annihilate the building and the men in it, he had tanks and planes that could do the job in minutes. He did not need to bother with tunnels.

The divisions and fractures opening up between the various Paris Resistance groups posed almost as much of a threat to their efforts as the ongoing aggression of German forces did. Disagreement about the truce nearly split the Resistance in two. The FFI, and Rol in particular, saw the truce as the product of negotiating with the enemy and akin to treason. "As long as Germans are in Paris," he thundered, "our duty is to fight them." The more the Germans kept up the shooting during the truce, the angrier Rol became; he later counted ninety-four members of his FFI killed during the ostensible hours of the truce. German soldiers and vehicles had also continued to fire randomly into buildings, especially in high combat areas like St. Michel.[27]

With every report of German violations of the truce terms, Rol grew more impatient. One of Rol's deputies, Maurice Kriegel-Valrimont, later recalled that the FFI leadership believed that the truce would strongly favor the Germans because it allowed them free movement of their men, tanks, and supplies around Paris. If the FFI honored the truce, the Germans could redeploy and be in a much stronger position once the fighting inevitably restarted. There was also nothing in the terms of the truce, for instance, to prevent the Germans from preparing demolitions of Parisian bridges, buildings, and monuments. As a result, Kriegel-Valrimont ordered his men to disregard the truce and keep fighting.[28]

These FFI leaders were not alone in their outrage at the truce. The communist leader André Tollet also opposed any truce unless its terms led directly to the departure of German forces from Paris. "The enemy is on the run," he said. He then asked, "Why accept a truce? We have nothing to gain." Léo Hamon, the socialist editor of the clandestine newspaper *Combat*, agreed, although he also understood that the truce gave the Resistance fighters much-needed breathing space. More critically, he realized, it gave them a chance to care for their wounded. He also saw a chance to use any time the truce bought to get a message to the Allies about the rapidly developing situation inside the city. Still, Hamon only agreed to the truce at the personal urging of Nordling, and only to the extent that he believed the Germans were honoring it as well.[29]

At the other end of the political spectrum, Chaban and most other Gaullist representatives supported the truce. Although Chaban saw clearly that the passionate disagreements over the truce could well split the fragile structure of the Paris Resistance, he believed that it was the only way to save the prefecture from the wrath of German tanks and airplanes. Consistent with his views throughout July and August, he saw the truce as a way to buy a few precious days for French and U.S. military units, allowing them to get to Paris so they could provide direct support for an uprising. At the moment, the Germans still had enough power to crush it.

Although American generals still had a far from complete understanding of what was happening inside Paris, the events of August 19 finally began to awaken their interest in the city. Vague reports began to filter into Allied headquarters saying that FFI members were roving the streets of Paris with weapons and engaging in combat with Germans. Reports of active fighting in the city deeply concerned the Americans, because they assumed that the much more heavily armed Germans would have little trouble massacring the now dangerously exposed FFI. Fighting inside Paris also carried the risk of drawing the Americans into the city at a time when they wanted to remain focused on crossing the Seine to the north in order to cut off avenues of retreat for large German formations. Nor had American concerns about feeding and supplying the city become any less acute.

French leaders, of course, were deeply concerned about events inside their beleaguered capital. The idea of combat inside Paris between unarmed citizens and the German Army was nightmarish to de Gaulle and Leclerc. Moreover, given the strategic and operational positioning of Allied forces, if the Allies decided to send units into Paris to protect the population, those units were more likely to be American than French. Despite repeated promises from Eisenhower, Patton, and Bradley that the French would have the honor of liberating Paris, the three closest corps to Paris were all American: Major General Wade H. Haislip's XV Corps was just 25 miles away and engaged in a river-crossing operation over the Seine; Major General Walton Walker's XX Corps was at Chartres, approximately 55 miles away; and Major General Gilbert Cook's XII Corps was at Orléans, approximately 80 miles away. Most elements of Leclerc's Deuxième Division Blindée, by contrast, were more than 140 miles away, still engaged in operations near Argentan. If the Allies were to liberate Paris quickly, it looked as if it would be the Americans who did it.[30]

The American high command had in fact begun to take its first active steps to deal with the problem of the liberation of the French capital. Still unsure of what exactly was going on inside the city, they settled for half measures. Bradley ordered the formation of a secret unit called the "T Force" that had orders to be ready to move into Paris quickly if the situation there deteriorated. Its small group of sixteen officers and seventy enlisted men, mostly special forces and intelligence operatives, were to make contact with members of the French Resistance, amass critical documents that could help him interpret the strategic situation, and identify high-value targets for interrogation, such as captured German and Vichy officers held by the FFI. They would also identify strategic locations that regular U.S. Army units would need to prioritize when they entered the city in large numbers. Some members of the T Force had already made limited contact with a handful of French Resistance members who had recently left Paris, and thus had some knowledge of events inside the capital. The T Force positioned itself at Le Mans and prepared to move to Rambouillet, just 30 miles southwest of Paris, where it would join up with 60 French soldiers who would serve as guides and translators.

Allied plans for the city worried officers like T Force's commander, Major William Hornaday, who wanted no part of the political battles taking place inside the city. Hornaday guessed that the Resistance figures he had met, all of whom were Gaullist, might be using the U.S. Army to prevent the communists from taking power, but he had no interest in getting sucked into that kind of vortex; nor did he have orders to favor one faction over another.

The Gaullists still feared that the Americans would renege on their promise to allow a French unit to liberate Paris. They also realized that they might be forced by circumstances to send the much better positioned American units into the city. Leclerc and de Gaulle met on August 19 to discuss just that possibility. De Gaulle knew that he held the legal title to the French government in exile, but that the FFI, to which he had only tenuous links, controlled the streets of Paris. He also knew that the Deuxième Division Blindée could not possibly hope to move on Paris without logistical support from the Americans. Leclerc understood the constraints as well, but he had already decided to move a portion of his division toward Paris using fuel and ammunition that his division had conserved, begged, and borrowed. Anything more, he told de Gaulle, was impossible: "I can't move the rest of my division," he said, "for reasons of supply and the desire not to overtly violate the rules of military subordination."[31]

Franco-American tensions were clearly building. Major General Leonard Gerow, Leclerc's corps commander, and General George Patton both wondered how much longer Leclerc would follow American orders. Leclerc had indeed begun to consider taking his orders directly from his political chain of command (meaning de Gaulle) rather than his military chain of command. Patton, however, had more sympathy for the French plight than either Gerow or the First Army commander, Lieutenant General Courtney Hodges, both of whom had grown tired of Leclerc's obsession with Paris. They still saw the city as strategically unimportant, and Gerow, in particular, came to despise Leclerc.[32]

Parisians, of course, knew nothing about these dramatic discussions. Most of them understood the importance of the day's events, but they could not discern where they might be leading. As she went to bed that night, one Parisienne compared the events of August 19 to the events of another day four years earlier. On that night, June 13, 1940, she and her fellow Parisians had known that their city would surrender to the Germans in the morning. Reflecting on that horrible memory, she wrote in her journal that the night of August 19 had a similar feeling of suspense, uncertainty, and silence. But there was one major difference. The silence of June 1940, she recalled, had been a "silence of death." More than four years later, with liberation approaching but danger still menacing, the city was living through a "silence of waiting." Waiting for what, she did not know. Across Paris, Yves Cazaux was also confiding his thoughts to his journal. "The storm," he wrote, "is about to burst."[33]

A storm did indeed burst the next morning, as rain showers poured down on Paris on the morning of August 20. The rain, combined with the truce, might have brought a measure of quiet to Paris on this Sunday morning, normally the calmest day of the week. Some Parisians tried their best to treat August 20 just like any other summer Sunday afternoon, even though events had moved far too fast for such normalcy to be possible. Despite the rain and the sporadic fighting, men still fished in the Seine, grandmothers strolled with their grandchildren through the gardens, and couples sat on park benches to enjoy the summer air. Young love in a time of war was the subject of Robert Doisneau's poignant photograph *Amour et Barbelés* (*Love and Barbed Wire*), taken just before the liberation in the Tuileries Gardens across from Choltitz's headquarters in the Hôtel Meurice. Even amid revolutionary change, the rhythm of Parisian life continued as it always had.

But if some Parisians were trying to live their lives as if everything were normal, others were risking their lives to create a new future for the city. Fighting continued all night in some parts of the city, especially in the Latin Quarter, where the casualties mounted. The fighting proved that neither side was respecting the truce. Rol continued to oppose the truce and challenged the authority of the Gaullists to negotiate it. "No order from any higher official has reached me about a cease-fire," he declared. "In consequence, as long as the Germans are in Paris, we will fight." Rol even told one associate that he feared the Gaullists might be setting up the FFI to be slaughtered as the members of the Polish Home Army in Warsaw had been.[34]

The Left scored a coup of its own early that morning when the daring Léo Hamon and a small group of socialists and communists took over the Hôtel de Ville, a long-standing symbol of revolutionary activity in Paris and the place from which Jacques Cazaux had witnessed the raising of the flag at the prefecture just the day before. Hamon had burst into the office of the prefect of the Seine and demanded his resignation, announcing to him that he was taking over the Hôtel de Ville in the name of the people of Paris. When the prefect demanded to see written orders to that effect, Hamon calmly replied, "We've got out of the habit of that kind of thing." He arrested the entire Paris municipal council, including Mayor Pierre Taittinger. The Gaullists now had control of the prefecture, the FFI had control of the streets, and the communists had control of the Hôtel de Ville.[35]

Rol could see that the last act of the Paris drama was about to unfold. In part to protect himself from the Germans and in part to set up a more effective command post, he closed down his hideout in a water and sewer authority building in northeast Paris and opened a new subterranean headquarters. He preferred to work underground, in part for security; underneath Paris sat a vast infrastructure that could not have been better designed for his purposes. Most of the city's sewer and telephone workers were Resistance members who knew this hidden world, with its miles of tunnels and hundreds of hiding places, intimately. The tunnels provided cover for snipers and

« Suivez-moi. Gardez votre confiance en
la France éternelle. »

"Follow me. Keep your faith in eternal France." This Vichy postcard with the image of Marshal Philippe Pétain appealed to conservative values and implicitly urged the French to reject both the Resistance and Charles de Gaulle. (UNITED STATES ARMY HERITAGE AND EDUCATION CENTER)

June 23, 1940: Hitler poses near the Eiffel Tower at the end of his only visit to Paris. The visit did not even last long enough for him to eat a meal in the French capital. (NATIONAL ARCHIVES)

German soldiers stand over the bodies of several dead members of the FFI. The angle of the photograph suggests that it was likely taken by a French observer watching carefully from an apartment window. (LIBRARY OF CONGRESS)

General Dietrich von Choltitz in 1944, by which time he was no longer the aggressive general he had been when directing the sieges of Rotterdam and Sevastopol. (BUNDESARCHIV BILD 183-E1210-0201-018)

American soldiers approaching Paris via a damaged French village. The fighting in Normandy and Falaise had been bloody and had distracted American attention from the problems of Paris. (UNITED STATES ARMY HERITAGE AND EDUCATION CENTER)

Allied bombers strike targets in Paris. Although Winston Churchill and others had qualms about bombing an occupied capital and adding to the misery of Parisians, Allied airmen insisted on striking what they saw as strategic targets of value to German industry. (LIBRARY OF CONGRESS)

Parisians line up behind a makeshift barricade in the crucial days of the uprising. The barricades were little military match for German tanks, but they did make German movements around the city much more difficult. (UNITED STATES ARMY HERITAGE AND EDUCATION CENTER)

Street fighting in Paris. Note that the woman to the left is wearing a German helmet, likely taken from a German casualty or prisoner. (LIBRARY OF CONGRESS)

An American-made M10 tank destroyer moves through the streets of Paris. Armored vehicles gave both physical and morale support to Frenchmen who had been fighting the Germans with whatever small arms they could find. (UNITED STATES ARMY HERITAGE AND EDUCATION CENTER)

An American armored vehicle rolls down the Avenue des Champs Élysées in front of the Arc de Triomphe. Finding enough gasoline to get tanks like these to Paris proved to be an enormous challenge. (NATIONAL ARCHIVES)

The French victory parade, which began even as thousands of Germans remained unaccounted for and the German air force still had planes at nearby Le Bourget airfield. Note the large French flag flying from the Arc de Triomphe. (LIBRARY OF CONGRESS)

An ecstatic scene near the Hôtel de Ville during the victory parade. Note the mix of Americans and Frenchmen in the crowd. (UNITED STATES ARMY HERITAGE AND EDUCATION CENTER)

French and German officers move through Paris together on an American-made Sherman tank to announce the surrender. The German looks none too pleased, but he is at least alive. (UNITED STATES ARMY HERITAGE AND EDUCATION CENTER)

Parisians gather to hurl insults at German prisoners. Afraid of what the mob might do to them, German soldiers were often among those happiest to see Allied soldiers arrive in the city. (LIBRARY OF CONGRESS)

German POWs being marched through Paris. Based on the dress uniforms of the French soldiers and the calm demeanor of the crowd, this photo was likely taken a few days after the emotions of the liberation had begun to ebb. (LIBRARY OF CONGRESS)

FFI commander Henri Rol-Tanguy inspecting members of his unit. Based on their uniforms, this photo was likely taken after the liberation, when many veterans of the FFI joined the regular French Army. (LIBRARY OF CONGRESS)

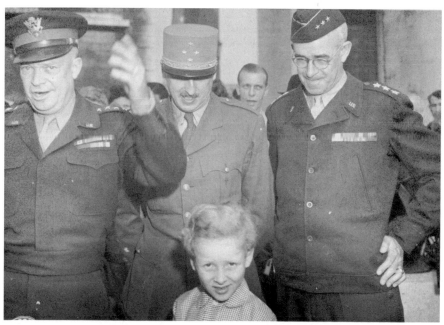

Left to right, Generals Dwight Eisenhower, Marie-Pierre Koenig, and Omar Bradley walk through Paris. Koenig was in nominal charge of the FFI during the uprising but had virtually no say in its day-to-day operations. (UNITED STATES ARMY HERITAGE AND EDUCATION CENTER)

An American soldier tours Versailles after the liberation. Americans found Paris and its wonders to be, in the words of journalist Ernie Pyle, "a champagne dream." (LIBRARY OF CONGRESS)

Charles de Gaulle (left) and Philippe Leclerc walk proudly through Paris. Although he was not a major player in the city's liberation, de Gaulle benefitted more than anyone else from the events of late August. (UNITED STATES ARMY HERITAGE AND EDUCATION CENTER)

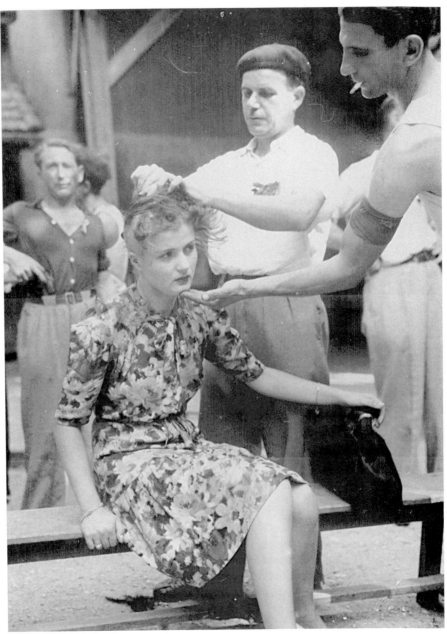

A "horizontal collaborator" having her head shaved in public. Women who had taken German lovers were often singled out for humiliations like these in the heady days following the liberation. (NATIONAL ARCHIVES)

Despite its liberation, the threat of German aircraft remained, as illustrated by an air raid the day after the parade. This antiaircraft gun emplacement near Notre Dame was a reminder that Paris was not yet safe. (UNITED STATES ARMY HERITAGE AND EDUCATION CENTER)

American soldiers found Parisian women particularly appealing. Most, however, were struck by how thin many of them looked and how desperate the food and fuel problem remained for months after the liberation. (UNITED STATES ARMY HERITAGE AND EDUCATION CENTER)

The Eiffel Tower lit up to celebrate the end of the war. Victory brought hope, even if the city was still short of food and other essentials. (UNITED STATES ARMY HERITAGE AND EDUCATION CENTER)

escape routes for Resistance members conducting guerrilla operations. Rol himself had worked on the ventilation systems in many Métro and sewer passageways and thereby knew this troglodyte world as well as anyone. The sewer system, Rol knew, had a separate telephone network that the Germans had tapped but only listened to twice a day, always at the same hours. It would provide the perfect communication system for him. He had decided to set up his tactical command post underneath the Denfert-Rochereau Métro station near one of the most extensive sections of the Paris catacombs. "It would be difficult," he noted, "to do better." The station's name, honoring a colonel who had defended the fortress of Belfort against the Prussians in 1870, also carried with it some symbolism for those who were historically minded.[36]

That afternoon, at around 2:45 p.m., the Gestapo arrested Alexandre Parodi and two of his Gaullist colleagues. Their first instinct was to shoot all three in the streets, but something in the behavior of their captives made the Gestapo think that they had arrested men of importance. At this point, a shadowy German intelligence official named Emil Bender intervened. Better known by his improbable nickname, Bobby, Bender was a member of a Paris-based German anti-Nazi group and may well have been a double agent working for the French Resistance. Bender urged the Gestapo to bring the men to the Hôtel Meurice to meet with Choltitz. At Bender's urging, the German commander agreed to the meeting, his first with Resistance members, and asked Nordling to attend. Choltitz asked them if they were in a position to speak for the Resistance and the provisional government. Parodi said that he was, but he gave the Germans a fake name and fake code name. Choltitz then asked Nordling if these were "the kind of gentlemen you urged me to negotiate with the other day." Parodi cut the Swedish consul off before he could reply, saying, "You know full well, Monsieur [Nordling], that I am the sole representative of the French government in Paris!" It was a brave proclamation, as it could well have led to his arrest, torture, or deportation. The Germans had killed people in Paris for much less.[37]

Instead, Choltitz extended an olive branch. He told Parodi that he needed order in the city and pledged not to fire on the French in any building they occupied if the French would promise not to harass German movements through the city. Then, hoping to establish a means of communication with the Resistance through these three men, he sweetened the deal even further. With Nordling observing the negotiations, Choltitz pledged to expedite food shipments into the hungry city if the Frenchmen would ensure that the FFI obeyed the ceasefire. Parodi bravely replied that Paris had starved for four years, and it would wait for another four days. Choltitz, following his belief that the violence in the city was the work of a few extremists, then ordered food brought in, despite Parodi's defiance, on the condition that it not be distributed to members of the Resistance. Nordling told him that he needed to accept the reality that "almost all of Paris is now in the Resistance." The meeting ended with Choltitz agreeing to release the men and extending his hand to Parodi. The Frenchman refused it and calmly walked out of the Hôtel Meurice with his two colleagues as free men.[38]

The Resistance was clearly making headway inside Paris, but its efforts still had little direct effect on the Allies. The Americans, who, as one Parisian noted in his journal, were "not at all pressing to make their entry into Paris," continued to divert their eyes from the city as much as they could. Eisenhower and de Gaulle met on Sunday morning, but the French leader failed to convince the supreme commander to redirect his forces toward Paris. It was an operation that American planners estimated would require five divisions and unknown tons of badly needed supplies. Eisenhower continued to stay focused on the drive to the east, hoping that if the Allies reached Reims they could cut off the German avenues of escape. Then, he argued, German troops "would just drop into our laps," and with them, Paris. De Gaulle responded by implying that he might assume control of French forces in France in his capacity as the head of the provisional government, but Eisenhower, knowing that he alone controlled the gasoline and ammunition supplies that the French needed, just smiled. Patton, who was indirectly involved in these strategic discussions, was no less determined than Eisenhower to keep driving east, despite his sympathies toward the French. In his characteristic manner he thundered, "They started their own goddamned insurrection. Now let them finish it."[39]

Leclerc tried once again to convince the Americans to let him drive on Paris. Scheduled to attend a Sunday lunch at First Army headquarters, he showed up at 10:30 a.m. to make his case to Lt. Gen. Hodges and his staff. William Sylvan, a member of Hodges's staff who attended the meeting, later recorded his impressions for the First Army's War Diary: "His arguments, which he presented incessantly, were to the effect that, roads and traffic and our plans notwithstanding, his division should run for Paris at once. He said he needed no maintenance, no more equipment, and that he was up to strength—and then, a few minutes later he admitted he needed all three. The General [Hodges] was not impressed with him or his arguments, and let him understand that he was to stay put until he gave orders otherwise."[40] This testy exchange showed both that Leclerc was determined to drive on the capital and that he lacked the ability to do so on his own. It also shows the high level of tension between Leclerc and his nominal superiors.

If the Americans were still unsure of the situation in Paris, the Germans were at long last awakening to the emergency. Kurt Hesse, the German general responsible for the defense of the Seine and the Oise region, and based in the Paris suburb of St. Cloud, noted that August 20 was the date of the first serious sense of crisis among the defenders. Outside Paris, six American divisions began a major advance out of the Loire Valley, with the exact destination unknown to German headquarters. From inside Paris, Hesse's headquarters began to receive reports from units whose commanders believed themselves encircled by FFI units. At German Supreme Headquarters in France on the same day, officers determined for the first time that "in Paris itself the situation became increasingly critical." Their war diary for that day expressed doubt that the Germans could hold the city, noting that "the initiative remained rather with the enemy." In their eyes, the German defense should have focused on the bridges in the Seine region, not on the city itself. Hitler's headquarters, however, had determined that holding Paris was of extreme importance, but refused to send new resources to the city.[41]

The fighting over the weekend had been some of the bloodiest in the long history of Paris. Saturday and Sunday had witnessed the deaths of 231 Frenchmen and the wounding of more than 800 more. The FFI moved through the city, setting up strongpoints on bridges and near intersections. This sort of warfare, where FFI fighters could go home for meals in shifts, provided the entire city with a kind of street theater that captivated Parisians. Nevertheless, this theater was violent and brutal, as the destruction and death throughout Paris clearly showed.[42]

Parisians continued to ask themselves where the Americans were and why they were not coming to their aid. "Où sont-ils?" were the words on everyone's lips. Even without help from the outside, the people of Paris had taken great strides to liberate themselves and restore much of their wounded sense of self. By nightfall, the Préfecture de Police, the Hôtel de Ville, the Interior Ministry in the infamous building on the Rue des Saussaies, and the Health, Finance, Economy, Education, and War ministries were all under the control of either the FFI or the Gaullists. Parisians could justifiably take great pride in the actions they had taken to liberate themselves.[43]

Nevertheless, the Germans had not exhausted all of their options. They still had thousands of soldiers, including many SS troops, who were supported by dozens of tanks and airplanes in the Paris region. If they intended to fight a pitched battle for Paris, they could bring this lethal might to bear against the Resistance fighters. The FFI needed to find a way to deny the Germans mobility through the city, both to impede their movements and to isolate the German strongpoints from one another.

To accomplish these feats, Rol relied on a traditional Parisian tactic. He called for the people of Paris to spend the night building the barricades that had been such a visible part of past periods of revolution in Paris. Bulletins spread across Paris on the 20th and 21st carrying the electrifying message "Tous aux Barricades!" ("Everyone to the Barricades"). The communists sent out their own flyers noting that the barricades could ensure that "not one Boche leaves the Paris region alive." An open battle for Paris had begun.[44]

7

THE DAYS OF THE
BARRICADES, AUGUST 21–22

THE WEEKEND'S DRAMATIC EVENTS HAD TRANSFORMED THE situation in and around Paris. What had begun as a strike of the Paris police rapidly developed into a full-scale insurrection that not even the leaders of the Resistance could fully control. Perhaps most importantly, the people of Paris were beginning to realize not just that the day of their liberation was rapidly approaching, but that they themselves might have a chance to play the key role in their own redemption. For a city that had been humiliated, occupied, and brutalized for four agonizing years, it was an empowering— almost intoxicating—sensation. Although he was not blind to the difficult days that lay ahead, Jacques Bardoux, the former French senator, basked in the notion that "Paris can liberate itself—a magnificent gesture worthy of two thousand years of history." FFI section leader Pierre Maudru also took pride in the courage of Parisians, noting, "Paris is not waiting for the arrival of the Allies. It will liberate itself. It will pay back the enemy for all he has done to this city for four years."[1]

In the past two days the Germans had also woken up to the severity of the situation. On Monday, August 21, the German high command war diary finally acknowledged that Paris had become untenable. This conclusion had important implications. With the loss of the city, the Germans knew, "the entire coastal front north of the Seine would be ripped open and the bases for the long-range warfare [sic] would be lost." The loss of the city, its bridges, and its transportation network would mean that the large German units west of Paris would not be able to retreat in good order to positions farther east. The Germans would need to defend Paris for as long as possible in order to allow for the escape of these westerly forces, but the high command acknowledged that "precautionary measures had heretofore not been authorized." The promised infantry reinforcements had not arrived. The German Army had even abandoned the idea of retreating units through the city as a show of force, preferring instead that they establish new positions east of the city as quickly as possible. Top German commanders understood how hopeless the situation was in Paris, but they still refused to rethink some of their most basic strategic assumptions. German officers in the Paris region struggled in vain to convince higher military officials in Berlin that the Americans were in fact bypassing Paris, thus rendering all of their plans to base their defense on the city itself irrelevant.[2]

Still, the German Army had little choice. The Germans could not merely give up the city. Paris remained an important symbol, and its fall would have dramatic reverberations throughout Europe and the world. American and British reporters were already beginning to angle to be the first Allied journalists to enter the liberated city. Thomas Wolf, the Fourth Infantry Division's war correspondent; A. J. Liebling of The New Yorker; and America's most famous war correspondent, Ernie Pyle, were all positioning themselves to be ready to rush in to Paris and broadcast news of its freedom. "To appreciate the mystique of Paris," Wolf later wrote, recalling the days before the liberation, "I think you had to have been born in the first quarter of the twentieth century." To Wolf and his generation, Paris had been the very center of European civilization. Indeed, the name of the city had been shorthand for freedom and democracy. Long after Berlin, Rome, and

Madrid had become hosts to fascist dictators, Paris had held against the tide, setting an example of resistance to tyranny to millions of people until its tragic fall in 1940. To many onlookers in Europe and across the world, there was no more important symbol of the impending end of the Nazis and the return of freedom to the western world than the Germans' eviction from the majestic City of Light.[3]

But Paris wasn't free yet. Nor could the German Army be expected to simply hand the French capital over to a band of guerrillas and irregulars whom they identified as terrorists. The German Army, with its intense professional self-identification, had a particular loathing for guerrillas and irregulars. For German higher headquarters to surrender the city to the FFI or even to representatives of Charles de Gaulle, whom they did not recognize in any official capacity, was simply unacceptable as either a matter of strategy or honor. Still, events in the city were moving rapidly, and German options were dwindling as quickly as their resources.

Choltitz knew that he was in an impossible situation. He had too few assets to hold the city against the uprising then spreading across the sprawling city, and he could not hope to combat the Allies if they ever decided to turn toward Paris. Only the indifference of the British and Americans to the French capital had left it in German hands this long. Yet at the same time, he knew that by offering the FFI a truce and opening even preliminary discussions with Resistance leaders in the city, he had put himself in a tenuous position. To go any further would be extremely dangerous. Raoul Nordling thought that the German commander was "visibly frightened by the fear that the SS or the Gestapo would denounce him as a soldier without courage." In the paranoid atmosphere of the German Army after the bomb plot at the "Wolf's Lair," such an accusation could lead to his arrest, demotion, or even execution.[4]

Inside the city, the truce barely held. Choltitz made an effort to sell it as being in the best interests of the Parisians themselves, a point the Resistance vehemently rejected. The Germans hung posters urging Parisians to respect the truce. "We are thinking of you," the

posters read. "Think of the fate of Paris." The FFI responded with
posters of their own that read, "No truce has been concluded between the French and the enemy commands." Noting that the Germans continued shooting in many parts of Paris despite the truce,
the FFI warned that "the lives of German prisoners in jails and hospitals will answer for any violence committed against the people of
Paris." As tension continued to build, each side accused the other of
repeated violations of the truce terms.[5] No one expected it to last for
much longer.

Members of the various factions of the Resistance itself, moreover,
continued to hurl accusations at one another over the issue of the
truce. At a Monday morning meeting of Resistance leaders, Chaban
once again urged Rol to support the truce, claiming that he had information (which was either erroneous or contrived to sway Rol) indicating that 150 German tanks were on the way to Paris. Honoring
the truce, he argued, was the only way to keep those tanks from
killing thousands of innocent people. Rol angrily shot back with his
oft-repeated statement that the liberation of Paris was worth
200,000 dead. The communist representative Pierre Villon was even
more irate than Rol. Villon, an Alsatian Jew who had risen to become
a leader of the military arm of the Resistance, had spent the war
years in hiding and wanted to hide no longer. He glared at Chaban
and told him, "This is the first time I have ever seen such cowardice
from a French general," a comment designed to insult the honor of
the man de Gaulle had recently named the youngest general in the
army. Villon also accused Chaban of having ulterior motives for
pushing the truce, charging, "[The Gaullists] fear the people. They are
stopping the battle in order to steal their victory. . . . [The truce] is in
the spirit of Munich, the spirit of Vichy, not the spirit of the Resistance." Villon ended by shouting, "Better Paris be destroyed like Warsaw than that she live through another 1940." While impassioned,
Villon's challenge to Chaban was more emotional than strategic; it
failed to move Chaban, who continued to urge his comrades to respect the truce. Most of the men at the meeting still disagreed with

Chaban, however, noting that the SS was not respecting the truce. FFI reports from across Paris warned that the Germans were using the time the truce bought to reposition their forces for a vigorous counterattack.[6]

It was obvious to Chaban that he was on the losing side of the argument. Most of the Resistance rank and file had no intention of honoring a truce that they believed the Germans were not themselves respecting. Moreover, they found the very idea of talking to the Germans a treasonous act. Chaban had made his point and could tell de Gaulle that he had done everything in his power to try to slow down the uprising, even if it continued apace. Events were spiraling dizzyingly out of his, or anyone else's, control. At the end of the meeting, the Resistance leaders decided to support the decisions made the day before to construct barricades throughout the city. Chaban noted that nothing in the truce forbade the construction of barricades, so he could still claim to be honoring the French side of the bargain, a point that won him little favor with the hard-liners like Villon.

All of the representatives at the meeting knew how powerful an emotional and political symbol barricades were to Paris. They had been a regular feature of Parisian revolutions and had figured famously and prominently in Victor Hugo's epic novel of the failed 1832 revolution, *Les Misérables*. Five years after that dramatic event, the Paris police noted that any group wishing to control France could do so by assembling "at certain key parts in the city the following items: two carts, some tables, chairs, bed frames and doors, several mattresses and some well-chosen rubbish." The need to reduce the potential power of barricades had helped to motivate the redesign of Paris by Baron Haussmann in the late nineteenth century. Haussmann razed entire neighborhoods, demolishing their narrow alleyways, and built in their place wide boulevards, in part to allow for the free flow of troops to put down rebellions. Despite the redesign, parts of Paris were still characterized by thin, narrow streets and alleyways. Many neighborhoods, such as St. Michel, the Latin Quarter, and the Marais, remained a warren of small, easily barricaded roads.[7]

Parisians had responded with enthusiasm to the call, erecting four hundred barricades in two days. By the end of the battle for Paris, the city had more than six hundred barricades in place. Most were built in the traditional Parisian style, using paving stones hacked out of the roads by the sweat and muscle of the neighborhood's young men. Anything that might help support a barricade was soon added, including disabled vehicles, felled trees, and broken pieces of furniture. Some barricades were just a few large branches stretched across a road. Others were as deep as six feet and as high as four feet. In many cases, Parisians added portraits of Hitler or other symbols of the German occupation to the front, thus requiring any German troops to open fire on photographs of the führer or Nazi flags if they attacked. It may have been a small token of resistance, but it was symbolic nonetheless. Other barricades flew French tricolors or improvised Soviet, British, or American flags.

The barricades served both symbolic and strategic purposes. From a symbolic standpoint, they showed that the city belonged to the FFI and to the people of Paris. The formation of barricades recalled heroic periods in French history and connected the events of 1944 to those of the historic days of 1789, 1830, and 1848. They showed that a battle was well and truly underway, and they served as a rallying point for neighborhood action. The construction of the barricades involved thousands of people, young and old, rich and poor, male and female. Even children participated, bringing supplies to the barricades' defenders and, like Victor Hugo's young hero Gavroche, often exposing themselves to danger in the process.

Sylvia Beach, an American expatriate who owned the Shakespeare and Company bookstore, marveled at the sights of the barricades in her neighborhood, writing: "The children engaged in our defense piled up furniture, stoves, dustbins, and so on at the foot of the Rue de l'Odéon, and behind these barricades youths with FFI armbands and a strange assortment of old-fashioned weapons aimed at the Germans stationed on the steps of the theater at the top of the street." The uprising that had begun as a movement of select, clandestine groups had now expanded to include a wide array of Parisians, all of whom fought for a common cause. The password of the St. Michel neighborhood's barricades was "Vengeance."[8]

The sight of entire communities openly working to defend themselves underscored the communal nature of the new struggle. Another famous Parisienne, Simone de Beauvoir, recalled children behind the barricades singing, *"Nous ne les reverrons plus / C'est fini, ils sont foutus"* (We will not see them again / It's all over, they are screwed). The barricades thus had an important symbolic purpose in a city desperate to recover some of its own self-respect. FFI member Jean Reybaz watched in wonder as children in his working-class neighborhood piled paving stones into the baskets of their bicycles and took them to barricades that needed reinforcement. Philippe Barat, an FFI commander who was in charge of the barricades in the critical St. Michel area, recalled that the neighborhood "was suddenly filled with a motley and strange crowd that formed a vast, marvelous fraternity. The rich and the poor, the aristocrat and the worker, came together so that the Germans would take from their capital the memory of a city that had a true soul." Even allowing for some exaggeration in the heat of the moment, Barat had a point. For the first time in four years (at least), the people of Paris were standing together. As Gilles Perrault, a teenager at the time, thoughtfully noted, many of the barricades were not as much an action aimed at the Germans as "a matter between us and our long humiliation."[9]

From a tactical perspective, the barricades were unlikely to present much of an obstacle to a determined German attack; nevertheless, they served an important military purpose. Barat noted that they provided Parisians, many of whom had never held a gun in their lives, a modicum of protection that was crucially important to sustaining their morale. The men in his FFI cell were desperately anxious to fight—on hearing of the truce they had screamed, "No truce! War to the Death! Now more than ever!" But they had no real experience of fighting and no idea how to combat the materially superior Germans. The barricades gave them a place to assemble and site their few weapons. One barricade in the St. Michel area, for example, had thirty-seven men defending it, but just two rifles and a revolver. Fighting together as a community gave Parisians a strength they would not have had as individuals or pairs. As a result, the barricades took on an importance far out of proportion to their tactical value. Barat wrote that "words cannot express the fever of combat, the intoxication, the enthusiasm" that people felt as they took up an active role in their own liberation.[10]

When properly located and reinforced, moreover, the barricades could still play a strategic role. FFI leaders knew that the Germans were unlikely to risk losing a precious tank to demolish a barricade that was inexpensive to construct and simple to rebuild. FFI section chiefs carefully determined where to construct the barricades and instructed people how best to defend them in order to achieve the maximum effect. Barat's area in St. Michel sat along the route between the German tank park in the Jardin du Luxembourg and the Préfecture de Police. It therefore dominated one of the most important streets in the city on these days, the Boulevard St. Michel. Barat was determined to make his neighborhood a bastion of the FFI and a death trap for any Germans who dared to cross.

Barat oversaw the establishment of nine major barricades in St. Michel. The most important, made up of overturned trucks, paving stones, and sandbags, went up just west of the Boulevard St. Michel on the Quai des Grands Augustins. It was more than ten feet high and almost six feet deep, making it undoubtedly one of the strongest barricades in the city. It successfully prevented the movement of German tanks along the Left Bank of the Seine, thus protecting the southern approaches to the Île de la Cité. Other barricades blocked off the Boulevard St. Michel and the Rue St. Jacques at both the river and along the Boulevard St. Germain. Two barricades near the prominent fountain of St. Michel (the protector of Paris) stretched halfway across the boulevard to keep the interior lines of communication around the Rue St. Severin open for the FFI. In this neighborhood, at least, the barricades were not constructed randomly, but according to a plan that made maximum use of their strength.[11]

Barricades located in less important areas or that were less sturdily constructed still had their own roles to play. The barricades canalized German movements, forcing them to move around the obstacles or engage them directly. When they chose the former, they moved into alleys and side streets, where FFI teams were waiting for them with Molotov cocktails and whatever other weapons they could amass. When they chose the latter, they had to stop, which left them open to attack. In either case, Resistance fighters ambushed them, seized prisoners of war, and, more crucially, captured badly needed German weapons and ammunition. The barricades also presented a new and unwelcome problem for the Germans, who had grown accustomed to open lines of communication.

The Germans, and for that matter the French, often had no idea which streets were open and which were barricaded. The result was a communications headache for the Germans that sowed confusion and fear, placing them in the uncomfortable role of being on the defensive amid a hostile population. The barricades isolated the German strongpoints from one another. German units saw their supplies and reinforcements choked off as the roads literally closed in around them. When the Germans came out of their strongpoints to clear barricades, they found themselves engaged in disorienting street fighting for which they had no training. German attacks rarely succeeded, because the Germans could not survive outside their strongpoints for long before being surrounded. Even when the Germans damaged the barricades, teams of neighborhood volunteers quickly repaired them.

The mass confusion in the streets impacted the Germans much more than it did the FFI. Rol's fighters could easily move in pairs or small groups through the streets without fear of being intercepted by either the Germans or the police, who were protecting the prefecture and the commissariats. They could also use the corridors of the Métro and the sewer system to move underground, where the Germans could not see them and the barricades did not inhibit them. From his headquarters underneath the Denfert-Rochereau Métro station, Rol could keep in contact with the neighborhoods and even direct reinforcements to threatened areas where necessary. Rol's staff marked each barricade on a giant map, giving the FFI an enormous intelligence advantage over the Germans. The prefecture, too, acted as a command post. Its fully functioning telephone system helped the FFI to direct reinforcements and supplies to crisis areas.[12]

The heady atmosphere in Paris transformed it into a new city as residents felt freedom for the first time in years. Rol's courageous wife, Cécile, recalled these days as the first time she could walk through the streets of Paris without having to look behind to see who was following her. Parisians finally felt safe enough to use the telephones and say in public what had been on their minds throughout the occupation. "One could say out loud that Hitler was a bastard and Pétain an old traitor," recalled one Parisian with joy. Others were inspired by the sight of the French police patrolling the area around the prefecture in a captured German armored car with the word "POLICE" painted hastily on its sides. "People stared at us stupefied," the driver of the vehicle later noted. "They couldn't believe their eyes. Everywhere we went they cheered us and applauded us." The FFI flew a large tricolor flag over the recently liberated Cherche-Midi prison and stretched another across an adjacent road. A German armored vehicle passing by shot it down, but thirty minutes later a new one took its place. That flag flew throughout the rest of the liberation.[13]

The Resistance leaders attempted to channel these newfound energies into the ongoing battle raging within the city. One communist proclamation urged Parisians to join the fight, saying that "the hour has come to chase out the invader, the hour has come to once again proclaim the Republic at the Hôtel de Ville, by Parisians themselves. TO ARMS CITIZENS!" The Communist Party also posted notices urging Parisians to disregard the false truce. "Paris wants to fight!" they read. And fight Paris did. All but three of the city's arrondissements saw action on August 21 and 22.

For the first time, the French had the initiative, and the Resistance groups in the city were not shy about exercising it. FFI members moved through the city, making maximum use of the absence of German Army patrols. They captured buildings of importance, including the telephone exchanges that the entire German Army in France depended upon for communications. They attacked Germans when the military situation was in their favor, and they made dozens of arrests of collaborators, including so-called horizontal collaborators, women who had had affairs with German officials and were often accused of being critical sources of information for the Germans. These women soon became a symbol of the more vengeful side of the liberation and *épuration*, the purging of French society that followed.[14]

Without the collaborators and the Paris police acting as their eyes and ears, the Germans were operationally blind and deaf. The FFI could thus move freely and attack almost anytime they wished, weapons permitting. Spreading the fighting to as many areas as he could was part of Rol's strategy to ease the pressure on the prefecture. FFI bands, despite their lack of arms, tried to pin down Germans in their strongholds, including the Prince Eugène barracks on the Place de la République, the crucial Place d'Italie traffic circle, and the Porte d'Orléans, to keep them from being able to move men and arms to threatened areas. By the morning of August 22, the Germans felt safe moving around the city only when they were in armored cars. The cars offered reasonable protection against small arms, yet were faster and less vulnerable to Molotov cocktails than tanks.[15]

The momentum of battle quickly swung in the FFI's favor. They captured the critically important Gare de l'Est, with its rail links to the east, although the nearly adjacent Gare du Nord remained in German hands. These operations also gave the FFI a chance to capture more prisoners of war and weapons stocks. They found many German soldiers willing to surrender; entire German strongpoints and their garrisons frequently threw up their hands after just a few minutes of combat. Isolated from support and in the middle of a vengeful population, they could often do little more. Once in French hands, they often spoke of how sick they were of the war and how worried they were for their families back in Germany. The steady accumulation of these prisoners, 650 of whom the FFI captured between August 19 and 22, allowed Rol to issue a bold proclamation that he would kill every German in FFI hands if the Germans began demolitions inside the city.[16]

Other German strongpoints, like the École Militaire and the Palais du Luxembourg, both well protected by tanks and concrete blockhouses, were too heavily defended for the FFI to assault with their small arms. Luxembourg's defenders, about three hundred dedicated SS troops, warned that they would blow up the palace with ten tons of explosives stored underneath before they would surrender, sending a shiver of fright throughout the neighborhood. Police soon began evacuations of all buildings within about three hundred yards of the palace, which included the homes of two expatriate American women of letters: Sylvia Beach, owner of Shakespeare and Company, who lived near the Place de l'Odéon, and the collaborationist and scholar of Shakespeare Clara Longworth de Chambrun, who had used her links to Pierre Laval (her son had married his daughter) to keep the American Library of Paris open through 1944. Despite their almost completely opposite politics, both women were directly threatened by the increasingly tense situation in their neighborhood.[17]

Some key places fell to the Resistance without a shot being fired in their defense. The Gaullist representative Alexandre Parodi, perhaps motivated by the fear that the FFI was growing too powerful, ordered the seizure of the Hôtel Matignon, the seventeenth-century mansion that serves as the official residence of the French prime minister. Parodi dispatched a young dedicated Gaullist named Yvon Morandat and his fiancée, Claire Walborn, to do the job. Parodi had told him not to risk a confrontation with the Matignon's security detail, whose allegiances were unknown. If there should be opposition, Parodi advised him, he should leave the area at once. "If there is opposition," Morandat boldly replied, "I'll leave in a coffin." In his excitement, Morandat had set off before checking a map, heading instinctively to the Avenue

Matignon on the wrong bank of the Seine. He and Walborn, who rode on the handlebars of his bicycle, were reduced to asking the only person on the streets, an elderly Frenchman walking his dog, for directions to the prime minister's residence.

After reversing direction through nearly deserted streets, they found the Hôtel Matignon, just steps away from the apartment on the Rue de Bellechasse where the Resistance leaders had met three long days earlier. With little more than his courage to protect him, Morandat talked his way past the Matignon's security guards and to the commander of the well-armed one-hundred-man bodyguard unit that had protected Pierre Laval until just a few days before. Walking up to the commander of the guard with his, and Claire Walborn's, FFI armbands clearly visible, he said, "I have come to occupy these premises in the name of the Provisional Government of the French Republic." To his astonishment, the commander announced his own pro-Republican politics, called the guard to attention, and said, "At your orders."[18]

A few hours later, Parodi hosted a meeting of the shadow Gaullist government in the office of the prime minister, with Walborn assuming the role of recording secretary. A French government, with a complete cabinet, was back in business, even as the German Army still controlled many key points across the city. The meeting focused mainly on the food crisis, unemployment, and the need to establish order once the Germans left. The ministers made no critical decisions, but the mere fact that the meeting happened at all sent a powerful message across Paris, especially after the left-leaning press voiced its tentative support. This support was crucial because the new French government, although provisional, was dominated by men loyal to de Gaulle, who vitally needed the support of the French Left to lend legitimacy to their efforts. Other leftist elements in Paris, notably the FFI, were still far from endorsing the Gaullist government. The FFI may have controlled the streets, but the Gaullists controlled both the police and the new mechanisms of government represented by the cabinet now openly meeting in the Hôtel Matignon. The FFI leadership knew about the meeting but did nothing to disrupt it, an indication that they were focused on defeating the Germans, not seizing power by means of a coup.[19]

Still, the Resistance could only do so much without weapons. Despite their success, the leaders of both the Gaullists and the FFI knew that the Germans would recover from their surprise and initial setbacks. When they did, they would be looking for revenge, and they would have at their disposal heavy weapons, including airplanes. Unlike Parisians, moreover, German soldiers were unlikely to care how many civilians were caught in the crossfire or how much of the city they devastated. The FFI would need material help from the Allies, and fast, or the Germans would have the chance to strike back with ferocity. Both the FFI and the Gaullists made every effort to make their desperate situation known to the Americans and to de Gaulle. Using radio transmitters, they sent out updates on the military situation in the capital. But they had no way of knowing if the Allies were monitoring the frequencies they were using. Rol, in particular, used the transmissions to beg for arms drops to keep the uprising going.

A French Resistance sympathizer, a doctor named Robert Monod, understood the problem and thought he knew a way to get in touch with the Allies. He conceived a daring plan to get across the lines and plead with the Americans for help. Monod had admired the courage behind the uprising, but on the 20th he had written, "We have to prepare for a German offensive. Tomorrow the battle will doubtless resume and be much more violent. . . . Left to themselves, what can the insurgents do without cannons, without tanks, without trained men against a large German garrison well protected in fortified strong points and possessing ultra-modern weapons?" Monod, like many other résistants, believed that the truce was a German ruse designed to buy time to redeploy and reinforce in preparation for a major attack. He also thought that asking the Allies to drop weapons into the city would only prolong a battle that the Resistance was certain to lose without outside help. What Paris needed was not American rifles dropped from the sky, but

American tanks. It was the only way, he thought, to prevent a massive bloodbath on the streets of Paris.[20]

Monod wrote down the outlines of his plan in the form of a letter to Rol and gave the letter to an FFI contact, asking him to find the FFI leader and deliver it to him. The message proposed the dispatch of a mission to Allied lines to inform the Americans about the desperate situation inside Paris. It noted that he, Monod, was perhaps the only man in the city who could make such a mission succeed, but he needed help. By late afternoon on the 20th, however, Monod still had no reply from Rol and no way of knowing if his messenger had even made it to see the FFI commander. He decided it was worth the risk to make a few phone calls to FFI contacts, always using code names, to convince Rol to support his daring plan. Finally, at 6:00 p.m., an FFI agent showed up at Monod's apartment with Rol's chief of staff, Major Roger Cocteau, code-named Gallois, and the news that Rol had agreed to the courageous scheme that Monod had outlined in his message. And Gallois was going to accompany him on the mission.

Monod could not believe his eyes. Gallois was perfect for the plan he had in mind. He and Monod were good friends (Monod had suspected, but did not know for sure, that Gallois was a senior leader in the FFI), and Gallois spoke fluent English. But Gallois's instructions showed that Rol was still thinking in terms different from those of Monod. Rol wanted the mission to urge the Americans to drop arms and supplies into the city at this critical moment. With the barricades proving their effectiveness, Rol concluded, the Americans could now drop weapons (and maybe even paratroopers) into areas fully under the control of the FFI. With those weapons, the FFI would have a fighting chance to liberate the city on their own and prevent a massive German retaliation. Gallois also told Monod that Rol no longer had faith that the Americans or the Free French Army tanks could get to Paris in time to help. Parisians, he thought, needed to liberate their city themselves.

Monod disagreed with Rol's interpretation of the situation, but he immediately accepted Gallois's help. Monod had planned the trip carefully. In his capacity as a surgeon and a local health inspector, he had access to gasoline and a pass that could get them through German lines. He also knew Red Cross doctors close to the front line near St. Cyr and Versailles who had worked with the U.S. Army's medical staff to treat wounded civilians on both sides of the line. Those contacts might prove useful in finding intermediaries with whom they could talk, should they be able to get across the lines safely. The two men developed a cover story that they were going to a sanitarium near Saint Nom la Bretèche, a small village about twenty miles northwest of Versailles and close to the front lines. Monod had been there before to help care for sick children, thus his return to the sanitarium would not strike the Germans as unusual. Gallois would disguise himself as a male nurse. If they could get past the German checkpoints and find their way safely to the sanitarium, Monod thought, they might be able to make contact with the Americans nearby.

They left at 5:00 the next morning, moving slowly toward the front lines. They had to leave Paris by the southern Porte d'Orléans, then turn west to go past checkpoints and around roads and bridges damaged by recent air raids. Along the way, Monod attempted to convince Gallois not to ask the Americans for weapons but to urge them to change their plans and send a division or more to the city at once. Only a strong Allied presence, the doctor argued, could save Paris from a catastrophic battle. They passed through the checkpoint at St. Cyr, then found themselves in an area empty of Germans as they approached the front lines. Instead of continuing northwest to the sanitarium, the doctor turned due west down the D11 highway toward the town of Neauphle le Château, home to a friend of Monod's and, coincidentally, home to Gallois's grandmother. The two men thus knew the region well and hoped that it might provide more direct access to the Americans.

By the time they had arrived and made contact with a local FFI leader, who was code-named Dominique, Monod had managed to win Gallois over to his point of view, convincing him to ask the

Americans for more than just air drops. Dominique promised to find them a local farmer, who he said could navigate them through mine-fields and past a squad of SS soldiers camped nearby. He told the men to park their car on a hill, then directed them to a field, where they were to await their guide. Sitting in the rainy, muddy field, Monod began to sense that something wasn't right. They felt, he recalled, like rabbits waiting for hunters. Fearing that their sixth sense was telling them that they had been double-crossed by Dominique, they headed carefully back to their car and used their knowledge of the area to make an escape. They then headed to the sanitarium, where Monod had contacts and felt safer.

If their sixth sense had indeed been right, their decision not to trust Dominique likely saved their lives and possibly the lives of thousands of Parisians as well. Once at the sanitarium, Monod introduced Gallois to a reliable FFI contact code-named Georges, who agreed to take Gallois to the American lines. Monod left Gallois there, telling him that if the Americans would not listen, then he should claim that he and Leclerc were old friends and ask to see him. If that bluff worked, then Gallois could make his case directly to the French general, a man he had never actually met but who Monod was sure would be sympathetic. Monod then returned to Paris and his badly understaffed hospital. Georges drove Gallois to a spot where the American and German lines were so close to one another that Gallois could see soldiers from both armies at the same time. He was sure that the Germans saw him crawling through the woods as he made his way toward the American lines, but concluded that they were afraid to shoot at him for fear of provoking an American response. He crossed the lines at 7:30 p.m. on August 21, tired, wet, and hungry.[21]

Gallois's remarkable journey continued as he left occupied France for the first time in four years. He crawled to some American soldiers and warned them about the presence of German soldiers nearby. "What the hell do you want us to do about it?" was their reaction, leaving Gallois wondering what kind of unit he had stumbled into. Eventually, he talked to an American lieutenant, who put him in a jeep with gum-chewing soldiers who were under orders not to talk to him. Gallois later recalled the oddity of not being able to speak English, a language he had worked hard to learn, with these curious Americans. The soldiers brought Gallois back to their regimental headquarters to meet with a lieutenant colonel who was connected to a military intelligence branch that specialized in the French Resistance. More than five hours of intense discussion served to convince the officer that the Frenchman in front of him was a genuine member of the Resistance with whom the American high command might want to speak. They got into another jeep and headed to a large American military camp, arriving in the middle of the night.[22]

Gallois did not know it, but he had arrived at a critical time. American planners had discovered that Leclerc had dispatched a detachment of his Deuxième Division Blindée toward Paris without permission, while the rest of the corps to which it belonged was moving to a rest area. The detachment contained ten tanks, ten armored personnel carriers, and ten armored cars. Gerow, as the corps commander, had received a terse message from army headquarters asking why troops under his command were not where they were supposed to be, followed by a none-too-subtle suggestion that he had failed to exercise effective command over his own unit. A furious Gerow ordered Leclerc to reverse the order and recall the detachment, but Leclerc refused, creating both a command and diplomatic crisis. Leclerc had, however, offered to come to discuss the matter with Gerow, Bradley, and Eisenhower, and he was in fact on his way to Allied headquarters when Gallois made his appearance.[23]

At the same time, Eisenhower's position on Paris was beginning to soften. He had determined that Allied forces would be "compelled to go into Paris" because of the incessant urgings of de Gaulle, who, Eisenhower knew, would likely be the head of the postwar French state. He was a man the Americans would need as an ally both in the final phases of the war and in the years that would follow. In any case, as Eisenhower had told General George Marshall, Paris "falls into our hands whether we like it or not" as soon as the Germans in the area surrendered or withdrew. The Allies would then need to assume responsibility for the city. Eisenhower also argued, consistent with Allied policy that predated the Normandy landings, that it would be best for all concerned to have a French unit accept that surrender, both to honor previous American promises and to ensure as smooth a transition as possible.[24]

The information Gallois brought with him reinforced these conclusions. Among the men who met with him was Harold Lyon, the commander of the American T Force. Lyon reported that the Frenchman brought with him five critical pieces of information: that the Paris police had begun an uprising on August 19; that barricades were being erected all across the city; that the FFI had control of the center of the city as well as its western bridges; that the German high command in the city had requested a truce; and that the truce was set to expire in a matter of a few hours. Lyon concluded from this information that the German garrison in Paris was close to surrendering and therefore that "the situation in Paris was an opportunity which the Allies had to take advantage of immediately."[25]

A colonel with whom Gallois had also met turned to an aide and mumbled something Gallois did not understand. The aide then left the room. A few minutes later, at 1:30 a.m. on August 22, a man in a general's uniform appeared before him. Sleepy and disheveled, the general turned to Gallois and said, "OK. I'm listening. What's your story?" Gallois, unsure who the man was but certain that he was someone of importance, explained why he had come as carefully and passionately as he could. The general listened thoughtfully, but then told Gallois that he would not change American plans. The goal of the Allied armies, he said, was "destroying Germans, not capturing capitals." The general then continued in a measured, professional tone, speaking to Gallois "as a soldier":

> You ought to know full well that our operations at this moment were not conceived lightly or without full reflection. We are obligated to follow our plans to the letter and not even a fortuitous or

unexpected event like this one can change these plans, even if the
event is of such extraordinary importance. Our objective is Berlin
and we want to end this war as quickly as possible. The immediate capture of Paris is not part of the plan and we are not moving
toward the capital; it is not a military objective, its capture would
be a burden, for we would have to assure the feeding of the population as well as the repair of the things the Germans destroyed.
We want to destroy the enemy not save cities. You should have
waited for orders from Allied headquarters before launching an
insurrection and not taken the initiative yourselves.

Gallois warned the general that France would never forgive the
United States if it did not help Paris in its hour of need. "I was bluff-
ing, because it wasn't at all true," he later recalled. "But I thought
that the idea might impress the Americans." It did not. After shaking
Gallois's hand, the American general turned and left the room.[26]

A dejected Gallois stood stunned and crestfallen. After all of his
efforts, and those of his comrades in Paris, he had failed in his mission. There would be no arms for Paris and no change of plans for
the Americans. Gallois then pleaded to be taken to see his "friend"
Leclerc, but the Americans said that they did not know where
Leclerc was, a statement that was probably true, given that Leclerc
had, in American eyes, effectively gone AWOL. Just as Gallois was
sinking into a state of depression, the general, George Patton, suddenly returned with a bottle of champagne and offered Gallois a
toast to victory. After clinking their glasses, Patton turned to Gallois
and said, "Are you ready to take a long voyage?" There was another
American general whom Patton thought Gallois should meet. Someone or something had changed Patton's mind. At 3:30 a.m., an
American major showed up with a jeep, and Gallois sped away once
more, not sure where he was going or who the general was who
wanted to see him.[27]

Gallois was not the only man trying to get to Allied lines. Another,
quite different, representative of Paris had come up with a similar

plan to make contact with the Americans and urge them to come to the city. Earlier that night, Choltitz had called Nordling and asked him to come to the Hôtel Meurice. After pouring a couple of glasses of whiskey ("Don't tell the English," he had joked), Choltitz told Nordling that the truce was not working. Furthermore, his encounter with Parodi the day before had convinced him that talking to the FFI was futile, because they were unable to control their own people. Nordling replied that only de Gaulle had the power to negotiate a lasting agreement that could end the fighting. "Why doesn't someone go to see him?" Choltitz asked. Nordling, who might have been forgiven for wondering how many whiskeys Choltitz had downed before his arrival, offered to go himself if the German general's offer was sincere.

Choltitz then told Nordling that he had received orders to begin demolitions in the city; the failure of the truce might leave him no option but to carry out those orders. What he needed, Choltitz said, was for the Allies to get to Paris so that he could surrender the city to a recognized authority. The German commander then took out a pass and wrote on it an authorization for "R. Nordling to leave Paris and its line of defense." As Nordling was officially a neutral diplomat, the pass should be all he would need to get through the lines, but Choltitz told him to take along a German officer, the same "Bobby" Bender who had played a key role in saving the lives of Parodi and his two comrades. If there was any trouble at checkpoints, Choltitz said, Bender could clear it up. "Go fast," Choltitz told Nordling. "Twenty-four, forty-eight hours are all you have. After that, I cannot promise you what will happen here."[28]

Although Choltitz had warned Nordling that he might be forced to carry out orders to demolish the city, it is clear that he lacked the means to do so. During the meeting, Choltitz had taken an official-looking document out of his tunic pocket that he claimed contained orders to destroy Paris, but he was careful not to let Nordling see it. In a few isolated places, like the Batignolles train station, FFI agents had discovered explosives and disabled them. There were also rumors spreading through the city that the Germans had placed explosives in the Palais du Luxembourg; these were the same rumors that were then prompting widespread evacuations of the surrounding areas. But the Germans were far from having the means to conduct widespread demolitions, especially given their limited mobility around the city.

Choltitz knew that his position was hopeless. Around the time he summoned Nordling, he learned that the 348th Division, which headquarters had promised to send to Paris, would go to the Calais region instead. Rather than more resources and reinforcements, he received empty missives urging him to hold the city at all costs. Down to just two days of rations and facing both an uprising and the possibility of an American drive on the city, Choltitz needed a way out of his increasingly desperate operational situation. "Ever since our enemies have refused to listen to and obey our Fuehrer," he angrily noted, "the whole war has gone badly." When Model ordered him to hold the city even if it cost 40 percent of his force, Choltitz replied that the "German high command was out of touch with reality." Lacking the means to carry out orders that he saw as impossible and unnecessary, Choltitz needed a miracle. The Nordling mission might just provide it.[29]

Nordling's extraordinary mission was complicated even further by the fact that he did not know de Gaulle or anyone close to him. He would need someone who could both arrange a meeting and vouch for his authenticity. He therefore decided to bring with him two French bankers who had connections to the French Resistance outside Paris, including a former head of the Banque d'Indochine, a man who knew de Gaulle. One of those bankers then convinced him to also bring the French-born British agent code-named Jade Amicol, who would travel in disguise as a Swiss Red Cross official and facilitate meetings with senior Allied leaders. Nordling thus had with him a strange assortment: a British agent and two French bankers, plus a German minder who would no doubt report back directly to Choltitz.[30]

The stress of these responsibilities, and the knowledge that he might well have the fate of Paris in his hands, finally caught up to Nordling. As he was making final preparations, he suddenly felt a pain in his chest and sank to his knees. He had suffered a heart attack that left him too weak to complete his critical mission. Even under these circumstances, however, Nordling's sharp mind kept working. The mission was too important to be halted, even by a heart attack. Lying in his bed, he thought of a way to save it. His pass permitted "R. Nordling" to cross German lines. Nordling called his brother, Rolf, and put him in charge of the mission to find Charles de Gaulle and tell him to hurry Allied troops to Paris.

Parisians, who knew nothing about these events, were not waiting for help from the outside. By the evening of August 21, symbols of impending liberation were beginning to appear everywhere. Parisians heard the first Resistance radio broadcasts that night, which ended with the playing of the *Marseillaise*. Resistance newspapers were openly on sale in kiosks that only days before had sold the newspapers of the Germans and Vichy. Within just a few hours, eight different Resistance newspapers were on sale, some of them new, and some of them, like the Communist Party's *L'Humanité*, prewar newspapers appearing in public for the first time in four years. Despite their shoddy look and low-quality paper, the newspapers had an electric effect on the city. "You cannot understand what they signified for us," recalled one Parisian. "We read in black and white things that had only been whispered for four years." To this man, the newspapers were a far more important symbol than the barricades. They meant that "we could believe in freedom."[31]

The most important of these newspapers, *Combat*, couched its messages in powerful terms. The paper's editorials, many of them written or edited by Albert Camus, announced that the left-leaning elements of the Resistance had much more in mind than simply removing the Germans from Paris. In its first issue for public sale published on the night of August 21, *Combat* pledged that "the stunned joy that we are beginning to read on Parisian faces is a joy we share . . . but the task of the men of the Resistance is not yet over." France, it argued, must not return to the France of 1939, because the prewar "ruling class had failed in all its duties." The only path for France, it said, was "a true peoples' and workers' democracy" that could counter the dominance of the moneyed classes. Anything less, *Combat* charged, would be a betrayal to France, especially given the number of wealthy Frenchmen who had eagerly collaborated with the occupiers. "Having begun with resistance, [we] want to end with Revolution." The following day, Camus urged Parisians to keep in their minds the image of "dead children, kicked and beaten into their own coffins," as they thought of the better, more egalitarian France they wanted to create. "We are not men of hate," he concluded, "but we must be men of justice."[32]

Combat reserved its strongest vitriol not for the Germans, who were obviously on the way out, but for the French collaborators who had made German rule possible. Resistance newspapers publicly identified the city's most notorious collaborators and reported on their whereabouts. The FFI arrested some, others fled (some under German protection), and a few committed suicide. One Parisian recognized that many of the most notorious collaborators were likely to escape punishment, either by exploiting their powerful connections or by fleeing the country. Those who had waited around long enough to be captured by the FFI, he felt, were likely to be those without money or connections, "those less guilty than their masters who will pay for their crimes and the crimes of those who abandoned them." With tremendous foresight, he wrote, "Even if silence and forgetfulness protect [the collaborator], history will not be silent forever." Many collaborators, including those with a great deal of blood on their hands, did indeed escape punishment for years or even decades before their crimes were exposed and punished.[33]

While Parisians were reading Resistance newspapers on the evening of August 22, Gallois arrived at a vast Allied military camp in a forest about 130 miles southwest of Paris near Le Mans. After taking a few hours to rest, eat, and clean up, he talked to a stream of American officers and quickly concluded that they had no sense of how desperate the situation was in Paris. Gallois did his best to impress upon them the seriousness of the military problem of the FFI, emphasizing that the truce was soon set to expire. When it did, the Germans would be free to attack with their full might, and the resulting tragedy might rival the terrible fate of Warsaw.[34]

Gallois's information led the Americans to draw a series of vital conclusions that led, at long last, to a change in American strategy. First, the Americans believed both that the German position in the city was feeble and that the FFI, in the words of the official U.S. Army history of these events, was "holding the city on bluff and nerve." The Americans deduced that if the Germans could not sweep aside a group of poorly organized and badly equipped civilians, then the Germans were ripe for plucking. They also concluded, however, that the Germans were probably rearming and preparing for a counter-offensive that might destroy the city as soon as the truce expired.[35]

Thus the Allies, who had deferred thinking about Paris for so long, now decided that they had to get to the city as quickly as possible. Eisenhower noted that the new thinking at Bradley's headquarters was that "we can and *must* walk in," an indication of both the new sense of urgency at his headquarters and the belief that if the Allies could rescue the FFI before the Germans brought in reinforcements, there need not be a major battle for Paris. Either because of Gallois's information or their own ability to read the strategic situation, the Americans made three critical decisions: to send a force into the city immediately in the hopes of accepting the German surrender, or at least taking over quickly from the departing Germans; to make sure that a French unit was the first Allied formation into the city; and to begin the immediate dispatch of 23,000 tons of food and 3,000 tons of coal to the beleaguered French capital. If the Allies could get forces to the city before the Germans could prepare a major counterattack, Eisenhower gambled, then "no great battle would take place" and the city would fall into Allied hands with a minimum of fighting. "The entry of one or two divisions," he presumed, "would accomplish the liberation of the city."[36]

Patton must have briefed his friend Bradley about the conversation with Gallois, because a few hours earlier, at 2:00 p.m. on August 22, Bradley had arrived unannounced at First Army headquarters with the momentous news that Paris was under the control of the FFI. "Paris could be avoided no longer," he told the assembled officers, because the Germans were preparing to violate a truce and attack. This news "demanded instantaneous action" on the part of the Allies in order to prevent terrible bloodshed. Bradley then departed, leaving it to flustered staff officers to figure out how to solve the problem. As one of them recalled, "The corps staff assembled in the war room . . . [followed by] the hasty assembling of maps, the hurried writing of movement orders, the determination of routes of march . . . [and] the careful instructions to the French, who have a casual manner of doing almost exactly what they please, regardless of orders." That final comment was undoubtedly designed to insult Leclerc, who had so recently disappeared without telling the staff where he was going.[37]

Although Bradley remained frustrated that his plan to go around Paris had been undermined by the news that Gallois had brought, he resigned himself to the path before him. Having briefed his staff officers, Bradley flew to Le Mans, where Gallois and Leclerc awaited him. His plane landed at 7:15 p.m. Leclerc, too anxious to wait for Bradley to descend from the cabin, grabbed the first man he saw with stars on his shoulders, Lieutenant General Edward Sibert. With the plane's engine still running, Sibert, Bradley's intelligence chief, yelled to Leclerc, "You win. They've decided to send you straight to Paris." Bradley then said to Gallois: "A grave decision has been made and we three bear the weight of responsibility for it: me, because I am giving the order to take Paris; General Leclerc, because he is the one who has to carry out this order; and you, because it is based on the information that you have brought that we have acted." Tired, but pleased that he had completed his extraordinary mission at last, Gallois briefed American officers for the next three hours before meeting with Gerow, who chewed him out for not being in uniform and ordered him to go to the American supply tent and get one. Then, wearing his new U.S. Army uniform, Gallois found a place to get a well-deserved night's sleep.[38]

For his part, Leclerc had finally received the orders he had waited so long to hear. Bradley, however, had given him clear instructions that "Paris was to be entered only if the degree of fighting could be overcome by light forces." If Leclerc encountered strong German resistance, he was to retreat, regroup, and await reinforcements. His orders also forbade him from using air or artillery inside Paris itself, both to protect the city and because the Americans assumed that such weapons would be unnecessary if the German position was as weak as they suspected. Finally, the Americans made it clear that Leclerc was to relieve the FFI and ensure that regular soldiers assumed the responsibility for security in the city as quickly as possible. Soon after Eisenhower and Bradley had approved the change in American strategy, Rolf Nordling arrived at American lines; the consistency of his information with that of Gallois reassured the Americans that they had made the right decision.[39]

Leclerc's greatest concern over the past few days had been finding a way to get his division from its bases at Fleuré, near Argentan, to the roads that commanded the approaches to Paris. To make the process move more quickly and perhaps force Eisenhower or Bradley's hand, Leclerc had not waited for orders to prepare his men. They had covered 120 miles the day before in anticipation of receiving an order to head for Paris—or in anticipation of going there even without orders. Even though they knew almost nothing about the enemy's forces or dispositions, Leclerc and his men were willing to take any risk necessary to liberate their capital. Before beginning the final drive, Leclerc had told one of his officers, "The cold logic of tactics cannot make General Gerow understand the importance of Paris for our people who have lived for four years without hope." Now Leclerc had orders and the full support of Bradley and Eisenhower.

But he still had to find a way to get his men into Paris before the Germans counterattacked.[40]

Knowing that he could never move his entire division quickly enough, Leclerc decided to send a small detachment of three tanks ahead of his main force. He chose as the unit's commander Captain Raymond Dronne, who had been with the Deuxième Division Blindée since 1940. Dronne had lived in Leipzig and Berlin before the war and had seen with his own eyes how terrible the Nazis truly were. Upon his return to France just before the outbreak of the war, he became convinced that his countrymen were not yet awake to the dangers they faced or the horrors that awaited them if the Nazis were not stopped. After the fall of France, he was among the small group of French officers to understand that Vichy would be little more than an auxiliary to the Germans. His loyalty to France now put him in the enviable position of leading a drive on to Paris. When Leclerc's orders to run for Paris with three tanks arrived, Dronne was trimming his red beard so that he would look good when the people of Paris saw the first Free French soldiers enter their city to liberate them.[41]

By the time night fell on August 22, the insurgents in Paris could well claim to have already done most of the hard work for Dronne, Leclerc, and Bradley. Although the situation was so confused that buildings on the same block flew the French tricolor and the swastika, the uprising had clearly gone a long way toward retaking the city. The FFI claimed to have effective control of seventy of Paris's eighty neighborhoods. The uprising had also made it impossible for the Germans to move through the city unimpeded or to carry out a program of demolition inside the city. The Germans maintained control of only a dozen of their original thirty-six strongpoints, although these included many strategically important buildings, including the Palais du Luxembourg, the École Militaire, and the Palais Bourbon, the home of the Assemblé Nationale.[42]

That night, two messages went out regarding Paris. The first, sent from Hitler to Choltitz, read, "Paris will be transformed into a heap of rubble. The general commanding in chief will defend the city to the last man, and, if necessary, be buried beneath it." It was a desperate message from a man who had long since lost any ability to control the situation in the French capital. Choltitz set it aside for the moment but knew that he would soon have to make a choice between fighting or surrendering. He knew nothing about the Gallois mission, and he had no idea where the Nordling mission was or if it would produce the desired results.

The second message came from Leclerc to the men of the Deuxième Division Blindée, some of whom had been with him since the unit's formation in Africa in 1940. Now that he was so close to his goal of liberating his suffering nation's capital, he was determined to make the most of the opportunity. His message implored his men to push as hard as they could and overcome any obstacles that might bar their way. "The general demands," it ended, "for this movement that can lead to the liberation of our capital, the full effort that he is certain he will obtain from everyone." The main force of Leclerc's armored division was set to enter the city the next day. The Allies were finally joining the battle for Paris.[43]

8

DELIVERANCE,
AUGUST 23–24

ANY HOPE THAT THE LIBERATION OF PARIS MIGHT HAPPEN
without further bloodshed or damage to the magnificent
buildings of the city literally went up in smoke on the morning of
August 23. Parisians, or at least those who were able to sleep that
night amid the sporadic sounds of gunfire, awoke to the sight of a
column of smoke towering above the Grand Palais, a massive structure completed in 1900 for the Universal Exposition of that year.
Sitting near the Avenue des Champs Élysées (on what is today the
Avenue Général Eisenhower and near the Franklin D. Roosevelt
Métro station), the Grand Palais, with its 250,000 square feet of exhibit space, remained open throughout the war to provide Parisians
with some entertainment and diversion. It had also hosted numerous exhibitions of Vichy and Nazi propaganda. On this Wednesday
it was hosting Europe's largest traveling circus. That a circus had
even been able to come to Paris that week is an indication of how
quickly events had transpired in the city in the previous few days.
Now that circus found itself in the middle of an active war zone.

That morning, a German detachment decided to attack the Grand Palais, probably in retaliation for an FFI ambush on a German car in that area the day before. The attack might also have been an attempt to rescue German prisoners of war rumored to be in the police station in the Grand Palais's basement. Or, it could have been the result of a misunderstanding about an order to clear a barricade nearby. In any case, unwilling to send tanks into the area without some preparation in this FFI-dominated neighborhood, the Germans decided to deploy a small remote-controlled tracked vehicle, known, incongruously enough, as a Goliath. Four feet long, two feet tall, and resembling a miniature World War I–era British tank, each Goliath could carry as many as two hundred pounds of explosives. Goliaths detonated upon a signal from operators who sat a safe distance away and controlled their machines by a telephone wire. The Germans had used Goliaths to blow up enemy tanks in Normandy until the Allies figured out that the best way to defend against them was to target the fragile cable with shrapnel shells.

On this day the Goliaths were to make their Parisian debut. In Normandy and elsewhere, they had proven their value against dense formations of infantry as well as against buildings and fixed defenses. Also known as "teletanks" or "mobile land mines," these early drones were a much more cost-effective weapon to use in urban settings than either tanks or armored personnel carriers. They also reduced the risks of German soldiers being captured. The Germans had used Goliaths with murderous effect against makeshift barricades in Warsaw. Ironically enough, the idea for the Goliaths was originally developed in a Paris factory. Now the small number of them that the Germans had at their disposal were to be unleashed against Paris as part of a new German approach to urban warfare.

The order to attack the Grand Palais did not come from Choltitz's headquarters, however. As the German commander knew, the building had little military value. The Germans, like everyone else in the city, knew that it was hosting a circus; many German officers had first-class tickets to that day's performance. The Palais and its basement jail were protected by policemen sympathetic to the uprising, but the building itself was not under the control of the FFI and was full not of soldiers, but of animals and ordinary criminals. There was only a single German being held there, a francophile baron who before the war had appeared in numerous equestrian shows in the Palais. His arrest had had nothing to do with the fighting underway, and he was so unthreatening that the French police even permitted him to move freely around the main hall. He was not confined to a cell with the prisoners in the jail, most of whom were prostitutes picked up in a recent raid.[1]

The Palais had no military utility at all. Nevertheless, out of confusion, vengeance, or both, the Germans attacked. The German baron was the first to recognize the strange device moving toward the Palais. He sounded the alarm, creating a panic as people sought to escape, and handlers struggled to release their animals from cages that would soon turn into death traps. The Goliath set off a massive explosion that German tanks followed with incendiary shells that caused multiple fires. Local German commanders initially forbade firefighters from extinguishing the massive blaze that ensued, sending panicked lions, tigers, prisoners of war, policemen, and prostitutes alike streaming out of the building in terror. As FFI leader Claude Roy, who witnessed the scene, recalled, "the firefighters arrived. Blinded by the smoke, those trapped inside ran for the basements. Some escaped, others did not. There was an odd mixture of firefighters, Germans, rescuers, and prisoners." Crazed and confused animals of every type ran out of the building into the streets, some of them on fire. Starving Parisians risked the fire and the wrath of the Germans, running into the Champs Élysées with knives and plates to carve into dead and dying horses for their meat, creating a truly hellish scene on one of the most famous and most beautiful avenues in the world.[2]

The Grand Palais was not the only structure burning on the morning of August 23. On the other side of Paris, the Germans had intentionally set fire to the massive flour mills in the far grittier Pantin neighborhood. This action was in response to rumors that the FFI was planning to attack it and seize the tons of grain stored there rather than let it be transported to Germany. The destruction of the Pantin granaries carried with it an especially bitter poignancy for Parisians, who were starving and badly in need of that grain. Word also reached the city that the Germans were blowing up stocks of ammunition in their main depots at Villeneuve-Saint-Georges and inside the Forêt de Sénard near Orly airfield to the south of the city. They were obviously planning to leave the Paris region, but no one knew what level of destruction they might be planning before they left. Fears began to spread that Paris might suffer the fate of towns like Oradur sur Glane, only on a much greater scale.[3]

Rumors that the Allies were approaching the gates of the city fueled the sense that the final reckoning was near. Despite their lack of weapons, the FFI fighters did not let up their pressure on the Germans. Nor did they count on receiving help from the outside. Most FFI leaders had long since learned not to base their plans on rumors of an Allied approach that seemed never to materialize. As one of them, lawyer Emmanuel Blanc, noted in his journal, "What is keeping the Americans? Every day we hear they are closer and closer, and every night we wait in vain. We hear they are at Versailles, they are at Fontainebleau, they are at Corbeil, they are at Melun. But Paris? When will they come to Paris?" More importantly, FFI leaders believed they were close to liberating the city by themselves, an achievement that they saw as erasing four long years of humiliation. As the Resistance newspaper *Action* remarked on August 23, "of course we want the Allies to arrive; but Paris is liberating itself. This is the source of our pride. Our friends will find their work done for them. We will receive them in a free city." Another Parisian rhetorically asked, "Is not [an FFI] brassard worth as much as a khaki uniform?" Resistance radio stations were already beginning to use the past tense, announcing during a midday broadcast that "Paris has liberated itself." Having begun the insurrection, Parisians were not willing to yield, even if they had to fight without allies or heavy weapons.[4]

Albert Camus's writings in *Combat* conveyed a sense of the intensity of the feeling inside the FFI: "On the fourth day of the insurrection, in the wake of the enemy's first retreat and a phony truce cut short by the murders of Frenchmen, the people of Paris will resume the fight. . . . The choice to kill was not ours. We were placed in a position where we had either to kill or bend our knees. And despite those who tried to put doubts in our minds, we know now, after four years of terrible struggle, that it is not in our blood to kneel."[5]

Camus's powerful words notwithstanding, ardor and will would not be enough to triumph. The situation for the FFI had grown increasingly desperate, in large part because of the lack of weapons and ammunition. After just a few days of fighting, the FFI was nearing the end of its meager resources. Resistance leaders estimated that 500 men on their side had been killed and that more than 2,000 were wounded and in need of medical assistance, an indication of the severity of the combat. With the Allies still reluctant to air-drop weapons into the city, the FFI had to take matters into its own hands. Philosopher Jean-Paul Sartre, a frequent contributor to *Combat*, noted the urgency of the situation in that newspaper's August 23 edition: "We all know the order: attack a German and take his revolver. With that revolver seize a rifle. With that rifle seize a car. With that car, seize a tank." Sartre estimated that 3,000 Parisians were actively involved in the fight against the Germans, and that 35,000 more would join if only arms could be found for them.[6]

The FFI kept fighting even as the material situation of the Parisians approached crisis levels. They raided wine shops run by people whom Resistance newspapers identified as collaborators to acquire more bottles for Molotov cocktails. They also learned to use their remaining resources more effectively. By August 23 they had learned to target the last vehicle in a convoy with their Molotov cocktails in order to block the retreat of the others. Along the Boulevard St. Michel, known as the "intersection of death," the FFI managed to disable a Tiger tank this way, creating an astonishing symbol of the power of the men of the street and essentially closing this critical artery off to

German movement. By the end of the day, the FFI had captured 8 German artillery pieces, 9 German armored vehicles, and 650 prisoners of war. They also engaged in some daring exploits, such as an attack on a tunnel along the Paris ring road that the Germans were using to store three truckloads of explosives. The FFI attacked both entrances to the tunnel simultaneously, trapping the German defenders inside and leaving them little choice but to surrender. That they did it mostly on bluff and with few weapons made the feat all the more remarkable. It also testified to the increasing unwillingness of the Germans to fight to the death for Paris.[7]

Although the FFI was rapidly depleting its resources, its ranks were growing every day, especially in working-class neighborhoods. Rumors that the Germans were planning to deport as many as 200,000 young men from Paris to factories in Germany sent thousands of Parisians into the FFI, creating chaos in the streets and headaches for Rol, who had no weapons to give them. Rounding up as many weapons as they could, the FFI in northeastern Paris focused on the major German strongpoint of the Prince Eugène barracks on the Place de la République. The largest single concentration of German soldiers in Paris, it housed 1,200 men. FFI members surrounded the exits from the building and trapped the Germans inside. They lacked the power to take the building, but their actions kept the Germans based there from coming to the aid of their comrades, especially at nearby strategic sites such as the Gare de l'Est and the Place de la Nation.[8]

All across the city the FFI members were becoming bolder and more daring. The new atmosphere on the city's streets was evident for all to see. On the Avenue Henri-Martin in the normally calm Passy neighborhood near the Bois de Boulogne, Charles Braibant watched in astonishment as a young woman bicycled toward a prone German rifleman, seemingly oblivious to his presence. His fear that she might ride into his line of fire and become an innocent victim soon turned to stunned amazement when he saw her take out a pistol, calmly shoot the sniper dead, then speed off, while another man raced from the safety of a doorway to seize the dead soldier's weapons. He also saw eight German soldiers captured and then summarily executed in the streets for trying to throw grenades into a crowd. Incidents like these spread fear through a German garrison unaccustomed to dealing with an openly hostile population. The FFI captured increasing numbers of German soldiers who were trying to escape from the city in civilian clothes. Hundreds of such men sought refuge from the vengeful crowds in the sprawling Bois de Boulogne and Bois de Vincennes on the city's edges. An FFI intelligence report given to Rol during this phase of the struggle noted that German morale was collapsing to the point that the FFI expected to be able to launch successful attacks on even well-defended strongpoints.[9]

The increasing German unwillingness to fight any longer for Paris stretched all the way to Choltitz, who saw no way out unless the Allies arrived in force. A battle in Paris, he had concluded, "would be a useless fight in a war already lost." In his eyes, surrendering to the Allies was a far better fate for him and his men than dying needlessly in the rubble of the city or surrendering to the dangerous mob he believed the FFI to be. German headquarters continued to pressure him to use explosives, like the ones the FFI captured in the ring-road tunnel, to begin demolitions of forty-five bridges and numerous key buildings. Choltitz never issued orders to carry out those demolitions, knowing full well that they had no military value and would simply waste what few resources he had left.[10]

In his memoirs Choltitz gave the impression that he considered orders to demolish Paris to be a violation of his honor. Most books that followed the war took him at his word, accepting his reluctance to harm Paris as an early step on the road to Franco-German reconciliation and making Choltitz a hero for saving the city. As a result, most writers have depicted him as a man who could have destroyed the city if he had wanted to, but instead chose not to carry out the orders of his insane führer. It is clear, however, that even if he had wanted to damage Paris, there is little he could have done. Choltitz responded slowly to the growing uprising in the city and seems never to have fully understood it. By the time he did begin to react, the FFI fighters were in control of much of Paris, thus preventing the Germans from carrying out any kind of widespread plan for demolition. Choltitz himself said as much in a 1954 interview with an East Berlin newspaper. When asked by an interviewer if humanitarian reasons had prevented him from carrying out orders to destroy Paris, Choltitz said no. The newspaper then suggested that the explanation for his decision to ignore the orders were "uniquely because he did not possess the necessary technical means" for destruction, a point Choltitz did not dispute. As a veteran of Stalingrad, Choltitz had personal connections to dozens of German generals who had died needlessly in that city following the irrational orders of German headquarters to stand in place rather than retreat. Choltitz had no intention of sharing the fate of those officers, or of ordering his men to die a pointless death to satisfy the pride of Hitler and his increasingly out-of-touch coterie.[11]

German headquarters continued to underestimate the FFI and badly misunderstand the larger strategic picture. Kurt Hesse, the German commander responsible for the Seine and Oise region, noted that even at this late date German strategists still assumed that the Americans "had pushed forward with strong armored units past Paris" with an eye toward "outflank[ing] the city eastwards in a wide circle." In other words, the Germans had not detected the change in Allied thinking or the shifting of two divisions (the Deuxième Division Blindée and the U.S. Fourth Infantry Division) toward Paris. Hesse also knew that the German garrison in the city was in no position to defend itself. It was filled not with frontline soldiers but with "badly trained and frequently ill people who were only fit for office work. They still tried their best but proved to be completely unusable." Ernest Hemingway recalled meeting German prisoners of war on the road to Paris who told him that they were office workers for the Paris garrison who had been given their first weapons only that morning. Given such a situation, Hesse saw no utility in the orders coming from German headquarters to stand and fight for Paris. Nor did he believe that orders to destroy the city could have been carried out in any case. In his opinion, the best course of action for Choltitz was the organization of a breakout and withdrawal from the city, but lacking orders to that effect, Choltitz had made no such preparations. Hesse saw that the general had already lost control of the city. Choltitz, he believed, "could not cope with the physical and mental demands of these days."[12]

Choltitz, furthermore, never fully understood the internecine nature of French politics, a handicap that further prevented him from coping with events inside the city. Politically, Paris was deeply fractured even when under foreign occupation, with the FFI and the communists on one side and the Gaullists on the other, but as a soldier who saw only military problems, Choltitz lacked the ability to see these fissures. Nor could any amount of Gestapo and SS torture have given him the insights he really needed on French politics. As a result, the German commander could not read the situation accurately; he did not know who spoke for whom inside Paris or whom to accept as a negotiating partner. He had become exasperated with Parisian politics, later confessing to an American interrogator that the complexity of the situation in Paris "surpassed all his expectations." He was glad, he said, to be rid of the responsibility of trying to figure out the inner workings of French politics. Choltitz, the interrogator determined, "was damn glad to get rid of the job of policing both Paris and the Frenchmen, both of which he apparently detests."[13]

Thus, although it may have been true that Choltitz was reluctant to compromise his honor by destroying parts of Paris, he was driven mostly by the need to make the best out of the bad situation he had inherited just a few weeks earlier. He could have ordered the Germans to fight much harder than he did, but he knew that his men, mostly reservists and second-line soldiers, lacked the ability to manage a situation spiraling dangerously out of control. He also thought that they might refuse orders to fight to the end. The large numbers of surrenders and desertions were a clear indication that many German soldiers were already giving up on their missions.

The Paris garrison, he knew, had neither the will nor the means to fight against an angry and vengeful population that was growing more militant by the hour. He also saw little point in accepting an offer from the Luftwaffe to begin air strikes on the city; such attacks would inevitably kill his own men or force him to evacuate the city to ensure their safety. An evacuation would make regaining control of the city much more difficult and would therefore defeat the purpose of continuing the German occupation.[14]

Choltitz therefore took the most logical course of action open to him, even if it was the unusual one of trying to contact his enemies to arrange a surrender. In doing so, he was also upholding his soldier's honor in seeking to ensure the safety of the soldiers serving under him, just as German officers in 1918 had done for young soldiers like him. Believing that the end was near for Germany, not just in Paris but across Europe, he saw his last duty as the protection of his soldiers from what he knew would be useless sacrifices. His true motives were less humanitarian than practical and were motivated in no small part by his deep fear of the Paris mob and by his realistic assessment of the situation that he and the men under his command faced.[15]

The mass confusion of events during these dramatic days further complicated the responses of people inside and outside of Paris. Midday on the 23rd, the BBC mistakenly announced that Paris had been liberated. An overeager BBC reporter, anxious to get his name on a major scoop, read a message saying that the Cité (meaning the island on which Notre Dame and the Préfecture de Police sit) was in FFI hands. Misinterpreting "Cité" for "City," he jumped too quickly to the wrong conclusion. Jubilation broke out in London. Mass confusion spread through Allied headquarters. Even General Pierre-Marie Koenig, the nominal commander of the FFI, began to celebrate. Church bells across Britain rang in joyous celebration, and both King George VI and Winston Churchill sent messages congratulating a bewildered Charles de Gaulle, who was at least gratified that George VI's message referred to him as "Your Excellency," which de Gaulle took to be a confirmation of Britain's recognition of his place at the head of the French government in exile. The celebrations stretched as far as New York City, where thousands of New Yorkers showered Rockefeller Plaza with confetti in celebration. "It was good to learn," said one Parisienne dryly of the "liberation" of her city, "because we knew nothing about it."[16] Parisians often had little information about the outside events that were shaping their future. Despite the premature announcement about the liberation, the BBC was usually a reliable source of information, although the limits on electricity meant that most Parisians did not have regular access to radio broadcasts.

Parisians, of course, still had to deal with their daily necessities, especially the quest for food. Jacques Bardoux, a former senator who was then trying to organize clandestine meetings of the members of the French Senate who were not in German prisons, walked past lines of sad, hungry Parisians waiting outside bakeries in the rain. "They are silent," he observed. "This is certainly not yet an atmosphere of liberation and victory." But despite their ongoing hardships, the mood was starting to change in the city. Bardoux knew, as did the hungry people in the bread line, that the Resistance was taking power from the Germans and that the Allies were finally coming. As one woman said to journalist Edith Thomas, "we may be hungry, but we are smiling."[17]

As the sun struggled to break through the rain and clouds during the early morning of August 24, the lead elements of the Deuxième Division Blindée were just twenty miles from Paris, moving through German opposition between Rambouillet and Versailles. French forces continued throughout the day to press on toward the city as quickly as they could. From the prefecture, Charles Luizet had managed to send a wireless message to Leclerc, once his roommate at the French military academy at St. Cyr, telling the French general that "the Resistance is at the limit of its resources and calls out for your help." Unable to offer any meaningful help, Leclerc opted for a symbolic gesture. At 5:00 p.m. on August 24, a small propeller airplane flown by a very reluctant pilot swooped down over the prefecture and dropped a leaflet signed by the French general that read, "Hold On. We are Coming." Although some policemen would undoubtedly have preferred that the plane had dropped arms or medical supplies, it was nevertheless a positive sign, providing a tremendous morale boost for the men in and around the prefecture. A short time later, the Paris police received an order to put on their dress uniforms in anticipation of giving arriving French and American soldiers a formal welcome. The order led to a series of triumphant cries and spontaneous hugs in the streets between the police and the residents of Paris.[18]

Despite the Allies' reassurances, the situation was still fraught with problems. De Gaulle and many others worried that if French forces did not secure the city quickly, the bloodshed could rapidly get out of control. De Gaulle was much less concerned about a German counterattack than the possibility of a civil war. After telling Leclerc how lucky he was to have the honor of commanding the division that would liberate Paris, de Gaulle had issued a solemn warning. "Go quickly," he told Leclerc. "We cannot have another Commune." To de Gaulle, the young Parisians on the barricades were not heroes but symbols of anarchy and a challenge to his own authority. Obsessed with the restoration of order and the legitimacy of the French republic, de Gaulle feared, not without reason, that the spirit of the uprising might well turn against him and his efforts to reconstitute the French state as quickly as possible. De Gaulle thus saw the need to move quickly and bring order to the city in the form of armed representatives of his own provisional government.[19]

De Gaulle was far from the only one who saw that Paris was in danger of suffering another Paris Commune, the two-month civil war that followed the Franco-Prussian War of 1870–1871. As many as fifty thousand people may have been killed during the violence of the notorious "Bloody Week" in late May 1871 alone. The Commune, and the mutual recriminations that followed, poisoned French politics for decades afterward. Many of the bitter political struggles in

France as late as 1944 had their direct origins in the harsh reprisals of the Right against the Left that followed in the wake of the Commune. While the constructions of barricades may have seemed like a symbol of liberty to the teenagers of St. Michel, they struck fear into the hearts of many of the city's older, more conservative residents, who saw in them the return of a dangerous specter from a distant and horrifying past.

The rhetoric of the Left in these heady days was certainly powerful, and whether or not the Left intended for it to be revolutionary, the Gaullists and even the Americans often read it as such. Free French general Alain de Boissieu, soon to be de Gaulle's son-in-law, recalled that de Gaulle and those working directly for him were sure that "the Communist party and its allies had already decided to take power and form, if at all possible, a Paris Commune, followed by a Revolutionary government that would control the capital before [de Gaulle's] arrival . . . with all the consequences one might imagine for the future." Observing events from her upscale apartment near the Palais du Luxembourg, Clara Longworth de Chambrun, an American who had married into a collaborationist French family, thought that the Resistance "craved revolution." She assumed that the communists would attempt a power grab as soon as the Germans left. She and most other members of the middle class shared de Gaulle's fear that the end of the war might be followed by a civil war such as the one that had rocked Germany in 1918 or, worse yet, by a communist-led coup. For her and many other conservatives, the FFI and the Resistance were not heroes, but an ill-formed mob that posed a threat to the return of democracy and capitalism. Frequent references to revolution and the "glorious weeks of the Commune" in the resistance newspapers only served to fuel those fears.[20]

The writings of Albert Camus, one of the most eloquent Resistance writers, provided a sense of the spirit that was animating the Left on August 24. Camus hoped to rebuild a better France out of the ashes of the past four years, but neither he, nor Rol, nor any other leading Resistance figure sought an armed conflict with the Gaullists.

They did, however, demand a settling of scores with the collaborationists (which included many members of Clara Longworth's family)
and a return for France to its historical roles. In his article for *Combat*
on the fourth day of the uprising, entitled "The Blood of Liberty," he
wrote:

> The barricades of liberty are once again built. We know too much
> to refuse the difficult destiny that we must fully accept. Paris
> fights today so that France can speak tomorrow. The people are in
> arms tonight because they want justice for tomorrow. . . . The
> Paris that fights tonight wants to command tomorrow, not for
> power but for justice. These are not words of regret but words of
> hope, a terrible hope of men isolated inside their own destiny. . . .
> This enormous Paris, hot and black, with its two storms, one in
> the sky and one in the streets, will become more than ever the lu-
> minous City of Light that is the envy of the world.[21]

Camus's writings, and those of many other Resistance figures, were
filled with Marxist and socialist rhetoric, but it spoke mainly of pun-
ishing those of all classes who had worked with the Germans and
Vichy. The spirit of vengeance, more than revolution, dominated these
days. In the same issue of *Combat*, Camus had also written, "No one
can hope that men who have fought for years in silence and for four
days now in a din of thunder and rifle fire will agree to the return of
the forces of resignation and injustice in any form whatsoever." For
Camus and many other members of the Resistance, there would have
to be a reckoning as soon as Paris was once again free. Whether that
reckoning would turn into a revolution remained an open question.[22]

Outside the city, French soldiers were making their final preparations for the advance on Paris. Holbrook Bradley, an American war
correspondent who had been in London for three weeks, returned to
the front and observed that "it was a different war," in large part because of the overriding enthusiasm of French and American soldiers
concerning the impending liberation of Paris. Emlen Etting, an Amer-

ican war artist, observed some of the soldiers of the Deuxième Division Blindée at Rambouillet, where, he wrote in a letter to his wife, the air was "electric with excitement and impatience." The Frenchmen wore American uniforms, but their red berets identified them as French and gave them "a jaunty touch." While he was with them, a report came in that lead elements of the French advance had seen the spire of the Eiffel Tower through a telescope. "A great elation came over us, and the name Paris in our talk made our hearts beat faster. Very soon now the heart of France would beat again."[23]

Raymond Dronne, who the day before had trimmed his beard to look his best for his entry into Paris, was by then a dirty, unkempt mess following a difficult day of combat and hurried movement. He and his men had encountered enemy resistance as they moved toward the western approaches to Paris, which the Germans were still guarding in force. Weather also played a role as the morning of August 24 opened with heavy thunderstorms that did not taper off until the afternoon. Having been told by Gerow's staff not to expect serious resistance, and having been warned not to fight a pitched battle with the few heavy weapons he had on hand, Dronne paused and radioed to Leclerc for advice. He did not want to stop his drive so close to Paris, but he also knew that he was not prepared for a large set-piece battle. The confusion so endemic to battlefields throughout history made it difficult for Dronne or any of the other Allied commanders to get a clear sense of the situation they were facing; in the haste to push toward Paris as quickly as possible, many staff officers did not even have accurate maps or reliable information on German positions. Leclerc assessed Dronne's predicament and ordered his entire division to change its route of march. Instead of approaching Paris from the west, by way of Versailles, he ordered his men to take the Orléans-Paris road, thus redirecting the advance into the city. Now it would come from the south, not the west, in the hopes of avoiding the strongest German positions.[24]

The decision infuriated an already irate Gerow. Still fuming at what he saw as Leclerc's insubordination days earlier, he was incensed to learn of the changes Leclerc had ordered. The new route of march for the French cut directly across the approach routes that the U.S. Fourth Infantry Division was supposed to use. Leclerc's orders thus tossed aside all of the careful supply and logistical details that the Americans had developed. Moreover, Leclerc's change of direction meant that the leading artillery and armor elements of the U.S. Army could not offer meaningful support if the French got bogged down in combat.

Leclerc's decision was most likely the result of his inexperience and lack of familiarity with the American staff system. It did, however, prove to be the correct one, as German positions south of the city were deeper, but weaker, than those to the west. Nevertheless, Gerow concluded that the only explanation for this kind of open defiance must lie in Leclerc's desire to make a statement of independence from his American chain of command. He thought Leclerc was trying to deliberately slow down the American approach to the city in order to keep the Yanks as far away from the liberation as possible. Delaying the U.S. Army's advance, however, would only give the Germans time to destroy the city and the communists time to put themselves in power. In Gerow's eyes, Leclerc, whom he called "that miserable man," was willing to gamble with the liberation of Paris to thumb his nose at his American commanders. Unable to sympathize with Leclerc's point of view, Gerow sent a message to Leclerc telling him that Allied units would go into Paris "with the French division or without it." Gerow later claimed that only his pressure on Leclerc forced the French to move closer to Paris, although in reality Leclerc paid little attention to the directive. Gerow never forgave Leclerc for making the change and blamed the French commander's decision for delaying the eventual Allied liberation of the city. It is clear, however, that his anger at Leclerc made it impossible for Gerow to assess the situation logically and impartially.[25]

Omar Bradley was less emotional than Gerow, but he, too, was angry. He considered Leclerc's insubordination and change of approach without consulting the Americans to be a poor way to repay their (admittedly tardy) change of heart about Paris. Neither he nor Gerow accepted Leclerc's argument that German resistance on the western approaches to the city was tougher than expected. Both American generals assumed that the French were spending too much time celebrating with the townspeople they were liberating. They also suspected that Leclerc's men were not using all necessary force to get to Paris as quickly as possible. Leclerc may not have wanted to fight a pitched battle on the outskirts of Paris, but he had the means at his disposal to do so; Bradley had emphasized that the restriction on the use of airplanes and artillery applied only to Paris itself, not the suburbs. Leclerc could have used heavy weapons to punch through the western German defenses rather than attempting to skirt them. Bradley failed, however, to understand that Leclerc's men might have a natural reluctance to fire on buildings—not out of concern for their architectural or artistic value, but because their countrymen might be inside.

The Americans grew angrier and angrier as each report from the front came in to their headquarters. Having been pestered by Leclerc and de Gaulle for so long over the issue of Paris, they simply could not understand why the French were not now moving more quickly. Only the day before, de Gaulle had written to Eisenhower to emphasize that "the great and urgent question is that of Paris. . . . If the Allied forces do not occupy Paris soon, grave disturbances may occur." Now the same Frenchmen who had made Paris such an issue seemed to be dragging their heels. Such a delay might be disastrous; based on the information that Gallois and Rolf Nordling had brought them, the Americans' greatest fear remained that the Germans would counterattack once the truce expired at noon the next day. Such an attack would cause widespread damage to the city and its people. The Americans did not know that both sides had effectively stopped honoring the truce already.[26]

The U.S. generals had political considerations on their minds as well. Gerow's headquarters had intelligence reports indicating that communist groups were preparing a coup once the truce expired. A civil war inside Paris was the worst-case scenario, as the Allies were ill-equipped to stop it from getting out of hand. Ernie Pyle, the famous American war correspondent, noted the fears among American generals that "another Stalingrad was developing. We could not bear to think of the destruction of Paris, yet at times it seemed desperately inevitable." Understandably enough, in American eyes, time was therefore the single most crucial factor in Paris's fate—and they were afraid that it was slipping hopelessly away.[27]

The Deuxième Division Blindée lost 71 men killed in action and 111 vehicles moving toward Paris, an indication that it did indeed see serious fighting. Pierre Bourdan, one of the division's tank commanders, recalled the toll that the rapid movement and fighting had taken on men and machines alike. He noted that his men were close to dropping from fatigue in the intense summer heat, but found the will to keep going. They were not initially motivated by the need to help the FFI uprising, about which they had heard only vague rumors. He and his fellow officers thought instead of the songs about their capital that they had sung in London for four long years. Now they had a chance to sing those songs not in English pubs but in Parisian cafés. American fears that they were moving too slowly did not affect the French at all. Bourdan and his men fully understood the urgency of their mission. As they approached the city, they met a group of men from the Resistance who told them how desperate the situation in Paris had become. Although Bourdan and his men had not slept for days, they pushed on so that the enemy would not be able to "inflict on the people of Paris a terrible vengeance" for the appearance of regular forces outside the city.[28]

But the Americans could not be placated. Gerow, in particular, sought to embarrass Leclerc by getting an American division into Paris first. Bradley, anxious to get the problem of Paris behind him so that he could resume his pursuit of the German Army, finally agreed that the Allies would not wait for Leclerc's troops to, in his words, "dance their way to Paris." Having had his fill of Paris, Bradley wanted results, regardless of whose feelings got hurt in the process.

"To hell with prestige," he told Gerow, "tell the Fourth [Infantry Division] to slam on in and take the liberation." Gerow gleefully sent a message to the division's commander, with a copy to Leclerc, stating that "precedence in favor of the French no longer applied." Gerow ordered the Americans, who had crossed the Seine that morning, to move into the city so quickly that they left without even acquiring decent maps of Paris. They would have to rely on the hazy recollections of World War I veterans and whatever local scouts they could find along the way.[29]

French forces had a head start and were now closer to the city. Leclerc urged his men forward, motivated more by the urgency of saving Paris than a rivalry with Gerow. Focused on the liberation, Leclerc kept one of his columns, commanded by Lieutenant Colonel Paul Girot de Langlade, on the western approach, using the road from Versailles. It faced a potential problem of crossing the Seine, if the Germans had demolished the bridges, but it also promised to distract the Germans and keep them from redirecting additional forces to the south. Three other columns took the southern approach, using parallel roads that permitted some mutual support. These columns would not face the problem of a major river crossing and were therefore likely to arrive quickly. The U.S. Fourth Infantry Division, meanwhile, turned to the east in order to prevent massive traffic jams on the roads south of the city. The Americans were to assemble to the south of Orly airfield, then turn north and enter Paris by its southeastern gates.

Not all of Bradley and Gerow's concerns about the French approach were entirely unfounded. All four French columns experienced delays caused by the delirious reception of locals, who showered them with food, wine, and flowers as they moved forward. Irwin Shaw, an American reporter who had found a unit of the Deuxième Division Blindée willing to let him come along, reported that their vehicles were "banked with flowers. . . . We had a small store of tomatoes and apples and bottles of wine that had been tossed to us as we slowly made our way through the crowds." The celebrations were understandable, but they caused delays at a time when speed was most needed. In most cases, French troops were able to explain their need to move quickly, but, inevitably, in some places they had difficulty moving through the cheering and adoring crowds. In a few places, the crowds slowed the French troops enough to make them inviting targets for German artillerists, although a few German shells were usually sufficient to sweep cheering civilians off the roads for at least a little while.[30]

Back in Paris, word spread like wildfire that French troops were in the suburbs. Paris had lived on rumors for four years, but these rumors were different. In a few places, telephone lines still connected the suburbs to the city, allowing elated relatives to call family members in Paris and report that they had seen French soldiers with their own eyes. Word of mouth thus spread the thrilling news through the city more quickly and effectively than any radio broadcast could have done.

All of this excitement notwithstanding, both sides inside Paris were feeling the desperation of their situations. Because of the uprising and the barricades, Choltitz could not communicate with his officers; nor could he safely move forces through the city to help his beleaguered garrisons. His staff had even told him not to leave the Hôtel Meurice, because they could not ensure his personal safety. German headquarters continued to urge him to hold the city, but gave him no resources and no real strategic guidance. A maniacal Hitler is supposed to have ordered a staff officer to send a message to Choltitz that read, "Is Paris Burning?" Choltitz later stated that he never saw such a message, and it is likely that the entire episode is apocryphal. Despite its later fame and use as a title of a feature film, there is no evidence that the words ever left Hitler's mouth. Whether Hitler said the words or not, Choltitz surely did not need yet another rambling message from Berlin to tell him what to do. Believing himself to be completely isolated and facing utter defeat, he had already determined to act independently of higher headquarters.[31]

Choltitz's situation was even worse than he realized. Neither he nor anyone in German Army Group B headquarters knew that elements of the Deuxième Division Blindée were just twenty miles away. With American airpower dominating the skies, the Germans could not observe Allied movements. Obsessed with building a new defensive line east of the city, they had failed to pick up on radio signals that would have indicated an Allied movement. Leclerc's shift from the western approaches to the southern ones also likely disguised the movement of Allied forces.

Leclerc wanted the lead column of the French advance to be that of Colonel Pierre Billotte, one of de Gaulle's favorite officers. He and his men were to enter the city through the southern Porte de Gentilly, one of the historical entrance gates into the city, and move immediately toward the Hôtel Meurice to obtain Choltitz's surrender, ideally ending the battle for Paris with a minimum of bloodshed. Billotte, however, ran into stiff German resistance west of Fresnes that he was unable to overcome before nightfall. Billotte wisely decided not to launch a night attack into a city he had yet to reconnoiter. Instead, he gathered his men and prepared to enter Paris early the next morning.[32]

Dronne made better progress, fighting his way toward the Porte d'Italie, one of the southern gates to the city just east of the Porte de Gentilly. His men compared themselves to crusaders seeing Jerusalem's walls as the goal of their long odyssey from Africa to Paris came into view at long last. Dronne then had with him three American-made Sherman tanks, six armored personnel carriers, and a handful of jeeps. He and his men had encountered stiff German resistance as well as delays caused by the ecstatic reception of locals. Not knowing where Billotte's forces were, he wanted to ensure a French presence in the city before nightfall to secure at least one of the city's gates, provide a morale boost to the people of Paris, and begin to gather intelligence to send back to Leclerc. He also had in the front of his mind the fearful example of Warsaw, a fate from which he hoped the arrival of the Deuxième Division Blindée could save Paris. Near the prison at Fresnes, Dronne met with General Alain de Boissieu,

one of de Gaulle's closest confidants. Boissieu gave him clear and unmistakable orders to "head directly to Paris and enter it. Do not let
anything stop you and go any way you wish. Tell the Parisians and
the Resistance not to lose courage, that tomorrow morning the entire
division will be in Paris."[33]

At 8:45 p.m., Dronne entered Paris through an undefended Porte
d'Italie. Locals, understandably afraid that his tanks were the vanguard of a German counterattack, at first ran and hid. When they
saw the French markings on the unfamiliar shapes of the American
Sherman tanks, however, they came rushing out to greet their countrymen. An Armenian-born Resistance member shouted to Dronne
and asked him where he wanted to go. Dronne paused. He had been
so focused on getting into Paris that he had not given any thought to
what he would do once he got there. Billotte was supposed to give
him his orders, but Billotte was not there, and he did not want to risk
breaking radio silence to find him. Dronne knew that he lacked the
combat power to take on any large German forces, but he also knew
that staying at the Porte d'Italie would minimize the symbolic and
morale value of the French entry.[34]

Thinking quickly, Dronne told the man that he would go to the
Hôtel de Ville, for him the "symbol of Paris's freedoms." With darkness rapidly falling, his new Resistance guide offered to steer him
around barricades and known German positions. They went east of
the Place d'Italie, then along the Rue Baudricourt and the Rue Nationale, to meet up with the Boulevard de l'Hôpital. Along the way,
they picked up an Alsatian girl in full Alsatian dress who leaped on
the hood of Dronne's command vehicle and refused repeated pleas to
descend. After they had crossed the Seine at the Pont d'Austerlitz, the
Alsatian girl finally jumped off his vehicle, and Dronne pushed on
without any opposition along the Quai Henri IV and the Quai des
Celestins. At 9:22 p.m., Dronne arrived at a quiet and nearly deserted
Place de l'Hôtel de Ville.[35]

Soon enough, however, shouts of joy shattered the silence. Word
that tanks driven by *French* soldiers were in the heart of Paris had

spread like wildfire. Church bells, including those in Notre Dame, began to ring in wild celebration. One Parisian thought the sight of the handful of tanks was "a hundred times more moving than the solemn victory parade of 1919." Dronne's arrival unleashed a storm of emotions and symbolically linked the FFI fighting inside the city with the regular forces fighting outside.

Jean Dutourd, a policeman who had fought in the Préfecture de Police, ran to the Hôtel de Ville upon hearing the news of the arrival of French tanks. He later wrote that Dronne "was welcomed like a prince, like Napoleon arriving from the island of Elba. He was more than a soldier; he was a symbol. In his person, *La France Combattante* joined hands with *La France Résistante*: Free France with slave France. From that moment on, there were no longer two Frances, but a single nation that was in the process of being reborn, that once again was going to be indivisible." Dronne's presence in Paris, and the promise of a reunified France fighting for a common purpose that he symbolized, had electrified the city. A journalist from the Resistance newspaper *Action* said that the ovation for Dronne was so loud that he expected the windows of the Hôtel de Ville to begin bursting.[36]

Dronne's arrival had important political ramifications as well. Georges Bidault, representing the political arm of the Resistance, and Alexandre Parodi, representing the provisional government, rushed to the Hôtel de Ville to meet Dronne. Bidault embraced Dronne and announced, "My dear captain, in the name of the ununiformed soldiers of France, I embrace you as the first uniformed soldier of France to enter Paris!" Now de Gaulle and his representatives in Paris had on their side a symbol of the French Army to complement Luizet's control of the police. In the eyes of the Gaullists, Dronne was not a revolutionary bandit like the members of the FFI, but a real soldier, a representative not only of what France had been but of what it would be again. He was another powerful link, along with Luizet, Parodi, and Yvon Morandat in the Hôtel Matignon, between de Gaulle and the levers of official power. Political power and military power in Paris were now both loyal to de Gaulle, a man who had yet to set foot in the capital. Tired and a bit overwhelmed by the scene before him, Dronne was the only man in the Place de l'Hôtel de Ville not smiling. What he really wanted was not an official reception but a meal, a bath, and a chance to trim his now scraggly beard.[37]

The FFI cells that controlled the power grid in the city turned the electricity on for an hour to allow Resistance radio stations to spread the news of Dronne's arrival, but they needn't have bothered. As one Parisian noted, "This time, there was no need for radio or newspapers. This time one could sense it. One could feel it: They were here." The radio broadcasters announced that the Hôtel de Ville was in French hands again and the Préfecture de Police was now safe. They told listeners that the first four French tanks to arrive at the prefecture were named Mort-Homme, Douaumont, Montfaucon, and Valmy. No Parisian needed to be reminded of the significance of those names. The first three honored battles from the last world war; Valmy honored one of the most famous battles in French history, fought in 1792 to safeguard the revolution against a combined Austro-Prussian army. Broadcasters also warned people to stay in their homes and shutter their windows as a defense against German snipers. The Germans, they announced, had not yet surrendered, and rumors abounded that large numbers of SS troops lurked in the city. The Germans, moreover, were still in control of the Jardin du Luxembourg, where numerous tanks were based, and they still had bombers at Le Bourget airfield. If they chose to use these forces to contest Dronne's entrance into the city, the results could be catastrophic. The ordeal of Paris was not over just yet.[38]

The end of that ordeal was, however, clearly coming into view. The western column of French troops had fought its way to the suburb of Boulogne-Billancourt by nightfall. The column, just two miles from the city line, was being showered with wine, food, flowers, and kisses by a delirious crowd. War artist Emlen Etting was with them. He later wrote: "Blue signs with bold white letters read: Paris 6 kilometers then 5, 4, 3. The mist evaporated and with it the doubts in the minds of the people along our path. Waving arms were accompanied by shouts of joy." Only by demolishing the western bridges over the Seine could the Germans forestall this column's arrival in Paris, but they had been unable to accomplish even that. Finding the Pont de Sèvres intact, the elated French troops knew they would undoubtedly enter the city in force the next morning.[39]

With the arrival of French troops and tanks, the uprising would stand a chance against any German counterattack. Philippe Barat, the FFI section chief in St. Michel, knew that the city was not yet out of danger, but he also knew what the arrival of regular forces meant: "Tomorrow, it is with them, under their orders, that we will fight. Tomorrow, the Krauts will be just a bad memory. Tomorrow is the dawn of liberty." Simone de Beauvoir also began to think hopefully, although she, too, knew that the days to come would be hard and contentious. "This victory," she wrote, "was to efface our old defeats, it was ours, and the future it opened up was ours, too." Whether that future was to be one of unity or violence still remained very much in doubt.[40]

Just a mile and a half from the Hôtel de Ville up the elegant Rue de Rivoli, the mood was quite different. Choltitz was there, wearing his best uniform at a small formal dinner for his staff in his golden cage at the Hôtel Meurice. The diners heard church bells ringing and also heard the distant sounds of voices singing *La Marseillaise*. When one of his staff officers had the temerity to ask why bells would be ringing at this late hour, Choltitz exploded, saying, "What else do you expect? You've been sitting here in your own little dream world for four years. What do you know about this war? You've seen nothing but your own pleasant life in Paris. You haven't seen what's happened to Germany in Russia and Normandy. . . . Gentlemen, I can tell you something that escaped you here in your nice life in Paris. Germany has lost the war, and we have lost it with her."[41]

Choltitz then placed a call to Army Group B headquarters in eastern France, holding the telephone out the window so the generals there could hear the sounds on the streets for themselves. They told Choltitz not to expect any help, not even in evacuating him or his staff from the city. They had no more resources to give him and no more orders to issue. Choltitz then asked an old friend, General Hans Speidel, to do what he could to look after Choltitz's family back in Germany, then hung up. The battle for Paris, he knew, was over, and Germany had lost. All that was left to do now was to salvage the lives of the men who remained under his command from the vengeance of the Paris crowd, a task that he did not anticipate would be easy to accomplish. That night, one of the staff officers present at the dinner confided to his diary, "I have just heard the bells of my own funeral."[42]

9

APOTHEOSIS,
AUGUST 25–27

"I HAD THOUGHT THAT FOR ME THERE COULD NEVER AGAIN BE any elation in war. But I had reckoned without the liberation of Paris." So wrote American journalist Ernie Pyle, a man who had seen more of the ugly side of World War II than almost any of his countrymen. The war had taken a severe psychological toll on Pyle and would continue to do so until he was killed in action on the island of Ie Shima, near Okinawa, in April 1945. Those who knew him watched as the horrors he saw, including a bloody friendly-fire incident and the deaths of dozens of men he had come to know, steadily wore at his nerves. Pyle was as much a victim of combat exhaustion as any soldier, and by late August 1944, he was close to the breaking point.

Nor had Paris been foremost in his mind. The city had hardly featured in his dispatches throughout the month of August. There were other stories to tell. Nevertheless, as the situation in Paris developed, he began to pay more and more attention to the city, which he feared might be destroyed in the act of its liberation. As that liberation approached and as the stories of heroism from the city reached Allied lines, Pyle, like most of his fellow war correspondents, knew that

Paris was rapidly becoming one of the most important stories of the century. He did not know if he would find the city in ruins or in ecstasy, but he knew that he had to be there to see it for himself.[1]

What he saw in Paris astonished and even rejuvenated him. Pyle came into the city on August 25, the day after Dronne and his small advance unit had entered the city from the south. That morning, three more French columns had entered: Colonel Paul Girot de Langlade's through the west via the Pont de Sèvres; Colonel Pierre Billotte's through the southern Porte de Gentilly; and Colonel Louis Dio's through the adjacent Porte d'Orléans. The U.S. Fourth Infantry Division also entered the city, through the same Porte d'Italie that Dronne had used the day before, turning east at the Bastille and heading for Vincennes and the eastern suburbs in the hopes of rapidly continuing the pursuit of the Germans. Leclerc himself had entered Paris at 7:45 that morning to the choruses of World War I veterans singing the victory songs of 1918. Four years before to the day, Leclerc had set off from Cameroon to join the Free French forces of Charles de Gaulle. Now he was leading an army of liberation into Paris.[2]

Forty-five minutes later, Billotte's men were on the Île de la Cité shaking hands with the policemen still defending the prefecture. Rumors soon spread that de Gaulle would be in the city by midday to assume control of the French government. Parisians were wild and delirious with happiness. Even a man as grizzled and as scarred by war as Pyle could happily write that it had been "a pandemonium of surely the greatest mass joy that had ever happened." August 25, he believed, would go down as "one of the great days of all time."[3]

It was indeed to be a day that no one who saw it would ever forget. The rain of the day before had cleared and taken with it the heat of August, leaving a dry, breezy, and sunny day that was ideal for celebration. For decades afterward Parisians recalled with immense pride the French flag that flew over the Eiffel Tower at 12:30 that afternoon, placed there by the same man whom the Germans had ordered to take it down four years earlier. An hour and a half later, Parisian firefighters hung a massive tricolor flag from the top of the Arc de Triomphe. The flag was there to welcome the men of Langlade's column when they appeared at the Place de l'Étoile (today also called the Place Charles de Gaulle) at 2:25 p.m.[4]

Parisians came out into the streets proudly displaying the national blue, white, and red. Men wore the colors in their clothes, women wore them in ribbons in their hair, and everyone waved them on flags. Parisian Pascale Moisson even saw a man walking his dog with a homemade tricolor collar and leash. Individual recollections of this day would fill volumes, as seemingly everyone who was there remembered particularly poignant memories. A disabled World War I veteran standing on the Avenue Henri Martin, for instance, gave his Legion of Honor medal to the first French officer he saw. The American journalist Irwin Shaw met a Jewish refugee who had hidden in the city for four years and who begged him to send a letter to his sister in New York City. When Shaw asked what he wanted to say, the man looked stunned, merely said, "Tell her I am alive," then wandered off into the crowd. More comically, Shaw also recorded the scene of a "very handsome twenty-year-old boy with a deep South Carolina accent" proudly showing off the list of "three or four dozen" addresses of Parisian girls that he had collected as his jeep drove through the streets of the city.[5]

The entrance into the city was the culmination of what one American soldier called "fifteen solid miles of cheering, deliriously happy people waiting to shake your hand, to kiss you, to shower you with food and wine." American historian S.L.A. Marshall later counted sixty-seven bottles of champagne given to him by Parisians on that day. Jeeps and tanks were soon covered in flowers. They were also covered with what Thomas Wolf called "the most beautiful girls I had ever seen." Wolf was far from alone in that judgment, although more than a few observers also noted how thin the women of Paris appeared. Charles Codman, an American who had lived in Paris before the war, wrote that the young women of Paris were "much prettier than I remember them," but he was also reflective enough to note, "I suppose they don't eat so much." BBC correspondent Robert

Reid, who was equally astounded by the sights of the city on that historic day, wrote, "It was one of those emotional experiences which rarely come to any man. . . . No human being could have remained unmoved and I saw many fighting men weep unashamedly that memorable afternoon."[6]

The celebrations were personal as well as patriotic. Jacques Bardoux watched as a mother and grandmother recognized their son/grandson in Langlade's column. They embraced and exchanged kisses, and for the first time in almost five years the women knew that he was alive. Now this son of Paris had come back to his tortured home as a savior to his family and his native city. The scene rendered Bardoux speechless and filled his eyes with tears. "I have seen my own people again," he wrote in his diary. "I now recognize them. I feel that they will rise again, with freedom leading them back to their grandeur. I can now die. I have seen, after five years of war and occupation, the City of Cities free itself."[7]

Soldiers rushed to telephones hoping to make contact with mothers, fathers, wives, and siblings living in the city. When that didn't work, they often passed pieces of paper into the crowd with the name and address of the person they were seeking and a note saying that they were alive and well, trusting the crowd to ensure that the notes got to their intended recipients. Not all the celebrations were joyous, as soldiers sometimes learned of relatives who had been killed or deported. Parisians equally learned from soldiers of loved ones who had died in battle. In one case, a soldier found his parents, but noted that his mother had lost fifty pounds and his father had lost thirty-five pounds since he had last seen them. The misery and hunger of Paris were evident to all even as the Parisians willingly shared with soldiers the best of what little they had.[8]

Although few people knew it, Paris was then on its last day of food reserves. *Newsweek*'s correspondent Kenneth Crawford watched as soldiers handed food back to the crowds, aware that Parisians could not afford to part with the precious apples, tomatoes, and other foods they had so ecstatically tossed to their liberators. Then he watched as the soldiers gave the crowd some of their own food, reversing the trend of the initial moments of euphoria. Crawford noted that even "dignified epicures gobbled up K rations," because "food was Paris's first need." *Time* war correspondent Charles C. Wertenbaker had a similar experience. He recalled that the dominant cry from the joyous Paris crowds was "Merci!" followed closely by, "Are you bringing food to us?"[9]

Food was not the only problem. There still remained the matter of getting the Germans out of Paris. Even while Parisians gleefully mingled with the liberating troops, the shooting in the streets continued, forcing the liberators to continue their drive into the city. The professional soldiers of the Allied armies knew that, the delirious joy on the streets of Paris notwithstanding, the Germans still maintained significant combat power in the city. On some streets there was ecstatic celebration, on others active combat. Charles Codman wrote to his wife to describe the odd contrast of fighting and celebration: "Champagne on every street corner. Then put-put-put-put machine gun fire. Into a doorway with your drinking companion. Put-put stops. Out again. More clinking of glasses and onto another quarter." Pierre Bourdan recalled "passing quickly from joy to anger," and being successively "shot at, cheered, photographed, then shot at again."[10]

Even as Parisians celebrated the end of the fighting, German soldiers shot into crowds from their strongpoints. Later in the day, Bourdan and his fellow officers were eating dinner in the home of a grateful Parisian family when sniper fire shattered their windows. Bourdan ran to the windows with a gun in one hand and an elegant linen napkin in the other. The odd juxtaposition of peace and war was commonplace. Pascale Moisson recalled simultaneously hearing church bells ringing in celebration and the reports of German 37 mm cannon. More romantically, the teenaged Gilles Perrault remembered seeing lipstick-streaked soldiers firing shots at Germans in between kisses from the local girls. "I suddenly felt a military vocation coming on," he recollected. Parisians, he noted, were too choked up to talk, but the men of the Deuxième Division Blindée had come to fight first and celebrate later. As one of them told him, "my boy, no emotions, we have serious work to do." Perrault knew then that "this was going to be a day worth living, even if it were the last."[11]

Despite the joy, those soldiers who talked to Perrault knew that Paris wasn't free just yet. Key remaining German strongpoints included the École Militaire opposite the Champ de Mars from the Eiffel Tower; the Quai d'Orsay; the Assemblée Nationale; the Kommandantur on the Place de l'Opéra; and the Hôtel Crillon and the Navy Ministry on the Place de la Concorde. The latter positions protected the Hôtel Meurice from any attack coming from the direction of the Champs Élysées. The two most important German positions remained the Palais du Luxembourg and the Prince Eugène barracks on the Place de la République. The prewar home to the French Senate, the Palais du Luxembourg was the Paris headquarters of the Luftwaffe during the war, and it was heavily guarded by hundreds of SS and regular German forces as well as by the tanks parked in the palace's magnificent gardens. Rumors continued to spread throughout the city that the Germans had placed several tons of explosives in the palace's underground passageways. Evacuations from the surrounding Odéon quarter continued in case the Germans decided to blow the palace up rather than surrender it.

The Prince Eugène barracks on the Place de la République, capable of housing more than three thousand men, presented a different kind of problem. Originally built by Napoleon III, the rectangular place had replaced a warren of narrow streets equally famous for its theaters and its antigovernment activity during the revolutions of 1830 and 1848. The placement of the barracks allowed the soldiers stationed there to use the wide avenues radiating from their quarters to deploy quickly to almost any spot in the working-class districts of northeastern Paris. A century later, those same districts, called the "red quarters," formed the core of the Parisian opposition to the German occupation. The strategic importance of the Prince Eugène barracks had hardly diminished in eighty years. For that reason, the FFI had targeted the location with enough men and weapons to prevent the garrison from leaving. They did not, however, have enough fire-power to force its surrender.[12]

Much of the fighting on August 25 was done with small arms, but it was intense nevertheless. Jacques Massu, then a battalion commander under Langlade, estimated that his men, covered in lipstick though they were, killed forty to forty-five German soldiers between their entry into the city and their arrival at the Arc de Triomphe. Combat intensified as his men moved down the Champs Élysées toward the Place de la Concorde, the scene of some of the bitterest fighting of the liberation. It was here that Irwin Shaw saw a member of the FFI proudly show off the helmet of a German soldier he had just killed, which was "full of brains and blood." It was also here that he saw the odd sight of an American soldier negotiating the surrender of a German detachment using the only language he knew that the Germans could understand—Yiddish.[13]

Also of great concern to the liberators was the *guerre des toits*, the war of the rooftops. Snipers fired repeatedly into the crowds that had gathered to welcome the Allies, often sending people scurrying for cover and causing hundreds of casualties. Exactly who did the shooting and why remains unclear, but most people at the time assumed it was the work of a few diehard members of the Vichy paramilitary force, the Milice. They may have been trying to kill leading FFI members to prevent them from assuming leadership roles in postwar France, or they may have just been trying to spoil the party. The staff of the U.S. First Army saw the sniping as evidence of an ongoing "war between French political parties, collaborationists and anti-collaborationists" that had to be stopped before it descended into outright civil war.[14]

The snipers created turmoil and chaos on the streets. Shaw recalled being repeatedly warned by the FFI to "watch the windows" as the snipers moved from building to building. "We watched the windows," he recalled, "with the old, uncomfortable feeling, which you had in any town where there were still snipers, that buildings are made with a ridiculously extravagant number of windows." If there was anything positive to note, Shaw observed that the snipers were on the whole not good shots. Their poor aim and amateur style led most Parisians to dismiss the notion advanced after the war that the shooters were German soldiers. Luizet, by contrast, was convinced that the shooters were Germans trying to cover the retreat of German forces out of the city. If that was indeed the case, their inaccuracy may have been a function of the generally low quality of German troops left in Paris at that late date.[15]

The fastest and least bloody route to ending the violence in Paris involved forcing Choltitz to order the surrender of German troops. With a surrender, the necessity to reduce each remaining German strongpoint by force would disappear. To avoid a prolonged pitched battle in the streets, de Gaulle wanted Billotte and Langlade to lead their armored columns to the center of the city and force Choltitz to surrender. By 9:00 a.m., Billotte and his men were across the Seine, pausing briefly at the Hôtel de Ville before turning west toward the Louvre and Choltitz's headquarters on the Rue de Rivoli. Using the telephone network at the Préfecture de Police and the policemen's direct line to the Swedish consulate, Billotte got a message to the general, whom he called "Sholtitz," through the ailing Nordling, demanding that the Germans surrender their remaining garrisons or risk their extermination. He had decided to name himself a general in the hope of impressing on Choltitz the size of the force headed to Paris. It didn't work. A deflated Choltitz, although unable to offer much in the way of military resistance to the French units surrounding his positions, responded that his soldier's honor prevented him from surrendering without a fight. "I don't accept ultimatums," was his laconic reply.[16]

Choltitz, who had been willing to contemplate surrender, hoped the French would attack him in force so that he could at least claim that he had yielded to superior forces. But Choltitz had other reasons to delay his surrender. His advisers warned him that masses of French and U.S. troops, supported by tanks, were on their way and suggested that he surrender immediately. Choltitz still refused. Whether out of a sense of honor or, more likely, his fear of being taken by the FFI mob, he wanted regular troops to attack him so that he could surrender to men in uniform. He and his soldiers would therefore be more likely to be treated according to the laws of war.

Billotte was even then unwittingly obliging him, directing street-by-street fighting along the Rue de Rivoli and the Quai du Louvre toward the Hôtel Meurice. The fighting had been intense enough to blow out the windows of the Meurice as Choltitz ate lunch. It was to be his last meal as commander of the city. Sometime after that lunch, he gave orders for his staff officers to put on their best uniforms and prepare to surrender, but only to regular uniformed French or U.S. soldiers.[17]

By 2:00 p.m., men under the command of Lieutenant Henri Karcher had fought their way to the outside of the Hôtel Meurice. While his soldiers covered him with machine-gun fire, Karcher and one other officer ran to the front door and tossed phosphorus grenades into the lobby, using a portrait of Hitler that hung behind the concierge's desk as an aiming point. In the confusion caused by the smoke and noise, six German officers surrendered. Karcher demanded that one of them tell him where Choltitz was. He then raced up the steps toward the office of the German military commander of the Paris district.

An odd story later spread that Karcher burst in and demanded to know if Choltitz spoke German. Choltitz was then supposed to have replied, "Yes, and probably better than you do." How the story began or why it persisted for so long is a mystery. Karcher had no need to know if Choltitz spoke German, a language the Frenchman himself did not speak. Instead, Karcher, logically enough, asked Choltitz if he understood French so that they might converse over surrender terms or if they needed to find a translator. Choltitz replied that he had a staff officer who understood French well enough for the purposes at hand. Through that interpreter he told Karcher that he would surrender himself and the entire Paris garrison if he and his men would be treated as regular soldiers and protected by the rules of warfare.

Karcher promised to protect him but told Choltitz that he had orders to escort him to the prefecture, where Leclerc was waiting.[18]

Karcher escorted Choltitz out of the Hôtel Meurice and into a wild mob. Word had spread that Choltitz had surrendered, and Parisians gathered to yell curses at him, spit in his direction, and, in some cases, try to tear him away from his French escort. One woman broke through the soldiers around Choltitz and smashed his cigar into his face. Karcher and his men did the best they could to protect Choltitz and his officers, but they might have failed against the angry crowd if a Red Cross nurse had not run to them and helped them into a waiting car. The crowd did, however, manage to grab Choltitz's suitcase, whose contents they ripped to pieces in their fits of anger. Choltitz later submitted a formal claim to the French government for compensation, which the government understandably denied.[19]

At 4:00 p.m., Choltitz arrived at the prefecture, where Leclerc was awaiting him in the billiard room. Rol and his deputy, Maurice Kriegel-Valrimont, had rushed to the prefecture as soon as they heard about the surrender, fearing that Leclerc was going to shut them—and the FFI—out of the proceedings. Rol and Kriegel-Valrimont arrived to find Choltitz meeting with Leclerc, Chaban (representing de Gaulle) and Major General Raymond Barton, the commander of the U.S. Fourth Infantry Division. Leclerc asked the two résistants to leave, arguing that the ceasefire was a military arrangement between uniformed soldiers only. Leclerc's staff officers were even then reading a German translation of the terms of the brief ceasefire agreement to Choltitz, who must have been quite curious about the heated exchanges in French between a general and a charismatic civilian who obviously had no intention of yielding; Choltitz had no idea that the civilian was in fact the man who had been directing the uprising against his forces. Barton, too, was curious, but he knew a delicate situation when he saw one. He left the room in order to avoid even the appearance that the U.S. government was supporting one side of this French political conflict.

Rol was incensed, not only because the terms, written in the name of the provisional government, were drawn up without his input, but because the document itself had no place for him to sign in his capacity as the leader of the FFI. In his eyes, his men had made this victory possible, and no ceasefire could be agreed without his consent. Rol further insisted that he did not take his orders from Leclerc and that therefore if he did not sign, his men would not be bound to agree to its terms. Leclerc was furious at the challenge to his authority, but he was more interested in ending the battle with the Germans in Paris than in starting one with the FFI. Charles Luizet, the Gaullist prefect of the Paris police, convinced Leclerc to allow Rol to sign the surrender document rather than risk further bloodshed in the city. The political problems could be solved later; first the shooting had to stop. Leclerc agreed and Rol signed. Then, in a gesture of reconciliation, Leclerc gave Kriegel-Valrimont the honor of driving Choltitz to the Montparnasse train station, where the agreement would be finalized in the presence of de Gaulle himself, who was expected within the hour. Kriegel-Valrimont later remembered that drive as "the greatest moment of my life."[20]

Leclerc ordered teams of French and German officers to drive through the city jointly announcing the ceasefire. One of those teams featured Philippe de Gaulle, Charles's son and an officer in the Deuxième Division Blindée. In some places, the teams succeeded in getting the Germans to come out peacefully in exchange for promises that French troops would protect the prisoners from the crowds that were gathering around them. In most cases surrendering Germans avoided being attacked by the crowd, although Jacques Bardoux estimated that forty Germans were killed by crowds on their way to captivity. Much more commonly, they were spit upon, and in some cases hit with stones or other objects, as they marched through the streets with their hands in the air. Irwin Shaw watched as the German officers tried to maintain some dignity "in the middle of a city full of voluble, newly liberated citizens, mostly women, who have hated you for four years and who spend half their time kissing your conquerors and the other half devising means of breaking through the ranks and taking a swipe at the highest officer in your column." All German prisoners were serenaded with endless choruses of *La Marseillaise*. But despite the unbridled enmity, Shaw and other observers rightly noted that Parisians were saving their real hatred not for the Germans but for the collaborators among them.[21]

Not all German strongpoints surrendered peacefully. By the time teams of officers had arrived on the Place de la République, the FFI had taken control of all of the outer defenses of the Prince Eugène barracks and were preparing an attack on the building itself. The Germans and French had to work together to find an agreement whereby the Germans inside would voluntarily surrender rather than fight to the finish. At the Palais Bourbon across the Seine from the bloody fighting on the Place de la Concorde, the Germans refused to accept the announcement of the ceasefire, believing it to be an FFI trick. They insisted that they would surrender only to Americans. Some American officers from the Fourth Infantry Division were quickly located in eastern Paris, which led to the surrender of 530 Germans following combat so intense that the Palais, the home to the lower house of the French Parliament, was on fire.

In some cases, French and German teams intervened in the fighting just in time. Near the Place de la République on the Rue du Temple, Raymond Dronnc found the Germans heavily defending their last telephone and telegraph station. After losing a number of his men in the act of taking the building, he discovered that the Germans had mined it for demolition. Dronne had arrived just in time to force the engineers to defuse their explosives at gunpoint. His actions may well have saved the building and the surrounding area from a major explosion. The surrender of the 176 Germans in the luxurious Hôtel Crillon on the Place de la Concorde went much more smoothly, as they neatly stacked their arms in the cloakroom and calmly walked outside with their hands raised.[22]

The final German strongpoint to yield was the Palais du Luxembourg, which was guarded by SS troops. Its garrison had seven hundred men and ten tanks at their disposal, plus the building itself, which was as imposing as any fortress. Leclerc had been adamant in upholding Eisenhower's order that no artillery should be used inside the city itself, but he was ready to make an exception to capture this last island of German resistance. Boissieu, the senior officer on the scene, gave orders to fire on the building's cupola if French troops had evidence that the Germans were using it for observation. Finally, at 7:35 p.m., even the fanatical SS troops inside saw that any resistance would be futile and surrendered. The last major German stronghold in Paris was gone, even as sniping continued. But an estimated 2,500 Germans who had put on civilian clothes tried to melt away, most of them in the vast Bois de Boulogne on the city's western edge. Almost all of them were apprehended in the next few days.[23]

With the German strongpoints falling or already taken, there only remained the formalities of the German surrender. By 4:30 p.m., Leclerc, Choltitz, and Rol were among a group in a small, packed office of the Gare Montparnasse, just a short walk from Rol's headquarters underneath the Denfert-Rochereau Métro station. Choltitz thought at one point that he, like Raoul Nordling a few days earlier, was having a heart attack and asked a French soldier for a glass of water so he could take his medicine. "My dear general," the soldier asked, "you aren't trying to poison yourself, are you?" A dejected Choltitz, the strain of the past few days clearly visible on his face, signed a new set of surrender papers, then headed off to two and a half years of captivity in England and in Mississippi. His war was over, as was the presence of the German Army in Paris.[24]

If the morning of August 25 belonged to Leclerc and his soldiers, the afternoon belonged to de Gaulle. For the next twenty-four hours he played his cards so skillfully and adroitly that he cemented both his political power in France and his independence from the Americans. With an air of drama surrounding him, de Gaulle had come to Paris without informing the Americans and, symbolically, in a French vehicle. He came in through the Porte d'Italie (as Dronne had done the night before) to such an ecstatic celebration and welcome that he almost couldn't move through the adoring crowds. Eventually his driver found a route to the Avenue du Maine and into the Montparnasse section of the city, which de Gaulle knew intimately from his time studying at a Jesuit school there. In more ways than one, he was coming home.[25]

De Gaulle moved with the air and confidence of a head of state, dominating the events that followed. At Montparnasse he angrily berated Leclerc for letting Rol, a civilian, sign the ceasefire documents. "Why do you think I named you interim military governor of Paris?" he thundered at Leclerc, "if not for *you* to accept von Choltitz's surrender?" But at the same time, he was gracious to Rol personally, shaking his hand and thanking him for his service to France. With these gestures de Gaulle sent the message that the proper political authority in France rested with him and not with the FFI. He also sent symbolic messages back to his alliance partners, demonstrating to the British and Americans that, now that France had been liberated, their political presence in the country was not needed. Every act he performed was laden with symbolism and carefully crafted to send the clear signal that the French government had returned and was back in control of Paris. The final surrender documents that Choltitz signed made no mention of the Americans or the Allied command structure, as Gerow and Bradley had wanted. Instead, Choltitz formally surrendered to the French government. Present to witness the signing was Gallois, who had managed to get to Paris with Leclerc's staff; his presence at this historic moment was a just reward for the role he had played in convincing the Americans to send the Deuxième Division Blindée to Paris.[26]

Everywhere de Gaulle went, he attracted massive, joyous crowds. Journalist Roger Stéphane, who had himself twice escaped from Nazi prisons, compared the general to a king, saying that de Gaulle "was like a sovereign returning home who was clearly marking that return for all to see." From Montparnasse, de Gaulle went directly to his old office in the War Ministry on the Rue St. Dominique. In doing so he was sending the message that there was still a war to be fought. He was also sending the message that he was still only the head of a provisional French government and, as such, he had no right to use the presidential residence, the Élysée Palace. Despite the urgings of some of his staff officers, de Gaulle refused to sleep or hold meetings there, saying that he was not the elected representative of the French people.[27]

De Gaulle found, much to his surprise, that the office he had left in 1940 had not changed at all. The Germans had not occupied the War Ministry, so the furniture and files were exactly as they had been four years earlier. The same butlers were there to bring him his food, and even the names on the telephones were the same. "Nothing was lacking, apart from the state," de Gaulle later wrote. "It was my task to set about it again." De Gaulle made the Rue St. Dominique his Paris headquarters for the duration of the war and the place from which he would begin to reassemble the French state. To outsiders, and even to many of those closest to him, he moved with an air of complete confidence and seemed to be in total control of events around him, but de Gaulle was also adeptly concealing the strain that he felt in confronting such an enormous task. His aides thought he was always more comfortable inside the army than in the world of politics, and he seems to have confirmed as much in a letter to his wife around this time. To her, he complained of the continued shooting in the streets ("This will not last long," he pledged) and signed it "Your Poor Charles," an indication of the weight of the responsibility he felt he could share only with her.[28]

"Poor Charles" did not take much time to feel sorry for himself. He had already begun to assure the stability of any future French government, and the task absorbed most of his attention in the first few days after the liberation. He urged Gaullist officials in Algiers and London to get to Paris within a week so that they could begin to reform a French government in the national capital. That process was likely to be difficult and contentious. The first decision was whether to reestablish the prewar Third Republic or begin writing a new constitution for a Fourth Republic. De Gaulle had definite ideas on that subject. He also arranged for the transfer of eight thousand small arms from the Americans to the Paris police force to replace their losses from the days of the uprising and to make sure that they would be in a position to exercise effective control over the city.[29]

As the transfer of arms indicated, de Gaulle had carefully thought through his next moves. Rol and the French communists wanted de Gaulle to go from the Rue St. Dominique to the Hôtel de Ville, both to proclaim the return of the French Republic and to thank the mostly left-leaning groups that had gathered at the historic site. De Gaulle, however, had other ideas. He went instead to the Préfecture de Police, remarking that he had no intention of being officially received by low-level city functionaries at the Hôtel de Ville. He would, instead, receive them when the proper time came. By going to the prefecture, and recognizing the role the police had played in the uprising, de Gaulle cemented his hold on the police force and ensured its loyalty to him in the heady days that followed.

Only after his meeting with the police did de Gaulle finally, and reluctantly, agree to go to the Hôtel de Ville. It was the right decision, as de Gaulle himself soon realized. As he recalled it, "along the way, the combatants, tears in their eyes, presented arms. Under a thunderous applause, I was escorted to the second floor. I was surrounded by numerous companions. Many had on their arms the insignia of the FFI. All wore the Cross of Lorraine." The symbols of the uprising and the symbols of his own Free France movement had merged. French officials at the Hôtel de Ville urged him to declare the return of the French Republic, but de Gaulle refused, saying that because the Vichy government had been illegitimate, the French Republic had never ceased to exist. De Gaulle then stepped up to the balcony of the Hôtel de Ville, the place from which previous French republics had been announced. He leaned out toward a crowd so adoring that even the leftist *Franc Tireur* called it "an homage from the people" to the man "whom they had followed with such unwavering loyalty. In de Gaulle the soul and spirit of France are at once united." De Gaulle basked in the adulation of the crowd, leaning so far forward that Georges Bidault, the Resistance's political representative, reached out and grabbed his belt for fear that he might fall.[30]

De Gaulle had not intended to come to the Hôtel de Ville or make any public pronouncements. He had no speech to read. But the moment required his words and, by most accounts, he gave the best speech of his life:

> Paris! Paris outraged! Paris broken! Paris martyred! But Paris liberated! Liberated by itself, liberated by its people with the help of the French armies, with the support and the help of all France, of the France that fights, of the only France, of the real France, of the eternal France!
>
> Since the enemy which held Paris has capitulated into our hands, France returns to Paris, to her home. She returns bloody, but quite resolute. She returns there enlightened by the immense lesson, but more certain than ever of her duties and of her rights.
>
> I speak of her duties first, and I will sum them all up by saying that for now it is a matter of the duties of war. The enemy is staggering, but he is not beaten yet. He remains on our soil.
>
> It will not even be enough that we have, with the help of our dear and admirable Allies, chased him from our home for us to consider ourselves satisfied after what has happened. We want to enter his territory as is fitting, as victors.
>
> This is why the French vanguard has entered Paris with guns blazing. This is why the great French army from Italy has landed in the south and is advancing rapidly up the Rhône valley. This is why our brave and dear forces of the interior are going to arm themselves with modern weapons. It is for this revenge, this vengeance and justice, that we will keep fighting until the last day, until the day of total and complete victory.
>
> This duty of war, all the men who are here and all those who hear us in France know that it demands national unity. We, who

have lived the greatest hours of our history, we have nothing else
to wish than to show ourselves, up to the end, worthy of France.
Vive la France![31]

It was a stirring speech, and some of its words live on, inscribed
on the statue of de Gaulle that now sits on the Champs Élysées near
the Grand Palais, which, as de Gaulle spoke, was still smoking. Even
when speaking extemporaneously, de Gaulle had been careful. He
did not mention the communists or the Resistance by name and only
referred to the FFI obliquely. These omissions were deliberate, as de
Gaulle wanted to underscore the point that political authority derived only from the provisional government and not from organizations outside the structure of the state. De Gaulle was, in effect,
disconnecting the Paris Resistance from the formal authority structure of France, although, if they noticed this maneuvering, the members of the Resistance seemed not to mind. They shouted, "Vive de
Gaulle!" and "Vive la France!" with as much emotion as anyone.
Franc Tireur went as far as to claim that chanting "Vive de Gaulle"
was also a chant in favor of "the heroes of the Resistance and of the
martyrs of the Gestapo and Vichy."[32]

One of de Gaulle's biographers called the speech a "blend of
strength, diversity, and ruthlessness." Above all, it was a call for order
and unity at a time when France was desperately in need of both. At
dinner after the speech, de Gaulle and Leclerc discussed the possibility
of a Commune on the model of 1871 arising anew in Paris. Given the
uncertain political situation and the tenuous food supply, it may well
have been a reasonable worry. To prevent it, de Gaulle planned to use
the Paris police, if necessary, to force the members of the FFI to disarm
or join the regular French Army. An armed FFI, de Gaulle feared, was
a threat to the stability of postwar France. In his eyes, the FFI could
no longer be permitted to have a military presence of its own.[33]

Most Parisians had their eyes not on political problems but on enjoying their new freedom. Ecstatic celebrations lasted well into the
night. They were carried around the world by radio, inspiring celebra-

tions on every continent. Paris, which a correspondent for *Life* magazine called "the second capital of every nation," was free once again. "Whenever the City of Light changes hands," the magazine noted, "Western civilization shifts its political balance. So it has been for seven centuries; so it was in 1940; so it was [today]." Now that Paris was free, the correspondent thought that people could finally begin to hope that a "decent postwar world" might atone for the sufferings of the past five years.[34]

Members of the Deuxième Division Blindée did not have to look far to find men wanting to share their wine or women willing to feed them, wash their clothes, and offer them beds for the night. As Suzanne Massu, a female member of the FFI, noted, "Many Parisian women were too charitable to let our lads spend their first night in the capital alone." The adolescent Gilles Perrault heard the sounds of "hundreds of men and women" in the division's encampments in the Tuileries that night, and Ernie Pyle, looking over a city he described as a "champagne dream," told a fellow correspondent, "Any G.I. who doesn't get laid tonight is a sissy." An entire generation of Parisians met their future spouses during the celebrations. The postwar baby boom had begun.[35]

At the end of this historic day, two eloquent writers tried to find words to describe the meaning of it all. Albert Camus, in an article for *Combat* entitled "The Night of Truth," told his fellow Parisians, "Those who never despaired of themselves or their country can find tonight under this sky their recompense." To Camus and so many others, this day was to signal the start of a new France, more just and more noble than the prewar France. Andrzej Bobkowski, the expatriate Pole who had lived in Paris for most of the war, was thrilled that his new city had avoided the tragic fate of his native Warsaw and that the Americans were, at long last, bringing food and medicine into Paris. "Everything passed exactly as I imagined it in my dreams. The Germans have not blown up anything. As if through a fog, I can see an endless line of new trucks bringing soldiers in green uniforms." This overwhelming scene was marred only

by the number of ambulances moving through the city to care for
the wounded. As both men knew, Paris was free, but not yet completely out of danger.[36]

Up to this point, de Gaulle had been a relatively minor player in
the military events surrounding the liberation of Paris, but he was
about to become its greatest beneficiary. As dawn broke on the morning of August 26, celebrants began nursing their hangovers—but
snipers were still shooting from their rooftops. Paris's first full day of
freedom would be marred by continued bloodshed but also crowned
by one of the most dramatic and inspirational events in its long history. The sun rose warm and bright over Paris that morning, and de
Gaulle was planning the finishing touches on the most theatrical and
symbolic act of his career.

Although two thousand German soldiers remained unaccounted
for and German bombers remained near the city at Le Bourget airfield, de Gaulle was planning a massive victory parade to confirm the
freedom of Paris and his role as France's leader. Some, including most
of the Americans on Eisenhower's staff, thought the parade was too
big a risk, given the continuing German presence in the area, but de
Gaulle insisted that the risks were worth the potential reward. By the
end of the day, he had become, for a time at least, more closely connected to his people than any other leader in the world.

On this day, de Gaulle offered something to everyone in Paris. To
members of the FFI he may have seemed a rival and a link to the prewar conservative order that had caused the collapse of 1940, but he
also had with him the army that protected them from a German
counterattack and the link to the Americans who could guarantee
food and coal. To members of the middle class, he represented order
and protection from the working-class mobs they still feared. Indeed,
leaders of the FFI caustically noted that many of the people in the
crowd at the Hôtel de Ville who were welcoming de Gaulle had also
been there in April to give Pétain a warm welcome. There was more
truth to the comparison than de Gaulle may have liked. Despite their
differences, both men stood for the stability and order that the city's

bourgeoisie craved. To Parisians across the political spectrum, de Gaulle represented the possibility of a rebirth of France in all of its grandeur, real and imagined. He was the man of the June 18, 1940, radio broadcast from London; he was France's first résistant. De Gaulle himself must surely have known that, given the political history of France, this honeymoon would not last long. "The iron was hot," he later noted. "I struck."[37]

As he had the day before, de Gaulle carefully controlled and orchestrated every move of the victory parade. He ordered Leclerc to prepare the Deuxième Division Blindée to march down the Champs Élysées with him as an honor guard, giving Leclerc the treat of disobeying Gerow's orders that the division move out of Paris and rejoin his corps. "You are not to take orders coming from other sources. . . . The troops under your command will not take part in the parade either this afternoon or at any other time except on orders signed by me personally," Gerow had written that morning. Three times Gerow gave the orders for Leclerc to leave the city, and three times Leclerc disobeyed him. The division, Leclerc emphasized, now belonged to France and took its orders only from the head of its provisional government. Gerow, predictably enough, was livid, but Eisenhower was more understanding, writing, "We shouldn't blame them for being a bit hysterical."[38]

At 3:00 p.m., while some elements of the French and American armies were still engaged in rooting out snipers and stubborn pockets of German forces who refused to observe the ceasefire, de Gaulle appeared at the Arc de Triomphe. Amid the wild enthusiasm of one of the largest crowds in Paris's history, he placed a garland of flowers shaped like the Cross of Lorraine (symbol of both his Free France movement and of the FFI) at the tomb of the unknown soldier that sits beneath the Arc. Then he relit the tomb's eternal flame, which the Germans had extinguished in 1940. As de Gaulle turned to the crowd, a band started to play *La Marseillaise*. Thousands of Frenchmen lining both sides of the Champs Élysées and sitting in its many windows sang their national anthem with one teary voice.

For the first time in public in four years, de Gaulle's face showed a smile.[39]

Then, at 3:18 p.m., de Gaulle began to march down the most famous street in Europe leading a massive procession. Maurice Kriegel-Valrimont and Rol began the parade with General Alphonse Juin, one of the heroes of the Free French campaign in Italy. Juin was confused and uncomfortable next to these strange ununiformed soldiers, but the sight of senior army officers and FFI leaders together sent a message of unity to the city. In keeping with de Gaulle's plans for disbanding the Resistance, however, the regular army dominated the proceedings, with Pierre-Marie Koenig and Leclerc marching closest to de Gaulle and underscoring the central role that the army had played and would play in the future of France. Politicians stayed one rank back. Once, when Georges Bidault, the man who had grabbed de Gaulle's belt at the Hôtel de Ville, made the mistake of trying to march closer to the front, de Gaulle calmly said, "Monsieur, step back please." De Gaulle also chastised another French official for smoking during the parade. Nothing, it seemed, would happen without de Gaulle's careful orchestration.[40]

But de Gaulle could not control everything. The first sign of trouble came as the procession approached a jam-packed Place de la Concorde. Once the scene of the beheading of Louis XVI, it was, in 1944 as now, a place of immense symbolism for France and its history. On this day it was full of Parisians in their best clothes. The windows surrounding the plaza were decked out with the flags of France, the United Kingdom, the United States, and the USSR. Evidence of recent fighting there belied the English translation that some American reporters used for it, the "Place of Peace." So, too, did the reception de Gaulle received there. As he stepped onto the historic square, shots rang out, sending onlookers and even the combat veterans of the Deuxième Division Blindée scurrying for cover. De Gaulle, however, did not break his stride. As Parisians dusted themselves off and came to their feet, they watched in astonishment as he calmly walked through the square and got into a car that was waiting to take him to Notre Dame for a *Te Deum*, a hymn of praise. Pascale Moisson, who was on the Place de la Concorde that day, looked up after taking cover to see de Gaulle for the first time. His face, Moisson recalled, "inspired confidence and compassion at the same time. It was the face of a hero."[41]

Once he was on the Île de la Cité, de Gaulle stepped out of his car and walked toward Notre Dame. Thousands of Parisians moved toward him to touch him and greet him, presenting a security challenge to the police outside the cathedral. Then, as de Gaulle approached a group of young men and women from the Resistance, shots rang out from the towers of Notre Dame. Bursts of machine-gun fire sent the crowd scurrying for any cover they could find, and a panic ensued as police began to return fire.

As he had at the Place de la Concorde, de Gaulle kept his pace, calmly walking into the cathedral. A reporter from the Parisian daily *Le Figaro* was right next to him and dove for cover. He looked up to see de Gaulle walking steadily toward the doors of Notre Dame: "Not a muscle moved on his face. He was perfectly calm. The Parisian crowd watched in stunned amazement," he later wrote. The BBC's Robert Reid was close by as well, struggling to stand back up as the crowd overwhelmed him. The general walked "straight ahead without hesitation" showing not the least fear, he said into his microphone. "It was the most extraordinary example of courage that I've ever seen."[42]

The shooting, however, continued inside the cathedral, seemingly coming from the towers and behind the pipe organ. Reid watched as a priest took children in his arms and carried them to safety. FFI members, policemen, and soldiers returned fire as the cathedral echoed with the sound of gunfire. Helen Kirkpatrick, a reporter from the *Chicago Daily News* who was standing next to Koenig, feared that "a great massacre was bound to take place." But she watched in awe as she noticed the "coolness, imperturbability, and apparent unconcern" of the senior officers present. Men fell wounded, and "there was a smell of cordite throughout the cathedral" from all the shooting, but the *Te Deum* continued, with de Gaulle leading the ceremony. He and the senior officers of the French military then turned and coolly walked out of the cathedral, even as "there were blinding flashes . . . [and] pieces of stone ricocheting around the place."[43]

No one then or now knows exactly who did the shooting. Kirkpatrick watched as four men in grey were escorted out of the cathedral. She assumed that they were Milice members trying to assassinate de Gaulle, but Reid thought that they "looked obviously German." Kirkpatrick also heard that a German sniper had been arrested for the shooting on the Place de la Concorde. De Gaulle himself discounted the theory that the shooters were trying to kill him. He blamed the shootings on too many guns and too much emotion among the youth in the city. All the more reason, he concluded, to get the weapons off the streets and the FFI under regular army discipline as quickly as possible. Harold Lyon, the American T Force commander, agreed, noting that FFI members "were racing around . . . waving firearms and firing at anything, in or on a building, that moved."[44]

Whatever caused the shooting, the incidents, and de Gaulle's cool response to them, put an end to any doubts about whose city Paris was. De Gaulle's poise and bravery only contributed to the ovation he received, helping to confirm him as the unquestioned master of Paris. The lawyer Emmanuel Blanc recalled that the general received "the hurrahs of an entire city drunk with happiness." He had also fulfilled the pledge he had made to Paris in 1940 that "one day, I promise you, our unified forces . . . in common with our Allies, will return freedom to the world and grandeur to the nation." De Gaulle, for four years just a voice on the radio promising liberation, was now a living, breathing representation not of France's humiliating past but the glorious future it might still have. Paraphrasing La Marseillaise, Pascale Moisson concluded that it was thanks to de Gaulle that "ce jour de gloire est arrivé" (the day of glory has arrived).[45]

One last episode highlighted the nature of the new Paris and the new France. Two days after the French victory parade, on August 28,

Gerow proposed a ceremony to hand official control of Paris from the Americans to the French. Koenig refused, arguing that the French had had control since August 25 and could not therefore accept the Americans giving the French something that was rightfully theirs. The Americans settled for their own parade through the city the next day, which residents cheered and celebrated. Parisians would not forget the Americans' critical contributions to the liberation of the city or their role in keeping it fed in the months that followed.[46]

The Americans may not have been native sons, but they appeared to Simone de Beauvoir as "freedom incarnate." Strong, smiling, and "so sure of themselves," they brought with them an optimism about the future that Parisians themselves had long since lost. They also brought food and other badly needed supplies, turning Paris into a city of American cigarettes, instant coffee, and Spam, all of which were welcome. Eisenhower had already decided to make Paris a major American rest and recreation site, in large part to ensure a flow of American money into the destitute city. "We treated them as Allies and friends," Brigadier General Pleas Rogers, a senior American supply officer, said of the Parisians. "I think you can say sincerely that we were made very welcome."[47]

Difficult days were still ahead for Paris, a reality underscored by a German air raid on the city the night of August 26 that killed 213 people, wounded 914 more, and damaged 597 buildings just hours after the end of the victory parade; the Germans were not finished killing Parisians just yet. Food and health remained important concerns as well. American medical officials who came into the city found that more than half of Parisian children had rickets caused by malnutrition, and serious illnesses were up 67 percent from the prewar years. Infant mortality was twice what it had been in 1939, and even among the children who had survived, delayed growth and anemia were endemic. Among adults, the problems were hardly less severe. The French Army turned away half of the 200,000 members of the FFI who attempted to volunteer, mostly because of malnutrition-related health problems.[48]

There were also funerals to plan and heroes to mourn. Even before the liberation was complete, Parisians had begun to mark in chalk and paint the locations where Frenchmen had died to liberate their capital. Small makeshift shrines telling passersby to incline their heads or remove their hats in honor of a Frenchman who had died on the spot were sometimes replaced by the permanent markers that are still visible across Paris. Some of the most poignant appear near the Préfecture de Police and on the northeast corner of the Place de la Concorde. They are better reminders of the cost of the liberation than the official figures of 1,482 members of the FFI and 581 French civilians killed. Additionally, 3,467 members of the FFI and 2,012 civilians were wounded in action. The official figures also list 2,887 Germans killed, 4,911 wounded, and 4,312 taken prisoner.[49]

The liberation had brought together Parisians of all stripes. Many hoped that this atmosphere of camaraderie might produce a long-lasting sense of unity within France. The events of August held out the possibility that France might escape its violent and contentious political past. Charles Braibant, for example, rejoiced in the idea of France "being restored to the first-rank of nations" and working with the world community "to bring our dreams of peace to life." Raymond Dronne knew better. He later recalled his feelings during that memorable and historic week: "Parisians believed that once liberated, all their problems would just disappear. . . . I knew that they failed to understand that when a country is ruined and brought to its knees, it takes years of work—hard work—to put it back together. And this, in their joy, Parisians failed to understand." The physical trauma to the city was plain to see, but the psychological and cultural effects of the occupation were less visible. Paris was free, even if France was not, but its problems were not behind it.[50]

CONCLUSION

T HE LIBERATION OF PARIS, JOYOUS AS IT WAS, DID NOT END
the war for France or for the Allies. Many Parisians, however,
found the prospect of final victory over the Axis almost anticlimac-
tic next to the drama that had surrounded the liberation of their
city. Simone de Beauvoir, for example, noted that "we had not
awaited [V-E Day], as we had the Liberation, in a fever of anxiety."
Although the German Army remained far from defeated after the liberation of Paris, many observers confidently predicted that the end of
the war would come in 1944. Charles de Gaulle and most other senior French leaders wanted France to play a determining role in the
final Allied victory, both to atone for France's collapse in 1940 and to
assure France a prominent voice in the postwar world. To fulfill this
wish, however, de Gaulle needed a rapidly expanded French Army.
This foreign policy goal was consistent with his domestic goal of dis-
arming the FFI and neutralizing the threat to his authority posed by
ununiformed and undisciplined bands of armed young men, many of
whom held political views diametrically opposed to his own.[1]

Thus de Gaulle summarily ordered the dissolution of the FFI and
the communist Comité Parisien de la Libération on August 28. His
disdain for the FFI was obvious for all to see. Daniel Mayer, a socialist

veteran of the FFI, watched as de Gaulle talked to some wounded résistants in the days immediately following the liberation. He was dismayed to witness a conversation between de Gaulle and one
particularly well-respected wounded FFI veteran. De Gaulle asked the
man what he had done before the war. When he answered that he
had been a law professor, de Gaulle curtly replied, "Good. You can
now go back to your post." Mayer thought de Gaulle's dismissal of
the FFI and its role in the liberation was "not very charitable." It was,
however, entirely consistent with de Gaulle's political plans.[2]

Despite the fears of the middle and upper classes, the FFI accepted
its dissolution peacefully, if with some sadness at the lack of official
recognition of its central role in the liberation of Paris. Maurice
Kriegel-Valrimont noted morosely that so few FFI leaders were invited to join the provisional government that their initials might well
stand for "Forces Françaises Inemployées" (Unemployable French
Forces). Still, the men of the FFI were not finished serving France.
More than 11,000 former members of the FFI enlisted in the French
Army after August 1944, indicating that the group's true goal all
along had indeed been to liberate France, not to incite a revolution in
the streets. As Kriegel-Valrimont recalled of the FFI's relationship
with the Gaullists and other moderate opposition groups, "yes, there
were points of disagreement, but no one was under any illusions: in
the face of treason, collaboration, and a betrayal of the nation, we
were all on the same side."[3]

Rol himself helped to organize a battalion of dedicated FFI members that joined the French Army as part of the 151st Infantry Regiment. The regiment had the honor of leading the Second Infantry
Division's parade celebrating V-E Day. As a legacy of their experience
together during the liberation, the battalion, which Rol commanded,
used handshakes instead of salutes and had an unusually high level of
camaraderie. Its adherence to the French Army structure indicated its
willingness to work within the system, as Rol's own career also
showed. In June 1945, Rol received the Croix de la Libération from
de Gaulle himself. The award, which de Gaulle created in 1940, is the

second highest honor France can bestow. Rol later commanded the French occupation garrison in the German city of Coblenz, at the conclusion of which he received the Legion of Honor award.[4]

Rol's continued leadership in the French Army was typical of most of the core members of the FFI. But thousands of men claiming FFI status were undoubtedly the latecomers to the Resistance and were known derisively as the RMA (Résistants du Mois d'Août, or Resisters of the Month of August) or, even more derisively, Les Septembristes. Some had joined the FFI late but in all sincerity to help in the liberation, but others had signed up at the last minute in an attempt to cover up their collaboration with the Vichy regime or the Germans, a practice known in Paris as "buying a traitor's insurance policy." Soon virtually all Frenchmen were claiming membership in the FFI, and with secrecy having been so central a feature of the Resistance, it was difficult to gainsay anyone's claims.

Dissolving the FFI was part of de Gaulle's plan to form a loyal and functioning French government as quickly as he could. He saw potential threats from both the Right and the Left and moved quickly to parry them. On August 30, he suspended the political rights of all members of Parliament who had voted to grant power to Pétain in 1940, thus minimizing the chance of collaborationists resuming their offices until officials of the new government investigated and adjudicated each case. On September 9, with German troops still in possession of much of eastern France, de Gaulle assembled a new provisional government with himself at the head. He established twenty-one ministries, only one of which (the Ministry for Air) went to a communist. Four more ministries went to socialists, two to the center-right Radical Party, and the rest to reliable Gaullists. By that time, both de Gaulle and the Americans believed that the danger of a communist coup had passed.[5]

With an overwhelming majority in France's new government, the support of the U.S. Army, and a loyal Paris police force, de Gaulle had the effective control over the levers of government that he had long wanted. His most important asset, however, was his personal prestige, which the liberation had raised to a level not seen in France since Napoleon, if even then. American officer Pleas Rogers went to hear de Gaulle speak in mid-September, by which time the ecstasy over the liberation had begun to ebb. Still, the crowd gave de Gaulle an ovation so overwhelming that he could not speak over it. His aides could only calm the crowd and give de Gaulle a chance to speak by playing *La Marseillaise*.[6]

De Gaulle owed some of his power, ironically enough, to the willingness of the FFI to cooperate with him. Their acquiescence to his rule put de Gaulle in a position of tremendous strength in relation to the Americans, who still withheld official recognition until a nationwide election could be held. With the fears of a communist coup fading, the Americans, who had plenty of other problems to face, began to show less concern over the postwar status of France. De Gaulle could thus fully resist their plans for an occupation of France or parts of the French Empire. He could demonstrate that an effective—if still only provisional—French government representative of the French people was in place. As a result, France emerged from the war more independent of its alliance partners than even de Gaulle might have dared to dream. On August 27, the day after de Gaulle's victory parade, news reached Paris confirming France's new position alongside the Allies. At the Dumbarton Oaks Conference, the Washington, D.C., gathering that eventually gave rise to the United Nations, representatives from the United States, Britain, China, and the Soviet Union had determined that France was to be one of the five great powers of the postwar world, an important symbol to Frenchmen looking forward to their nation's future.[7]

In large part because of the unity that followed the liberation, France had been spared the horrors of civil war, such as the one between communists and republicans that broke out in Greece in 1946. This accomplishment must not be taken lightly, as hatreds and mutual suspicions certainly existed in sufficient quantity to spark such a war. De Gaulle's firm hand and the willingness of the FFI to cooperate with the new government rather than confronting it go a long way toward explaining how France managed to face the remainder of the war with a degree of unity that would certainly have astonished anyone looking forward from the perspective of 1939 or even 1943. Many on the French Right have argued that the communists did not rise only because Stalin, unwilling to confront the United States over France, did not order a revolution. That conclusion, however, is unduly harsh; the spirit of reconciliation was strong enough to overcome a great deal of internecine animosity, at least temporarily. De Gaulle even granted an amnesty to French Communist Party leader Maurice Thorez, who returned to Paris in November 1944 from Moscow, where he had spent the war years after deserting from the French Army in 1939.

Despite these gestures of reconciliation, there remained the issue of the épuration, or purging. Few doubted that the Resistance would take some measure of vengeance on the collaborators, but no one knew how many people they would target or how violent the épuration would become before the forces of order could contain it. Also at issue was the tricky question of how to define collaboration. Eventually these questions would be taken up by official government boards of inquiry, but many Parisians were unwilling to wait or to put their faith in a government that had not yet been elected by the French people. The French government eventually investigated 900,000 people and meted out a wide variety of punishments, including 6,760 death sentences, almost 6,000 of which were eventually commuted.

Almost immediately after the Germans left, however, the first phase of the épuration, called the *épuration sauvage*, began. Involving as many as 9,000 summary executions across France, the épuration sauvage was controversial from the start. To those on the Left it represented a necessary cleansing of France's demons by the heroes of the Resistance. To those on the Right and in the center, such as the expatriate Briton Sisley Huddleston, it was more akin to a wave of crime by "bands of men answerable to no one, their connection with the Resistance often dubious and of recent date," and reminiscent of

the Great Terror of the French Revolution or even the Nazis themselves. To de Gaulle, it was a direct challenge to the authority of the
state he was trying to establish and therefore needed to be stopped.[8]

But too much emotion flowed through Paris in the heady days
following the liberation to contain the pent-up feelings of
vengeance that had simmered for four long and horrifying years.
Bands of armed men roamed the streets looking for collaborators
and taking the law into their own hands. Despite their Croix de
Lorraine brassards, most such men had only tenuous connections to
the FFI, whose most dedicated men had joined the army. These
groups arrested more than 10,000 Parisians and sent them to the
same Vel d'Hiv sports arena and prisons at Drancy and Fresnes that
had recently held thousands of Jews. When, for example, they could
not find collaborationist Robert Brasillach, they arrested his parents and held them until Brasillach turned himself in. The collaborationist actress Mary Marquet arrived at her cell at Drancy to find
bits of yellow cloth on the floor. Only after staring at them for a
while did she realize what they were: the remnants of Jewish stars
that prisoners had torn off their clothing with their bare hands as
they were rescued.[9]

These prisoners were, in one sense, lucky, as they avoided summary execution. Some fully expected to be killed. Parisian newspapers printed the names and addresses of collaborationists; one
Parisian saw the lists and thought they looked like a prewar society
column. Some prisoners arrived at their jail cells to find mobs shouting for them to be shot. The communist newspaper *L'Humanité* insisted that Drancy and Fresnes were too good for the most notorious
collaborationists; Pierre Taittinger went instead to the horrid medieval dungeon on the Quai de l'Horloge. Upon his arrival, his jailer
called out to the crowd, "You are about to see a gang of collaborators, agents of the Boche, traitors!" The members of the crowd, wearing hammer and sickle armbands, yelled out for the prisoners to be
executed. Most prisoners, including Taittinger, were eventually released by the government, but others languished in terrible condi-

tions; some were executed with only the thinnest semblance of a fair trial. Within a few weeks, even many of the épuration sauvage's most ardent supporters came to be appalled at its excessive violence, extralegality, and frequent targeting of people for personal instead of political purposes.[10]

The most symbolic acts of the épuration sauvage involved the phenomenon known as *la tonte*, the shaving of the heads of women known to have had affairs with Germans. Some of these women were accused of passing on critical intelligence to their German lovers, while many more were guilty of inappropriate romantic dalliances with the occupiers. As the French actress Arletty famously noted when confronted with her public affairs with German officers, "My heart is French but my ass is international." Most Parisians were reasonably tolerant of discreet affairs by unmarried women who had fallen in love with relatively harmless German noncombat troops, or of women who had used their liaisons to survive. But in the intensely emotional days after the liberation, few Parisians were in a mood to forgive those, like Arletty and Coco Chanel, who had lived conspicuous lives of extreme luxury at the hands of the occupiers in exchange for sex; both women lived extravagantly in the Ritz Hotel with their German lovers "while the rest of France went hungry." In the end, women like Chanel and Arletty, with money and connections, avoided the public spectacle of the shearing, and within a few years their indiscretions had been forgiven or forgotten. Less wealthy women had no such resources to protect them from the mobs.[11]

The affairs involved questions of the loyalty of French women, the symbolic emasculation of French men, and the ease with which many Frenchmen and women had worked with their occupiers. They also posed social questions, given that an estimated 100,000 to 200,000 *enfants de Boche* ("children of the Hun") were either born or about to be born, almost all of them out of wedlock. Especially difficult questions arose when French deportees or prisoners of war returned emaciated and sickly from German camps to find that their wives or sweethearts had given birth to babies fathered by Germans.

Many French women, most often those accused of not only having affairs with Germans but also denouncing fellow Frenchmen, became the subject of especially public humiliations. Thousands of women had their heads shaved, sometimes with a swastika-shaped patch of hair left behind. American colonel Brenton Wallace witnessed the shavings of several French women in a Parisian square. He left this account:

> One at a time, the women were brought forward to the edge of an open veranda on the second floor of a building, so that all could see them. An old, gray-haired woman called something to the crowd for each woman exhibited—probably naming her and telling what she had done in consorting with the enemy. And as she finished, the crowd yelled and booed.
>
> Then the girl would be thrust into a chair and held while hair clippers went quickly about her head, shearing her down to the scalp. Then she was hauled up and again exhibited to the crowd, her head white and nearly bald. . . . All this delighted the crowd, which roared its laughter, mingled with loud boos.[12]

Other women carried signs through the streets indicating specific crimes, like the woman who marched with a placard reading, "A Fait Fusilé Mon Mari" (Had my husband executed). Such women were paraded through the streets while men and women spat at them and tore at their clothes. Pascale Moisson watched as a crowd gathered around a group of women with shaved heads in the working-class district north of the Gare du Nord. The police refused to protect them, leading Moisson to fear that the women would be lynched as voices in the crowd called out, "Shaving them is not enough! They can wear wigs and no one will be any the wiser. We must mark them permanently, on their faces!" Not everyone in Paris was so vindictive, however. Rol was among those who were appalled by the shavings. He ordered posters put up in Paris denouncing the practice and urged FFI members still in Paris to put a stop to it.[13]

The épuration sauvage was about catharsis as much as revenge, but it could not erase the traumas of the previous four years. City residents remained jumpy and jittery at the sounds of boots walking behind them or an unexpected ring of their doorbell. Well into the winter following liberation, Parisians still had trouble adjusting to their new freedom. When Simone de Beauvoir heard about the start of a German counteroffensive in December 1944 (known to Americans as the Battle of the Bulge), she found herself fearful of the Germans once again. "In a flash I saw them reentering Paris in triumph," she recalled. Louis Rehr, an American pilot based in Paris at the time, remarked that Parisian prostitutes "got rid of their English phrasebooks and dusted off their German versions" in preparation for the Wehrmacht's return. This time the fear was all the greater than it had been in 1940 because Parisians knew much more about Nazi barbarities.[14]

Paris also remained on the thin edge of survival for months. British war correspondent Catherine Gavin noted that the first Christmas in a peacetime Paris since 1938 was not joyous but "miserable, without food or warmth," and Janet Flanner, a veteran American journalist, commented that Paris was "living largely on vegetables and mostly without heat." Without coal, the city was so cold that in January 1945 a recent arrival saw a glass of water on his kitchen table freeze. He also noted that there was so little gas that it took eighteen minutes to boil a cup of water. Some Parisians had taken to riding the Métro all day to avoid the sting of the winter. Others spent the days in museums. One Englishman saw a group of Frenchmen in the Louvre huddled together. Admiring France's love of art even in such troubled times, he approached to see what piece had so captivated them only to discover that they were huddled around a heat vent.[15]

Food remained the most elemental and intractable problem. Apples, carrots, and potatoes, available even in the desperate months of spring 1944, had disappeared. The liberation of Paris had helped to ease the food crisis, but not nearly enough. American war correspondents found that black markets with outrageous prices thrived for months after the liberation and that bread lines, blackouts, and a lack of fuel were still commonplace. Even the black market ran out of essentials like butter and sugar. During a spring 1945 visit to Portugal, Simone de Beauvoir was amazed at the opulence of the stores in Lisbon, a city that few Parisians before the war would have associated with luxury. The Portuguese capital seemed to her "part of another age" with its unrationed groceries and markets full of vegetables, meat, and fish. Before returning to Paris, she filled her suitcases with over a hundred pounds of food because of the poverty in Paris to which she knew she was returning. As late as October 1945, by which time the war was over, she still found she never had enough to eat; she was considering leaving Paris for North Africa, where she assumed she could find plentiful food and avoid another winter without coal.[16]

Knowing that the Allies were diverting supplies to make what everyone hoped would be the final push for victory in Europe tempered the complaints of most Parisians after the liberation, but it did little to quell their stomachs or heat their homes. Parisians, still getting an average of just 1,200 calories a day as late as January 1945, were surviving in large part off the generosity of the Americans, who brought money, coffee, cigarettes, and, most importantly, food. Half of all supplies brought into the city during the first fall and winter after the liberation came directly from U.S. Army stocks.[17]

Not until the Marshall Plan began to pump money into the French economy after the war did Paris attain normal levels of food and fuel. Until then, the dollars of the Americans on R&R kept Paris afloat. GIs came to Paris, a city they called their "silver foxhole," ready to spend freely in nightclubs and buy perfume and clothes for their wives, mothers, and girlfriends. Americans found Paris, and its women, to be irresistible. *Life* magazine noted that "Paris' greatest revelation was that, in privation, it had produced one of the prettiest crops of girls in the memory of living men." With an odd cheerfulness, it noted that "for four years they had not eaten too much or loafed. And, above all, they all had been obliged for four years to travel by bicycle. Bicycling in Paris was in fact the greatest leg show in the world." Photo captions in American magazines showed American MPs "taken into custody by a pair of French girls" in front of the Eiffel Tower and noted that "until this moment [GIs] did not appreciate the [War] Department's advice" to learn French.[18]

For most American servicemen who visited Paris during this time, R&R afforded their first exposure to the city's museums, cabarets, and nightlife. Their money bought them anything they wanted, including first-class guided sightseeing trips to Versailles or around the battle sites of the liberation, meals so sumptuous that they embarrassed men who knew how badly most of the city was suffering, and even personal shoppers who rented themselves out by the day. Most Americans also noted how easy it was to attract hungry Parisian women with only a few words of high-school French. Whether out of gratitude, necessity, or both, Americans were popular. Unlike the Germans, they paid with money not stolen from the French economy. The GIs were also generous with their cigarettes, their chocolate, and their food, helping to smooth over the obvious contrast in wealth and power between liberator and liberated.[19]

Little wonder, then, that Americans found the city so charming. For them, *Life* magazine noted, visiting Paris was "like rediscovering the faith that there is a heaven." American news reports claimed that the city was back to normal six days after the liberation and that Paris was liberated "just in time for the fall [fashion] season," as if Paris's biggest problems involved haute couture. This flippant, almost dismissive, American popular depiction of a Paris that had seemingly only suffered to give GIs pretty girls to stare at and sleep with helps to explain why Americans, then and now, have failed to appreciate the true history of Paris in World War II. For the French, of course, such a glib attitude was unimaginable.[20]

Even before the Germans left the city, the battle of words had begun over who should receive the credit for liberating it. The Americans and the Gaullists may have disagreed about grand strategy, but they were fully in agreement that they had rescued the people of

Paris, who may have been heroic but, according to American war correspondents, "were not quite strong enough to free their city by themselves." The parade on August 26 and the one by the Americans three days later were in part designed to underscore this version of history and the political implications that came with it. A Paris rescued by de Gaulle and his American allies justified the right of the Gaullists to govern postwar France. It is also true, of course, that the late arrival of Allied forces into the city meant that they did not see with their own eyes all of the bravery that the FFI had displayed in the days, weeks, and months before the liberation. Senior American leaders said the right words in public, but only grudgingly gave the FFI fighters their due. Dwight Eisenhower, in his first visit to the liberated city, praised Paris's residents, saying, "We shared your joy. Liberty has returned to one of its traditional homes. The glory of having freed the capital belongs to Frenchmen." Ever the politician, he could equally have been referring to the FFI, de Gaulle, or Leclerc's Deuxième Division Blindée.[21]

Although the Americans and Gaullists weren't willing to fully acknowledge the contributions of the Resistance, the French Left thought it obvious that the FFI had done the work necessary to secure the arrival of the Allies. As Jean-Paul Sartre observed, "If you do not proclaim that Paris liberated itself, you risk becoming an enemy of the people." The two sides of the debate clung tenaciously to their versions of the story. Given the heated political implications of the developing history of the liberation, it is perhaps not surprising to note that precious few people understood that Paris needed both the FFI and the Deuxième Division Blindée, plus some outside help, to throw off the shackles of the Nazi occupation.[22]

Visiting the city today, it is difficult to imagine in the mind's eye the dramatic events of the summer of 1944. A few memorials to this history exist, including a museum to Leclerc and Jean Moulin atop the Gare Montparnasse, bullet holes on the face of the École Militaire, and a large marker on the exterior wall of the Préfecture de Police that faces Notre Dame. All over Paris one can also see plaques and markers to fallen members of the Paris police or the FFI as well as to the deportees killed in German death camps. One can also still see the luxurious Ritz hotel on the Place Vendôme and the mansions of the Avenue Foch, homes to some of the city's wealthiest collaborators. These landmarks stand together as memorials to a city divided in 1944 along class and political lines.

The story of Paris in 1944 centers around the efforts of those who freed the city from its darkest hours. In 1837, Victor Hugo wrote in one of his poems of love to Paris:

> City that a storm envelops!
> It is her, alas, that night and day,
> Awakens the European giant
> With her bell and her drum . . .
> Paris always cries and growls,
> No one knows the profound question's answer
> Of what the noise of the world would lose
> If ever Paris fell silent.

For four terrible years the world got its answer as Paris did indeed fall silent. When at long last the city regained its voice, the cries of joy, freedom, and revenge echoed across the entire world.[23]

ACKNOWLEDGMENTS

THE 1942 CLASSIC *CASABLANCA* APPEARED IN AMERICAN theaters even as Paris sat under the boot of Nazi occupation. Not by accident, Ilsa left Rick in Paris (not Amsterdam or Brussels or some other occupied city) to set in motion one of the greatest cinematic love stories of all time. It was also for Paris, not her native Oslo, that Ilsa was saving the blue dress she was wearing on the day she and Rick had last seen each other. Paris had that kind of hold on people in 1942. Its occupation stood for the occupation of free cities everywhere. Its liberation meant the liberation of free people across the globe.

I had studied Paris, its history, its culture, and its language, since my first French classes in sixth grade. But I had never actually seen it until my wife, Barbara, took me there on our honeymoon. Tired from jet lag and annoyed by the difficulties of international travel that I now accept as normal, I did not immediately fall in love with it as I had with other cities I had visited. But, thanks to her, I soon did. We have been back to Paris many times since and have had the good fortune to spend two extended trips there. I thus start by thanking Barbara, without whom I might never have known Paris, let alone written this book.

I must also thank the two people who turned this project into reality. My agent, Geri Thoma, helped me to shape an idea into something coherent, and my editor, Lara Heimert, has been a source of encouragement and support. Ben Jones, himself a scholar of the French Resistance, asked me the question that got me thinking about a book on Paris. John Grenier, Rob Citino, and Bill Astore all read parts of this book and shared their ideas with me. David Zabecki helped me clear up some points on the German side, as Dominique Laurent and Laurent Henninger did for the French, although I hasten to note that any mistakes in this book are mine, not theirs. Jim Helis, David Bennett, Tami Davis Biddle, Craig Nation, Major General Gregg Martin, Chris Keller, Louise Arnold-Friend, Michael Lynch, John Winegardner, and Jessie Faller-Parrett all provided much-needed sounding boards.

For research assistance, nothing surpasses the Army Heritage and Education Center in Carlisle, Pennsylvania. In addition to those whom I have thanked above, I must single out Richard Sommers, Steve Bye, Gary Johnson, Jessica Sheets, Carol Funck, and the entire staff of AHEC. There is no place I'd rather work. I must also thank the staffs of the Archives Nationales and the Bibliothèque Nationale de France in Paris; the Library of Congress; the British Library; and the Hunt Library at Carnegie Mellon University. Thanks also to Andrzej Nieuvasny for pointing me to some helpful sources.

For their wonderful hospitality in Paris on many visits, I wish to thank our close friends Virginie Peccavy and Jean-Christophe Noël. Coming to Paris is, of course, always a joy, but seeing friends there makes it even better.

NOTES

Introduction

1. *Life*, September 4, 1944, 26; Omar N. Bradley, *A Soldier's Story* (New York: Modern Library, 1999), 384; Albert Camus, *Actuelles: Chroniques, 1944–1948* (Paris: Gallimard, 1950), 19.

2. *Time*, September 4, 1944, 34, 40.

3. Robert Aron, *France Reborn* (New York: Scribner's, 1964), 226–227.

4. Sisley Huddleston, *France: The Tragic Years, 1939–1947. An Eyewitness Account of War, Occupation, and Liberation* (New York: Devin-Adair, 1955), 240. Huddleston was a fiercely anticommunist British journalist who lived in the south of France for much of the war.

5. Positive feelings toward Pétain remained prevalent in France even after the full extent of Vichy's crimes had become widely known. As late as 1966, more than half of respondents to a national opinion poll said that Pétain "did some good," while only 17 percent said he "did some harm." See Henry Rousso, *The Vichy Syndrome: History and Memory in France Since 1944* (Cambridge: Harvard University Press, 1991), 288.

6. Recall the famous scene at the end of *Casablanca* when Claude Rains throws away a bottle of Vichy water and joins a Free French unit in Morocco.

7. Matthew Cobb, *The Resistance: The French Fight Against the Nazis* (London: Pocket Books, 2009), 38; Agnès Humbert saw the pamphlet and wondered if the people who wrote it will "ever know what they have done for us, and probably for thousands of others? A glimmer of light in the darkness." See Agnès Humbert, *Résistance: A Woman's Journal of Struggle and Defiance in Occupied France* (New York: Bloomsbury, 2008), 14.

8. The most controversial events include the trial of Maurice Papon, who had managed to hide his role in the deportations of Bordeaux's Jews during the war to become both prefect of Paris and a member of the cabinet of President Valéry Giscard d'Estaing. Papon was finally discovered, tried, and found guilty, but not until 1998. Three years earlier, President Jacques Chirac had apologized for the role of the Paris police in rounding up the city's Jews, and during the election of 1981, the socialist and former *résistant* François Mitterrand had to answer for his role as a Vichy administrator in the war's early years. A photograph of Mitterrand and Pétain in Vichy in 1942 proved to be especially embarrassing. See Rousso, *The Vichy Syndrome*, for more.

9. Ironically, he was standing in the shadows of the Musée de l'Homme, whose personnel formed one of the first effective Resistance cells in Paris. See Martin Blumeson, *The Vildé Affair: Beginnings of the French Resistance* (London: Hale, 1978). See also the opening chapters of Humbert, *Résistance*. She was a member of that cell. For more on Hitler's visit to Paris, see Graham Robb, *Parisians: An Adventure History of Paris* (New York: W. W. Norton, 2010), 247–268.

10. Jean Bruller, writing under the pseudonym Vercors, in *Life*, November 6, 1944, 55.

11. Huddleston, *France: The Tragic Years*, 240.

12. Humbert, *Résistance*. Chapter 5 contains a chilling account of her time as a prisoner at Fresnes.

13. Huddleston, *France: The Tragic Years*, 262; Ian Ousby, *Occupation: The Ordeal of France* (New York: Cooper Square, 2000), 267–268.

14. Quoted in Ousby, *Occupation*, 77.

15. Cobb, *The Resistance*, 64. Allied casualty estimates in North Africa vary. American sources say that Vichy forces inflicted 1,469 casualties, including 526 killed in action. British sources claim 2,225 casualties, including

1,100 killed in action. Vichy casualties are estimated at 3,000. See Rick Atkinson, *An Army at Dawn: The War in North Africa, 1942–1943* (New York: Holt, 2003), 159.

16. The head of the forced labor program for Europe, Fritz Sauckel, was tried and found guilty at Nuremberg. He was hanged in 1946.

17. Maurice Kriegel-Valrimont, *Mémoires Rebelles* (Paris: Éditions Odile Jacob, 1999), 45.

18. Bir Hakeim is commemorated today by a Métro stop near the Eiffel Tower. French participation in Italy is commemorated today in monuments on the Place d'Italie in the southeastern part of Paris.

19. Hamon led a raid on the central STO files in Paris, using incendiary devices to burn the files and any trace the Germans had of the identity of the men therein. He later sent a basket of food to a young French guard they had to overpower, along with a note that read, "You risked your life—next time, make sure it is for, and not against, France. Get well soon." Cobb, *The Resistance*, 197–198; Henri Michel, *Paris Résistant* (Paris: Albin Michel, 1982), 239.

20. Agnès Humbert left a description of the Rue des Saussaies interrogation chambers in *Résistance*, 48–53 and 66–67.

21. Eric Hazan, *The Invention of Paris: A History in Footsteps* (London: Verso, 2010), 231. On November 11, 2010, French President Nicolas Sarkozy inaugurated a memorial tablet to the students under the Arc near the eternal flame of the unknown soldier.

22. Cobb, *The Resistance*, 231. Near the Avenue Foch, on the Avenue Henri Martin, stood another building the Gestapo used as a torture chamber.

23. "Boche" was a pejorative French term for Germans loosely translated as "Hun" or "Kraut."

24. To his credit, Suhard did oppose Vichy's racial laws, the deportations of Jews, and the STO. In recognition of these positions, the French government approved his burial in the Notre Dame crypt after his death in 1949.

Chapter One

1. Paris is divided into twenty arrondissements, each of which has four *quartiers*. Andrzej Bobkowski counted nine air-raid alerts that night in the

Montparnasse section in the south of the city. See his *En Guerre et en Paix: Journal, 1940–1944* (Paris: Editions Noir sur Blanc, 1991), 554.

2. Gilles Perrault and Pierre Azéma, *Paris Under the Occupation* (Paris: Vendôme, 1987), 46.

3. Jacques Bardoux, *La Délivrance de Paris: Journal d'un Sénateur, Octobre 1943–Octobre 1944* (Paris: Fayard, 1958), 252–254. Paris did, in fact, have four more air raids that night. After the war, the provisional French government temporarily suspended Bardoux's eligibility to serve in government as a result of his vote in favor of the Vichy regime in 1940. In June 1945, a judicial panel restored his right to run for public office. He was reelected to the Chamber of Deputies and served in that role from 1946 to 1955. His grandson, Valéry Giscard d'Estaing, was president of the French Republic from 1974 to 1981.

4. Marguerite Duras, *The War: A Memoir* (New York: Pantheon, 1986), 73; Jean Galtier-Boissière, *Mon Journal Pendant L'Occupation* (Paris: La Jeune Parque, 1944), 237.

5. "1944: D-Day Marks Start of Europe Invasion," BBC, On This Day, June 6, http://news.bbc.co.uk/onthisday/hi/dates/stories/june/6/newsid _3499000/3499352.stm; Pierre Bourget, *Paris, Année 44: Occupation—Libération—Épuration* (Paris: Plon, 1984), 64; Jacqueline Gaussen-Salmon, *Une Prière dans la Nuit: Journal d'une Femme Peinture sous l'Occupation* (Paris: Documents Payot, 1992), 192; Charles Braibant, *La Guerre à Paris* (Paris: Corrêa, 1945), 489; Yves Cazaux, *Journal Secret de la Libération* (Paris: Alban Michel, 1979), 13.

6. Victoria Kent, *Quatre Ans à Paris* (Paris: Editions le Livre du Jour, 1947), 193; Henri Michel, *La Libération de Paris* (Brussels: Editions Complexe, 1980), 167.

7. Ernst Jünger, *Second Journal Parisien, Journal III, 1943–1945* (Paris: Christian Bourgeois, 1980), 301.

8. Pierre Bourget and Charles Lacretelle, *Sur les Murs de Paris et de France* (Paris: Hachette Réalités, 1980), 172.

9. Olivier Wieviorka, *Normandy: The Landings to the Liberation of Paris* (Cambridge: The Belknap Press of Harvard University Press, 2008), 203.

10. Claude Roy and the Comité Parisien de la Libération, *Paris: Les Heures Glorieuses, Août, 1944* (Montrouge: n.p., 1945), 57.

11. The Dieppe operation, whose strategic goals remain a source of historical debate, cost the Allies 4,384 casualties out of a total landing force of almost 6,000 men, most of them Canadian.

12. Matthew Cobb, *The Resistance: The French Fight Against the Nazis* (London: Pocket Books, 2008), 38.

13. Braibant, *La Guerre à Paris*, 498; Wieviorka, *Normandy*, 238.

14. Perrault, *Paris Under the Occupation*, 48. Perrault did not mention the death camps in Germany, an indication that he did not know about them.

15. Quoted in Cobb, *The Resistance*, 250; Yvon Morandat to Emmanuel d'Astier, June 14, 1944, Archives Nationales de France, 72AJ/234/VI, pièce 13.

16. Galtier-Boissière, *Mon Journal*, 238–239.

17. Wieviorka, *Normandy*, 124–125.

18. Jean-Pierre Azéma, *From Munich to the Liberation, 1938–1944* (Cambridge: Cambridge University Press, 1984), 179.

19. Cunningham, quoted in Andrew Roberts, *Masters and Commanders: How Four Titans Won the War in the West 1941–1945* (New York: Harper Perennial, 2008), 476; Wieviorka, *Normandy*, 125–130. See also Tami Davis Biddle, *Rhetoric and Reality in Air Warfare: The Evolution of British and American Ideas About Strategic Bombing, 1914–1945* (Princeton, NJ: Princeton University Press, 2004), chapter 5; Stephen A. Bourque, "Operational Fires: Lisieux and Saint-Lô—The Destruction of Two Norman Towns on D-Day," *Canadian Military History* 19, no. 2 (2010): 25–40; Eddy Florentin, *Quand les Alliés Bombardaient la France* (Paris: Perrin, 1997).

20. Wieviorka, *Normandy*, 131; Dominique Veillon, *Vivre et Survivre en France, 1939–1947* (Paris: Payot et Rivages, 1995), 265; Charles Glass, *Americans in Paris: Life and Death Under the Nazi Occupation, 1940–1944* (London: HarperPress, 2009), 353; Bardoux, *La Délivrance de Paris*, 248.

21. Veillon, *Vivre et Survivre*, 267.

22. Alice-Leone Moats, *No Passport for Paris* (New York: G. P. Putnam's Sons, 1945), 237–239.

23. Ibid., 203; Sisley Huddleston, *France: The Tragic Years, 1939–1947, An Eyewitness Account of War, Occupation, and Liberation* (New York: Devin-Adair, 1955), 243; Bardoux, *La Délivrance de Paris*, 268.

24. Huddleston, *France: The Tragic Years*, 248.

25. Thomas Childers, *In the Shadows of War: An American Pilot's Odyssey Through Occupied France and the Camps of Nazi Germany* (New York: Henry Holt, 2002), 185; Huddleston, *France: The Tragic Years*, 274; Moats, *No Passport for Paris*, 217.

26. Wieviorka, *Normandy*, 242.

27. Georges Mazeaud, quoted in Robert Gildea, *Marianne in Chains: Daily Life in the Heart of France During the German Occupation* (New York: Metropolitan Books, 2002), 90–92; Huddleston, *France: The Tragic Years*, 247.

28. Robert Aron, *France Reborn* (New York: Scribner's, 1964), 226.

29. Bardoux, *La Délivrance de Paris*, 215; A. J. Liebling, "Letter from Paris," *New Yorker* 20 (September 9, 1944), 42.

30. Allan Mitchell, *Nazi Paris: The History of an Occupation, 1940–1944* (New York: Berghahn, 2008), 143; Aron, *France Reborn*, 227; Braibant, *La Guerre à Paris*, 498.

31. Gaussen-Salmon, *Une Prière dans la Nuit*, 216; Janet Flanner, *Paris Journal, 1944–1965* (New York: Atheneum, 1965), 5; Catherine Gavin, *Liberated France* (New York: St. Martin's, 1955), 50. Gavin was a British journalist who was among the first correspondents in the city after its liberation.

32. Bobkowski, *En Guerre et en Paix*, 571, 580.

33. Moats, *No Passport for Paris*, 206–207.

34. Bobkowski, *En Guerre et en Paix*, 581.

35. Aron, *France Reborn*, 249. Pierre Cambronne was one of Napoleon's officers at Waterloo. After the battle, when the pursuing English and Hanoverians demanded that he surrender, he supposedly shouted *"Merde!"* although he claimed that he said the much more poetic "The Guard dies but does not surrender." Victor Hugo used the *"Merde!"* anecdote as a symbol of French heroism in his famous novel *Les Misérables*. Hugo apologized for using profanity in the book but called it "the most beautiful word perhaps that a Frenchman has ever uttered," thereby cementing Cambronne's name

as a rough French equivalent to the English "screw you!" Bienvenue does mean "welcome" in French, but the station, attached to the Gare Montparnasse, is actually named for Fulgence Bienvenüe (note the slightly different spelling), one of the chief engineers of the Paris Métro.

36. Huddleston, *France: The Tragic Years*, 246; Duras, *The War*, 96; Michel, *Paris Résistant*, 288; Morandat to d'Astier, June 14, 1944, Archives Nationales de France, 72AJ/234/VI, pièce 17. Most sources list the official exchange rate as 50 francs to the dollar, but Alice Moats found that her dollars bought her 400 francs each, so that is the rate of exchange I have used here. Compare the price of butter in Paris, equivalent to about $33 per pound, to that in the United States, where butter was also rationed. On the American black market in 1944, butter cost around $1.25 per pound. My thanks to Kelly Cantrell for helping me on this topic.

37. Childers, *In the Shadows of War*, 181; Bourget, *Paris, Année 44*, 45.

38. Duras, *The War*, 89; Moats, *No Passport for Paris*, 218.

39. Moats, *No Passport for Paris*, 228–229, 243.

40. Bardoux, *La Délivrance de Paris*, 277; Gaussen-Salmon, *Une Prière dans la Nuit*, 205.

41. Mitchell, *Nazi Paris*, 145; Richard D. E. Burton, *Blood in the City: Violence and Revolution in Paris, 1789–1945* (Ithaca, NY: Cornell University Press, 2001), 215. Burton noted that although the extreme Right often accused the Jews of Paris of being "foreigners," despite their very high level of assimilation, Jews were in fact overrepresented in the French Army in 1940 as they had been throughout World War I. The largest roundups of Parisian Jews occurred in July 1942, when Vichy police crammed 13,000 Jews (4,000 of whom were children) into the Vélodrome d'Hiver (known colloquially as the Vel d'Hiv), a bicycle racetrack. There were just two doctors on hand to treat the Jews, almost all of whom died in death camps before the end of the war.

42. Bardoux, *La Délivrance de Paris*, 212.

43. The French decided to leave Oradur sur Glane in the ghost-town state in which it was left by the SS. It stands today as living testimony to the horrors of the Nazi occupation.

44. Quoted in Cobb, *The Resistance*, 252. In Tulle, the Germans hung 99 townspeople at random, stopping only when they ran out of rope. They deported 150 more to Dachau, only 48 of whom survived the war.

45. Raymond Massiet, *La Préparation de l'Insurrection et la Bataille de Paris* (Paris: Payot, 1945), 32; Kathleen Cannel, quoted in Glass, *Americans in Paris*, 351.

46. Moats, *No Passport for Paris*, 246; Perrault, *Paris Under the Occupation*, 46.

Chapter Two

1. Patrick Marnham, *Resistance and Betrayal: The Death and Life of the Greatest Hero of the French Resistance* (New York: Random House, 2000), 129–132.

2. Agnès Humbert, *Résistance: A Woman's Journal of Struggle and Defiance in Occupied France* (New York: Bloomsbury, 2008), 7, 21.

3. Hilary Footitt and John Simmonds, "The Politics of Liberation: France 1943–1945," in Michael Scriven and Peter Wagstaff, eds., *War and Society in Twentieth-Century France* (Oxford: Berg, 1991), 105.

4. Matthew Cobb, *The Resistance: The French Fight Against the Nazis* (London: Pocket Books, 2009), 143.

5. See the work of Robert Paxton, especially his *Vichy France: Old Guard and New Order, 1940–1944* (London: Barrie and Jenkins, 1972).

6. Ian Ousby, *Occupation: The Ordeal of France, 1940–1944* (New York: Cooper Square Press, 2000), 240.

7. The death of Moulin, and the possible identity of the informer(s), remains a topic of heated debate, and no one knows the details for certain. After the war, one of Moulin's associates, René Hardy, was twice tried and acquitted of having betrayed him to the Gestapo. Hardy's escape from the meeting at which the Gestapo arrested Moulin and others aroused enough suspicion that another leading Resistance figure tried to poison Hardy, but failed.

8. Marguerite Duras, *The War: A Memoir* (New York: Pantheon, 1986), 33.

9. Quoted in Cobb, *The Resistance*, 140.

10. Jean-Pierre Azéma, *From Munich to the Liberation, 1938–1944* (Cambridge: Cambridge University Press, 1984), 186.

11. Claude Roy and the Comité Parisien de la Libération, *Paris: Les Heures Glorieuses Août 1944* (Montrouge: n.p., 1945), 7.

12. Willis Thornton, *The Liberation of Paris* (London: Rupert Hart-Davis, 1963), 103–104.

13. Azéma, *From Munich to the Liberation*, 178.

14. Martin Blumenson, *Breakout and Pursuit*. The US Army in World War II: The European Theater of Operations (Washington, DC: Center of Military History, 1961), 594–595.

15. Cobb, *The Resistance*, 129.

16. Forrest Pogue, *The Supreme Command*. The US Army in World War II: The European Theater of Operations (Washington, DC: Center of Military History, 1954), 239.

17. Jacqueline Lévi-Valensi, ed. *Camus at* Combat: *Writing 1944–1947* (Princeton, NJ: Princeton University Press, 2006), 11–13.

18. Thomas Childers, *In the Shadows of War: An American Pilot's Odyssey Through Occupied France and the Camps of Nazi Germany* (New York: Holt, 2002), 186.

19. Jacques Soustelle, in Philippe Raguenau and Eddy Florentin, eds., *Paris Libéré: Ils Étaient Là!* (Paris: France-Empire, 1994), 267.

20. Oral history of FFI commander Maurice Kriegel-Valrimont, in Philippe Raguenau and Eddy Florentin, eds., *Paris Libéré: Ils Étaient Là!* (Paris: France-Empire, 1994), 93.

21. Colonel [Henri] Rol-Tanguy and Roger Bourderon, *La Libération de Paris: Les Cent Documents* (Paris: Hachette, 1994), 25. Like many Resistance figures, Rol-Tanguy hyphenated his name after the war to include both his surname and his Resistance nom de guerre. He chose Rol to honor a fallen comrade from his unit in Spain.

22. FFI report of April 15, 1944, quoted in Rol-Tanguy and Bourderon, *La Libération de Paris*, 76. Hereafter I will use FFI to describe the members of all of the Resistance groups active in Paris under Rol's nominal authority, including the Francs-Tireurs et Partisans.

23. Rol-Tanguy and Bourderon, *La Libération de Paris*, 140; Adrien Dansette, *Histoire de la Libération de Paris* (Paris: Fayard, 1946), 51.

24. Dansette, *Histoire de la Libération de Paris*, 36.

25. He later hyphenated his name to Chaban-Delmas and went on to a remarkable political career, serving as mayor of Bordeaux from 1947 until 1995 and simultaneously serving as a deputy and prime minister of France from 1969 to 1972.

26. Richard D.E. Burton, *Blood in the City: Violence and Revolution in Paris, 1789–1945* (Ithaca, NY: Cornell University Press, 2001), 233.

27. Alice-Leone Moats, *No Passport for Paris* (New York: G. P. Putnam's Sons, 1945), 246.

28. Ernst Jünger, *Second Journal Parisien, Journal III, 1943–1945* (Paris: Christian Bourgois, 1980), 303; Gilles Perrault and Pierre Azéma, *Paris Under the Occupation* (Paris: Vendôme, 1987), 48.

29. Larry Collins and Dominique Lapierre, *Is Paris Burning?* (New York: Simon and Schuster, 1965), 37; Jünger, *Second Journal Parisien*, 305.

30. Ousby, *Occupation*, 271.

31. Marie Granet, *Le Journal "Défense de la France"* (Paris: Presses Universitaires de France, 1961), 261–262.

32. Alexandre Arnoux, "Fièvre de Paris," in Jacques Kim, *La Libération de Paris: Les Journées Historiques* (Paris: OPG, 1944), n.p.

33. Moats, *No Passport for Paris*, 222.

Chapter Three

1. Omar N. Bradley, *A General's Life: An Autobiography by General of the Army Omar N. Bradley* (New York: Simon and Schuster, 1983), 308.

2. Philippe Ragueneau and Eddy Florentin, eds., *Paris Libéré: Ils Étaient Là!* (Paris: France-Empire, 1994), 18.

3. Olivier Wieviorka, *Normandy: The Landings to the Liberation of Paris* (Cambridge: The Belknap Press of Harvard University Press, 2008), 217.

4. Jean-Pierre Azéma, *From Munich to the Liberation, 1938–1944* (Cambridge: Cambridge University Press, 1984), 185; Thomas Childers, *In the Shadows of War: An American Pilot's Odyssey Through Occupied France and the Camps of Nazi Germany* (New York: Henry Holt, 2002),

178; Le Comité Parisien de Libération, *Paris: Les Heures Glorieuses, Août 1944* (Montrouge: n.p., 1945), 73–77.

5. Charles de Gaulle, *Lettres, Notes, et Carnets*, vol. 5, *Juin 1943 à Mai 1945* (Paris: Plon, 1983), 262; Hilary Footitt and John Simmonds, *France 1943–1945* (New York: Holmes and Meier, 1988), 104.

6. "De Gaulle in U. S.," *Life*, July 24, 1944, 35; Quoted in Willis Thornton, *The Liberation of Paris* (London: Rupert Hart-Davis, 1963), 123.

7. Generalleutnant Freiherr von Boineburg, "Northern France," Foreign Military Studies D739.F6713, no. A-967, United States Army Heritage and Education Center, Carlisle, Pennsylvania, 1.

8. Freiherr Wilhelm von Boineburg, "Organization for the Defense of Greater Paris," Foreign Military Studies D739.F6713, no. B-015, United States Army Heritage and Education Center, Carlisle, Pennsylvania, 1–3.

9. Kurt Hold, "First Army Organization and Replacements," Foreign Military Studies D739.F6713, no. B-732, United States Army Heritage and Education Center, Carlisle, Pennsylvania, 10.

10. Raoul Nordling, *Sauver Paris: Mémoirs du Consul de Suède, 1905–1944* (Paris: Éditions Complexe, 2002), 78; Kurt Hesse, "Defense of Paris, Summer, 1944," Foreign Military Studies D739.F6713, no. B-611, United States Army Heritage and Education Center, Carlisle, Pennsylvania, 5–6.

11. Hesse, "Defense of Paris," 9. See also Albert Emmench, "Northern France," vol. 7, "The [German] First Army (11 August to 15 September 1944)," Foreign Military Studies D739.F6713, no. B-728, United States Army Heritage and Education Center, Carlisle, Pennsylvania, 3.

12. Wieviorka, *Normandy*, 8.

13. Martin Blumenson, *Breakout and Pursuit*. The US Army in World War II: The European Theater of Operations (Washington, DC: Center of Military History, 1961), 591.

14. Larry Collins and Dominique Lapierre, *Is Paris Burning?* (New York: Simon and Schuster, 1965), 19–20.

15. For all the jeering that the Maginot Line has taken from amateurs and armchair strategists, it should be remembered that in 1940 the Germans feared it enough to go around it rather than attack it. The Allies feared it enough to take the gamble of parachuting men into Holland via Operation

Market Garden in an attempt to outflank the line. When the Allies did attack the Maginot Line in the winter of 1944–1945, they found it tough going indeed.

16. Blumenson, *Breakout and Pursuit*, 590; Omar Bradley, *A Soldier's Story* (New York: Modern Library, 1999), 384.

17. Dwight Eisenhower, *Crusade in Europe* (Garden City, NJ: Doubleday, 1949), 296.

18. Carlo D'Este, *World War II in the Mediterranean, 1942–1945* (Chapel Hill, NC: Algonquin Books, 1990), 175–177.

19. Eisenhower, *Crusade in Europe*, 296.

20. Bradley, *A Soldier's Story*, 385; Azéma, *From Munich to the Liberation*, 178.

21. Bradley, *A Soldier's Story*, 384; Collins and Lapierre, *Is Paris Burning?*, 14; Maurice Kriegel-Valrimont, *Mémoirs Rebelles* (Paris: Éditions Odile Jacob, 1999), 64.

22. Jacques Bardoux, *La Délivrance de Paris: Journal d'un Sénateur, Octobre 1943–Octobre 1944* (Paris: Fayard, 1958), 298–299; Yves Cazaux, *Journal Secret de la Libération* (Paris: Alain Michel, 1979), 64.

23. Footitt and Simmonds, *France*, 109; Edith Thomas, *La Libération de Paris* (Paris: Mellottée, 1945), 16.

24. Ragueneau and Florentin, eds., *Paris Libéré*, 45.

25. Allan Mitchell, *Nazi Paris: The History of an Occupation, 1940–1944* (New York: Beghahn, 2008), 140–141.

26. Henri Michel, *La Libération de Paris* (Brussels: Éditions Complexe, 1980), 41–47.

27. Nordling, *Sauver Paris*, 80; Thornton, *The Liberation of Paris*, 114; Bardoux, *La Délivrance de Paris*, 299–300, 309.

28. Stauffenberg was the great-grandson of Count August von Gneisenau, a legendary Prussian general who had fought Napoleon and helped to design the reform of the Prussian Army in the early nineteenth century.

29. Hesse, "Defense of Paris," 17.

30. The bomb plot is too complex to deal with in detail here. For more information, see Danny Orbach, "Criticism Reconsidered: The German Resis-

tance to Hitler in Critical German Scholarship," *Journal of Military History* 75, no. 2 (2011): 565–590, and Joachim C. Fest, *Plotting Hitler's Death: The Story of the German Resistance* (New York: Metropolitan, 1996).

31. Gerhard Heller, *Un Allemand à Paris* (Paris: Éditions du Seuil, 1981). At the Battle of Valmy, Revolutionary citizen-based French forces defeated the professionals of Prussia and Austria, supposedly because their newfound revolutionary ardor gave them superior motivation. The battle seemed to usher in the era of men fighting for liberty instead of dynastic aims.

32. Bardoux, *La Délivrance de Paris*, 313.

33. Fest, *Plotting Hitler's Death*, 278.

34. Ernst Jünger, *Second Journal Parisien, Journal III, 1943–1945* (Paris: Christian Bourgois, 1980), 314.

35. Colonel Rol-Tanguy and Roger Bourderon, *Libération de Paris: Les Cent Documents* (Paris: Hachette, 1994), 158.

36. Jean Galtier-Boissière, *Mon Journal Pendant l'Occupation* (Paris: La Jeune Parc, 1944), 246; Marguerite Duras, *The War: A Memoir* (New York: Pantheon, 1986), 82–83; Charles Braibant, *La Guerre à Paris* (Paris: Corrêa, 1945), 513.

37. Wilhelm von Boineburg, "Northern France," 3; Boineburg, "Organization for the Defense of Greater Paris," 7–8; Emmench, "Northern France," 7. See also Hold, "First Army Organization and Replacements," 10, which says that German assets "could not possibly suffice for a successful defense of Paris."

38. Blumenson, *Breakout and Pursuit*, 234, 182.

39. Ibid., 335.

Chapter Four

1. Larry Collins and Dominique Lapierre, *Is Paris Burning?* (New York: Simon and Schuster, 1965), 35; Dietrich von Choltitz, *De Sébastopol à Paris: Un Soldat Parmi des Soldats* (Paris: Aubanel, 1964), 204–205.

2. Martin Blumenson, *Breakout and Pursuit*. The US Army in World War II: The European Theater of Operations (Washington, DC: Center of Military History, 1961), 592; Collins and Lapierre, *Is Paris Burning?*, 36.

3. Collins and Lapierre, *Is Paris Burning?*, 46–47; Sönke Neitzel, ed., *Tapping Hitler's Generals: Transcripts of Secret Conversations, 1942–1945* (London: Frontline, 2007), 367.

4. Marcelle Adler-Bresse, "Von Choltitz: A-t-il Changé d'Avis?" *Revue d'Histoire de la Deuxième Guerre Mondiale* 19 (1955): 116.

5. Raoul Nordling, *Sauver Paris: Mémoirs du Consul de Suède, 1905–1945* (Paris: Editions Complexe, 2002), 79.

6. Choltitz, *De Sébastopol à Paris*, 203; Robert Aron, *France Reborn* (New York: Scribner's 1964), 237.

7. Choltitz, *De Sébastopol à Paris*, 208, 195.

8. Gerhard Heller, *Un Allemand à Paris* (Paris: Éditions du Seuil, 1981), 184.

9. Gilles Perrault and Pierre Azéma, *Paris Under the Occupation* (Paris: Vendôme, 1987), 50. On the German Army, see Robert M. Citino, *Death of the Wehrmacht: The German Campaigns of 1942* (Lawrence: University Press of Kansas, 2007). There is a lot of questionable historical work on the German Army in World War II. Citino's work, along with that of Omer Bartov, Geoff Megargee, and Dennis Showalter, should be a serious researcher's first stop.

10. James A. Wood, ed., *Army of the West: The Weekly Reports of German Army Group B from Normandy to the West Wall* (Mechanicsburg, PA: Stackpole Books, 2007), 81, 158.

11. Choltitz, *De Sébastopol à Paris*, 9–10.

12. Andrzej Bobkowski, *En Guerre et en Paix: Journal 1940–1944* (Paris: Editions Noirs sur Blanc, 1991), 604; Jacques Bardoux, *La Délivrance de Paris: Journal d'un Sénateur, Octobre 1943–Octobre 1944* (Paris: Fayard, 1958), 345; Willis Thornton, *The Liberation of Paris* (London: Rupert Hart-Davis, 1963), 139.

13. Henri Rol-Tanguy and Roger Bourderon, *Libération de Paris: Les Cent Documents* (Paris: Hachette, 1994), 59–60.

14. Ibid., 164; Maurice Kriegel-Valrimont, *Mémoirs Rebelles* (Paris: Éditions Odile Jacob, 1999), 63.

15. Olivier Wieviorka, *Normandy: The Landings to the Liberation of Paris* (Cambridge: The Belknap Press of Harvard University Press, 2008), 280–281.

16. Quoted in Carlo D'Este, *Eisenhower: A Soldier's Life* (New York: Holt, 2002), 572; Wood, ed., *Army of the West*, 191.

17. Wood, ed., *Army of the West*, 187.

18. Blumenson, *Breakout and Pursuit*, 593.

19. Matthew Cobb, *The Resistance: The French Fight Against the Nazis* (London: Pocket Books, 2009), 258.

20. Collins and Lapierre, *Is Paris Burning?*, 68, 89; Kurt Hesse, "Defense of Paris, Summer, 1944," Foreign Military Studies D739.F6713, no. B-611, United States Army Heritage and Education Center, Carlisle, Pennsylvania, 18.

21. Martin Blumenson, "The Liberation of Paris," *World War II* 15, no. 3 (2000), accessed online through Academic Search Premier.

22. William Hornaday to Richard Sommers, November 11, 1971, William Hornaday Papers, Box 35, folder 14, p. 2, United States Army Heritage and Education Center, Carlisle, Pennsylvania. Hornaday was an aide to Bradley. The letter recounted a conversation with Gerow from 1949. I am indebted to Dr. Sommers for alerting me to the existence of this and other collections.

23. Bobkowski, *En Guerre et en Paix*, 605.

24. Charles Braibant, *La Guerre à Paris* (Paris: Corrêa, 1945), 529; Edith Thomas, *La Libération de Paris* (Paris: Mellottée, 1945), 23.

25. Bobkowski, *En Guerre et en Paix*, 601; Yves Cazaux, *Journal Secret de la Libération* (Paris: Albin Michel, 1979), 135; Braibant, *La Guerre à Paris*, 533; Richard D.E. Burton, *Blood in the City: Violence and Revolution in Paris, 1789–1945* (Ithaca, NY: Cornell University Press, 2001), 234.

26. Henri Michel, *Paris Résistant* (Paris: Albin Michel, 1982), 302; Rol-Tanguy and Bourderon, *Libération de Paris*, 176.

27. Rol-Tanguy and Bourderon, *Libération de Paris*, 177.

28. Michel, *Paris Résistant*, footnote on 304.

29. Philippe Nivet and Yvan Combeau, *Histoire Politique de Paris au XXe Siècle* (Paris: Presses Universitaires de France, 2000), 162–163.

30. Jean Galtier-Boissière, *Mon Journal Pendant L'Occupation* (Paris: La Jeune Parque, 1944), 251; Catherine Garvin, *Liberated France* (New York: St. Martin's, 1955), 43.

31. Léautaud is quoted in Herbert R. Lottman, *The People's Anger: Justice and Revenge in Post-Liberation France* (London: Hutchinson, 1986), 76.

32. Clara Longworth de Chambrun, *Shadows Lengthen: The Story of My Life* (New York: Scribner's, 1949), 216.

33. Marcel Jouhandeau, *Journal sous l'Occupation* (Paris: Gallimard, 1980). Jouhandeau was the author of the anti-Semitic tract *Le Péril Juif* in 1938. In 1941 he was among a group of collaborationist writers who went on a highly publicized tour of Germany paid for by Joseph Goebbels. He survived the war unharmed and died of natural causes in 1979.

34. Gilbert Joseph, *Une Si Douce Occupation: Simone de Beauvoir, Jean-Paul Sartre, 1940–1944* (Paris: A. Michel, 1991), 348.

35. Léon Werth, *Déposition* (Paris: Grasset, 1946), 550; Louis Chavet, "Journal d'un Témoin," and Alexandre Arnoux, "Fièvre de Paris," in Jacques Kim, *Libération de Paris: Les Journées Historiques* (Paris: L'O.P.C., 1944), n.p.

36. Bobkowski, *En Guerre et en Paix*, 597, 603.

37. Henri Michel, *La Libération de Paris* (Brussels: Editions Complexe, 1980), 33; Jacques Chaban-Delmas, *La Libération* (Paris: Paris Match, 1984), 26; Philippe Ragueneau and Eddy Florentin, eds., *Paris Libéré: Ils Étaient Là!* (Paris: France-Empire, 1994), 234.

38. Comité de Tourisme de Paris, "La Libération de Paris" (1945), United States Army Heritage and Education Center, Carlisle, Pennsylvania, D762.P3 L35 1945.

39. Choltitz, *De Sébastopol à Paris*, 7; Ragueneau and Florentin, eds., *Paris Libéré*, 136.

Chapter Five

1. Victor Hugo, in *Les Misérables*, quoted in Eric Hazan, *The Invention of Paris: A History in Footsteps* (London: Verso, 2010), 250.

2. Simon Kitson, "The Police in the Liberation of Paris," in Harry Roderick Kedward and Nancy Wood, eds. *The Liberation of France: Image and Event* (Oxford: Berg, 1995), 43. It appears that the unreliability of the police was an issue of concern to the Germans outside Paris in 1943 as well. See Robert Gildea, *Marianne in Chains: Daily Life in the Heart of France During the Occupation* (New York: Metropolitan Books, 2002), 269.

3. Maurice Rajsfus, *La Police de Vichy: Les Forces de l'Ordre Françaises au Service de la Gestapo, 1940–1944* (Paris: Les Éditions Cherche Midi, 1995), 240, 254, 261, 219.

4. Rajsfus, *La Police de Vichy*, 232.

5. Comité Parisien de la Libération, *Paris: Les Heures Glorieuses, Août 1944* (n.p., 1945), 92; Rajsfus, *La Police de Vichy*, 254.

6. Dietrich von Choltitz, *De Sébastopol à Paris: Un Soldat Parmi des Soldats* (Paris: Aubanel, 1964), 212.

7. Adrien Dansette, *La Libération de Paris* (Paris: Arthème Fayard, 1946), 91, 94, 136.

8. Rajsfus, *La Police de Vichy*, 251; Oral history of Henri and Cécile Rol-Tanguy, in Philippe Raguenau and Eddy Florentin, eds., *Paris Libéré: Ils Étaient Là!* (Paris: France-Empire, 1994), 47.

9. Raoul Nordling, *Sauver Paris: Mémoirs du Consul de Suède, 1905–1944* (Paris: Éditions Complexe, 2002), 93–94.

10. Gilles Perrault and Pierre Azéma, *Paris Under the Occupation* (Paris: Vendôme, 1987), 51.

11. Maurice Kriegel-Valrimont, *Mémoirs Rebelles* (Paris: Éditions Odile Jacob, 1999), 64.

12. Jean Galtier-Boissière, *Mon Journal Pendant l'Occupation* (Paris: La Jeune Parque, 1944), 251–252.

13. Yves Cazaux, *Journal Secret de la Libération* (Paris: Alban Michel, 1979), 135.

14. Rajsfus, *La Police de Vichy*, 238.

15. Richard D.E. Burton, *Blood in the City: Violence and Revolution in Paris, 1789–1945* (Ithaca, NY: Cornell University Press, 2001), 234.

16. Henri Michel, *Paris Résistant* (Paris: Albin Michel, 1982), 309.

17. Hilary Footitt and John Simmonds, *France 1943–1945* (New York: Holmes and Meier, 1988), 123.

18. Model went back east after his failures in the Battle of the Bulge. He shot himself in April 1945 rather than face a war crimes trial in the Soviet Union for the estimated 600,000 people he sent to death camps.

19. Larry Collins and Dominique Lapierre, *Is Paris Burning?* (New York: Simon and Schuster, 1965), 92.

20. André Desfeuilles, *Raoul Nordling et la Libération de Paris* (Paris: Institut Tessin, 1945). This document is Nordling's own oral history as recorded in June 1945.

21. After the war, Abetz was sentenced to twenty years of hard labor, although he only served six. He died in an auto accident in 1958.

22. Desfeuilles, *Raoul Nordling*, 8.

23. Laval was found guilty in October 1945 of treason and executed, although even many of Laval's critics alleged that the trial was rigged from the outset. Pétain's postwar story is much more complicated. He, too, was convicted and sentenced to death, but unlike Laval, he still had the sympathy of many people. Aging and becoming senile, he had his sentence commuted by the French government, which allowed him to live in relative comfort on the Île d'Yeu until his death in 1951 at the age of ninety-five. The Russians rescued Herriot from a German prison camp in 1945. He returned to his post as mayor of Lyon, where he emerged as an anticommunist and anti-Gaullist force in French radical politics. He held the presidency of the National Assembly from 1947 to 1954.

24. Henri Michel, *La Libération de Paris* (Brussels: Éditions Complexe, 1980), 34.

25. Charles Braibant, *La Guerre à Paris* (Paris: Corrêa, 1945), 535; Jacques Bardoux, *La Délivrance de Paris: Journal d'un Sénateur, Octobre 1943–Octobre 1944* (Paris: Fayard, 1958), 348.

26. Perrault and Azéma, *Paris Under the Occupation*, 50; Nordling, *Sauver Paris*, 96; Cazaux, *Journal Secret de la Libération*, 145–147.

27. Cazaux, *Journal Secret de la Libération*, 148.

28. Jean-Pierre Azéma, *From Munich to the Liberation, 1938–1944* (Cambridge: Cambridge University Press, 1984), 203; Footitt and Simmonds, *France 1943–1945*, 123.

29. Martin Blumenson, *Breakout and Pursuit*. The US Army in World War II: The European Theater of Operations (Washington, DC: Center of Military History, 1961), 595.

30. Braibant, *La Guerre à Paris*, 536.

31. Dansette, *La Libération de Paris*, 165.

32. Raymond Massiet, *La Préparation de l'Insurrection et la Bataille de Paris* (Paris: Payot, 1945), 111–113.

Chapter Six

1. Charles Braibant, *La Guerre à Paris* (Paris: Corrêa, 1945), 538–541.

2. Larry Collins and Dominique Lapierre, *Is Paris Burning?* (New York: Simon and Schuster, 1965), 105.

3. Yves Cazaux, *Journal Secret de la Libération* (Paris: Albin Michel, 1979), 153.

4. S. Campaux, ed., *Libération de Paris* (Paris: Payot, 1945), 27. Sources vary on the number of policemen in the Prefecture of Police on August 19 and 20, with the range being from 1,500 to 4,000. The latter number is most likely too high.

5. Collins and Lapierre, *Is Paris Burning?*, 111; Emmanuel Blanc, "Les Six Jours de Feu du Palais de Justice," in Campaux, ed., *Libération de Paris*, 46.

6. See the oral history of Roger Priou-Valjean, an organizer of the Paris police, in Philippe Raguenau and Eddy Florentin, eds., *Paris Libéré: Ils Étaient Là!* (Paris: France-Empire, 1994), esp. 71–73.

7. Adrien Dansette, *Histoire de la Libération de Paris* (Paris: Arthème Fayard, 1946), 178.

8. Ibid., 175.

9. Claude Roy, "Mine Eyes Have Seen," in A. J. Liebling, *The Republic of Silence* (New York: Harcourt, Brace, 1947), 449; Andrzej Bobkowski, *En Guerre et en Paix: Journal 1940–1944* (Paris: Editions Noir sur Blanc, 1991), 608; Raoul Nordling, *Sauver Paris: Mémoirs du Consul de Suède, 1905–1944* (Paris: Editions Complexe, 2002), 113; Jacques Bardoux, *La Délivrance de Paris: Journal d'un Sénateur, Octobre 1943–Octobre 1944* (Paris: Fayard, 1958), 351.

10. Général [Dietrich] von Choltitz, *De Sébastopol à Paris: Un Soldat Parmi des Soldats* (Paris: Aubanel, 1964), 231.

11. Martin Blumenson, *Breakout and Pursuit*. The US Army in World War II: The European Theater of Operations (Washington, DC: Center of Military History, 1961), 593.

12. Hilary Footitt and John Simmonds, *France 1943–1945* (New York: Holmes and Meier, 1988), 124; Colonel Rol-Tanguy and Roger Bourderon, *Libération de Paris: Les Cent Documents* (Paris: Hachette, 1994), 198.

13. Collins and Lapierre, *Is Paris Burning?*, 111.

14. Willis Thornton, *The Liberation of Paris* (London: Rupert Hart-Davis, 1963), 145.

15. Dansette, *Histoire de la Libération de Paris*, 178.

16. Roy, "Mine Eyes Have Seen," 454; Pierre Maudru, *Les Six Glorieuses de Paris* (Paris: Société Parisienne d'Edition, 1944), 38.

17. Thornton, *The Liberation of Paris*, 148; Ferdinand Dupuy, *La Libération de Paris Vue d'un Commissariat de Police* (Paris: Libraries-Imprimeries Réunis, 1944), 15.

18. Campaux, ed., *Libération de Paris*, 29; Dansette, *Histoire de la Libération de Paris*, 195.

19. Claude Roy and Le Comité Parisien de la Libération, *Paris: Les Heures Glorieuses, Août 1944* (Montrouge: n.p., 1945), 96.

20. André Desfeuilles, *Raoul Nordling et la Libération de Paris* (Paris: Institut Tessin, 1945), 12.

21. Quoted in Collins and Lapierre, *Is Paris Burning?*, 127.

22. Desfeuilles, *Raoul Nordling*, 13.

23. Nordling, *Sauver Paris*, 115.

24. Desfeuilles, *Raoul Nordling*, 14.

25. Ibid.; Robert Aron, *France Reborn* (New York: Scribner's, 1964), 268–269.

26. Nordling, *Sauver Paris*, 121.

27. Henri Michel, *La Libération de Paris* (Brussels: Éditions Complexes, 1980), 59.

28. Philippe Raguenau and Eddy Florentin, eds., *Paris Libéré: Ils Étaient Là!* (Paris: France-Empire, 1994), 51, 95.

29. Ibid., 125, 143.

30. Martin Blumenson, "The Liberation of Paris," *World War II* 15, no. 3 (2000).

31. William Hornaday, "The William T. Hornaday Papers," Vertical File 950, Bay 5, Row 190, Face A, Shelf 7, Box 35, Folder 14, United States

Army Heritage and Education Center, Carlisle, Pennsylvania, 2–3. See also Harold C. Lyon, "Operations of 'T Force', 12th Army Group, in the Liberation and Intelligence Exploitation of Paris, France, 25 August–6 September 1944 (Northern France Campaign)," Unit History 02–12 1949, United States Army Heritage and Education Center, Carlisle, Pennsylvania; André Martel, *Leclerc, un Homme, un Chef, une Épopée* (Paris: Charles-Lavauzelle, 1987), 63.

32. Hornaday, "Papers," 3

33. Victoria Kent, *Quatre Ans à Paris* (Paris: Editions le Livre du Jour, 1947), 201; Cazaux, *Journal Secret de la Libération*, 157.

34. Roy, *Paris*, 95.

35. Matthew Cobb, *The Resistance: The French Fight Against the Nazis* (London: Pocket Books, 2009), 261.

36. Michel, *La Libération de Paris*, 63.

37. Nordling, *Sauver Paris*, 129.

38. Dansette, *Histoire de la Libération de Paris*, 227; Aron, *France Reborn*, 271; Nordling, *Sauver Paris*, 130.

39. Dupuy, *La Libération de Paris*, 19; Collins and Lapierre, *Is Paris Burning?*, 143, 134.

40. Office of the Chief of Military History, Personal Papers of William Sylvan, United States Army Heritage and Education Center, Carlisle, Pennsylvania.

41. Joachim Ludewig, *Der deutsche Rückzug aus Frankreich 1944* (Berlin: Rombach, 1994), part B, I, section 3; Kurt Hesse, "Defense of Paris (Summer 1944) [Karlsruhe, Germany: Historical Division, Headquarters, US Army, Europe, 1947]," Foreign Military Studies MS# B-611, D739.F6713, United States Army Heritage and Education Center, Carlisle, Pennsylvania; OKW War Diary, 1 April–16 December 1944, Foreign Military Studies MS #B-034, Folder 2, United States Army Heritage and Education Center, Carlisle, Pennsylvania. I am deeply indebted to David Zabecki for making me aware of the Ludewig volume and for providing me with an English translation.

42. Jean Galtier-Boissière, *Mon Journal Pendant l'Occupation* (Paris: La Jeune Parque, 1944), 259.

43. Dupuy, *La Libération de Paris*, 19.

44. Footitt and Simmonds, *France 1943–1945*, 135.

Chapter Seven

1. Jacques Bardoux, *La Délivrance de Paris: Journal d'un Sénateur, Octobre 1943–Octobre 1944* (Paris: Fayard, 1958), 354; Pierre Maudru, *Les Six Glorieuses de Paris* (Paris: Société Parisienne d'Edition, 1944), 11.

2. OKW War Diary, 1 April–16 December 1944, Foreign Military Studies MS #B-034, Folder 2, United States Army Heritage and Education Center, Carlisle, Pennsylvania, 117–118; Joachim Ludewig, *Der deutsche Rückzug aus Frankreich 1944* (Berlin: Rombach, 1994), part B, II, section 1.

3. Thomas H. Wolf, "My Brush with History: The Liberation of Paris," *American Heritage* 45, no. 5 (1994): 29.

4. Raoul Nordling, *Sauver Paris: Mémoirs du Consul de Suède, 1905–1944* (Paris: Editions Complexe, 2002), 136.

5. Willis Thornton, *The Liberation of Paris* (London: Rupert Hart-Davis, 1963), 153, 157.

6. Adrien Dansette, *Histoire de la Libération de Paris* (Paris: Arthème Fayard, 1946), 246, 254–255; Larry Collins and Dominique Lapierre, *Is Paris Burning?* (New York: Simon and Schuster, 1965), 145; Thornton, *The Liberation of Paris*, 159, 173.

7. Graham Robb, *Parisians: An Adventure History of Paris* (New York: W. W. Norton, 2010), 107; Eric Hazan, *The Invention of Paris: A History in Footsteps* (London: Verso, 2010), 92.

8. Charles Glass, *Americans in Paris: Life and Death Under Nazi Occupation* (London: Harper Press, 2009), 387. Beach managed to keep the shop in the Rue de l'Odéon open until the fall of 1941; when she refused to sell a German officer her last copy of *Finnegans Wake*, as an act of vengeance, the officer had the shop closed. She moved her remaining books to an apartment nearby to prevent them from being confiscated by the Germans. She was interned for six months by German authorities but was allowed to stay in Paris upon her release. Philippe Barat, *Pavés Sanglants* (Paris: Armand Fleury, 1945), 76, 91.

9. Simone de Beauvoir, *Force of Circumstance* (New York: Putnam's, 1964), 3; Jean Reybaz, "Le Maquis St. Severin: Ou Comment Fut Libéré le Quartier St. Michel," in S. Campaux, ed., *Libération de Paris* (Paris: Payot, 1945), 76; Barat, *Pavés Sanglants*, 43; Gilles Perrault and Pierre Azéma, *Paris Under the Occupation* (Paris: Vendôme, 1987), 51.

10. Jean Amidieu du Clos, "Heures de Combat sur la Barricade de la Harpe," in S. Campaux, ed., *Libération de Paris* (Paris: Payot, 1945), 103; Barat, *Pavés Sanglants*, 69.

11. Raymond Massiet, *La Préparation de l'Insurrection et la Bataille de Paris* (Paris: Payot, 1945), 171. Massiet was himself a senior FFI leader and adviser to Rol; Barat, *Pavés Sanglants*, 66ff.

12. S. Campaux, ed., *Libération de Paris* (Paris: Payot, 1945), 33.

13. Oral history of Cécile and Henri Rol-Tanguy, in Philippe Raguneau and Eddy Florentin, eds., *Paris Libéré: Ils Étaient Là!* (Paris: France-Empire, 1994), 63; Campaux, ed., *Libération de Paris*, 37, 31; S. Dupin de Lacoste, *Les Journées d'Août* (Paris: L'Expansion Scientifique, 1945), 19.

14. Charles Braibant, *La Guerre à Paris* (Paris: Corrêa, 1945), 549; Maudru, *Les Six Glorieuses*, 34.

15. Claude Roy and Le Comité Parisien de la Libération, *Paris: Les Heures Glorieuses, Août 1944* (Montrouge: n.p., 1945), 86; Jean Galtier-Boissière, *Mon Journal Pendant l'Occupation* (Paris: Le Jeune Parque, 1944), 268.

16. Edith Thomas, *La Libération de Paris* (Paris: Mellottée, 1945), 71; Massiet, *La Préparation de l'Insurrection*, 138, 164, 224; Campaux, ed., *Libération de Paris*, 34.

17. Ferdinand Dupuy, *Le Libération de Paris Vue d'un Commissariat de Police* (Paris: Librairies Imprimeries Réunis, 1944), 24, 35.

18. Collins and Lapierre, *Is Paris Burning?*, 161–162.

19. Henri Michel, *La Libération de Paris* (Bruxelles: Editions Complexes, 1980), 73.

20. Robert Monod, *Les Heures Décisives de la Libération de Paris* (Paris: Editions Gilbert, 1947), 43.

21. Ibid., 51–55, 59; Dansette, *Histoire de la Libération de Paris*, 309–311.

22. Oral history of Roger Cocteau-Gallois, in Philippe Raguneau and Eddy Florentin, eds., *Paris Libéré: Ils Étaient Là!* (Paris: France-Empire, 1994), 216; "Le Récit de Gallois," in Robert Monod, *Les Heures Décisives de la Libération de Paris* (Paris: Editions Gilbert, 1947), 75–80.

23. Martin Blumenson, "The Liberation of Paris," *World War II* 15, no. 3 (2000).

24. Martin Blumenson, *Breakout and Pursuit*. The US Army in World War II: The European Theater of Operations (Washington, DC: Center of Military History, 1961), 601–603.

25. Harold C. Lyon, "Operations of 'T Force', 12th Army Group, in the Liberation and Intelligence Exploitation of Paris, France, 25 August–6 September 1944 (Northern France Campaign)," Unit History 02–12 1949, United States Army Heritage and Education Center, Carlisle, Pennsylvania.

26. Dansette, *Histoire de la Libération de Paris*, 312. Gallois's version of Patton's speech to him is in "Le Récit de Gallois," 77–78; Philippe Raguneau and Eddy Florentin, eds., *Paris Libéré: Ils Étaient Là!* (Paris: France-Empire, 1994), 218–219.

27. Dansette, *Histoire de la Libération de Paris*, 312; "Le Récit de Gallois," 78.

28. Collins and Lapierre, *Is Paris Burning?*, 188.

29. Blumenson, *Breakout and Pursuit*, 608.

30. Henri Michel, *Paris Résistant* (Paris: Albin Michel, 1982), 317.

31. Perrault and Azéma, *Paris Under the Occupation*, 52.

32. Jacqueline Lévi-Valensi, ed., *Camus at Combat: Writing 1944–1947* (Princeton, NJ: Princeton University Press, 2006), 12–13.

33. Dupin de Lacoste, *Les Journées d'Août*, 20–22.

34. "Le Récit de Gallois," 78–79.

35. Blumenson, *Breakout and Pursuit*, 604–605.

36. Forrest C. Pogue, *The Supreme Command*. The US Army in World War II: The European Theater of Operations (Washington, DC: Center of Military History, 1954), 240–241, emphasis in original; Blumenson, *Breakout and Pursuit*, 604–605; Martin Blumenson, *The Duel for France, 1944* (New York: Da Capo, 1963), 344; Dwight Eisenhower, *Crusade in Europe* (Garden City, NJ: Doubleday, 1949), 296.

37. Personal Papers of William Sylvan, US First Army War Diary, United States Army Heritage and Education Center, Carlisle, Pennsylvania, entry for August 22.

38. Omar Bradley, *A Soldier's Story* (New York: Modern Library, 1999), 392; Collins and Lapierre, *Is Paris Burning?*, 193; "Le Récit de Gallois," 79–80; Raguneau and Florentin, eds., *Paris Libéré*, 221.

39. Harold C. Lyon, "Operations of 'T Force', 12th Army Group, in the Liberation and Intelligence Exploitation of Paris, France, 25 August–6 September 1944 (Northern France Campaign)," Unit History 02–12 1949, United States Army Heritage and Education Center, Carlisle, Pennsylvania, 7.

40. Capt. Even, "La 2ième Division Blindée de son Débarquement en Normandie à la Libération de Paris," *Revue Historique de l'Armée*, March 1952, 116.

41. Oral history of Raymond Dronne, in Philippe Raguneau and Eddy Florentin, eds., *Paris Libéré: Ils Étaient Là!* (Paris: France-Empire, 1994), 229.

42. Oral history of André Tollet, in Philippe Raguneau and Eddy Florentin, eds., *Paris Libéré: Ils Étaient Là!* (Paris: France-Empire, 1994), 128. Tollet seems to have believed that the Germans never intended widescale demolitions in any case.

43. Robert Aron, *France Reborn* (New York: Scribner's, 1964), 279; "Le Récit de Gallois," 81.

Chapter Eight

1. Larry Collins and Dominique Lapierre, *Is Paris Burning?* (New York: Simon and Schuster, 1965), 145; Willis Thornton, *The Liberation of Paris* (London: Rupert Hart-Davis, 1963), 202–203.

2. Quoted in Christine Levisse-Touzé, *Paris Libéré, Paris Retrouvé* (Paris: Découvertes Gallimard, 2003), 51.

3. S. Dupin de Lacoste, *Les Journées d'Août* (Paris: L'Expansion Scientifique, 1945), 25.

4. Emmanuel Blanc, "Les Six Jours de Feu du Palais de Justice," in S. Campaux, ed., *La Libération de Paris* (Paris: Payot, 1945), 50–51; Lebar-Renaud, quoted in Campaux, ed., *La Libération de Paris*, 37; Jacques Kim, *La Libération de Paris: Les Journées Historiques* (Paris: L'O.P.G., 1944),

n.p.; Jean Eparvier, *A Paris sous la Botte des Nazis* (Paris: Editions Raymond Schall, 1944), 26.

5. Jacqueline Lévi-Valensi, ed., *Camus at Combat: Writing 1944–1947* (Princeton, NJ: Princeton University Press, 2006), 15.

6. This estimate comes from Collins and Lapierre, *Is Paris Burning?*, 145. There are no entirely reliable statistics on casualties at this stage of the uprising, but this number seems as reasonable a guess as any. Gilbert Joseph, *Une Si Douce Occupation: Simone de Beauvoir et Jean-Paul Sartre, 1940–1944* (Paris: A. Michel, 1991), 353–354, 358.

7. Jean Amidieu du Clos, "Heures de Combat sur la Barricade de la Harpe du 19 Août au 26 Août 1944," in S. Campaux, ed., *La Libération de Paris* (Paris: Payot, 1945), 105; Pierre Maudru, *Les Six Glorieuses de Paris* (Paris: Société Parisienne d'Edition, 1944), 40.

8. Today the barracks are called the Caserne Vérine and house the French Garde Républicaine. I would like to thank the young woman of the Garde who allowed me to take a brief walk around the courtyard. She had no idea of the events that had transpired there in 1944, although she told me she had always been curious about the old photographs and historical mementos inside. Robert Aron, *France Reborn* (New York: Scribner's, 1964), 283.

9. Joachim Ludewig, *Der deutsche Rückzug aus Frankreich 1944* (Berlin: Rombach, 1994), part B, II, section 2; Charles Braibant, *La Guerre à Paris* (Paris: Corrêa, 1945), 557; Colonel Rol-Tanguy and Roger Bourderon, *Libération de Paris: Les Cent Documents* (Paris: Hachette, 1994), 275.

10. Collins and Lapierre, *Is Paris Burning?*, 225; Général [Dietrich] von Choltitz, *De Sébastopol à Paris: Un Soldat Parmi des Soldats* (Paris: Aubanel, 1964), 240.

11. Marcelle Adler-Bresse, "Von Choltitz, A-t-il Changé d'Avis?" *Revue d'Histoire de la Deuxième Guerre Mondiale* 19 (1955): 116.

12. Kurt Hesse, "Defense of Paris (Summer 1944) [Karlsruhe, Germany: Historical Division, Headquarters, US Army, Europe, 1947]," Foreign Military Studies MS# B-611, D739.F6713, United States Army Heritage and Education Center, Carlisle, Pennsylvania, 17, 23–24; Ernest Hemingway,

"How We Came to Paris," in Samuel Hynes et al., eds., *Reporting World War II*, Part Two, *American Journalism, 1944–1946* (New York: Library of America, 1995), 247. The article originally appeared in *Collier's* in October 1944.

13. Martin Blumenson, *Breakout and Pursuit*. The US Army in World War II: The European Theater of Operations (Washington, DC: Center of Military History, 1961), 618.

14. Choltitz, *De Sébastopol à Paris*, 247.

15. Choltitz, *De Sébastopol à Paris*, 253, 255; Jean-Pierre Azéma, *From Munich to the Liberation, 1938–1944* (Cambridge: Cambridge University Press, 1984), 205–206. For more on the role of German officers in arranging surrenders at the end of World War I to protect their men from further harm in a lost cause, see Scott Stephenson, *The Final Battle: Soldiers of the Western Front and the German Revolution of 1918* (Cambridge: Cambridge University Press, 2009). Choltitz, a lieutenant on the western front in 1918, had undoubtedly learned from what he had seen firsthand at the end of that war.

16. "The Battle for Paris," *Newsweek*, September 11, 1944, 31; *Life*, September 4, 1944, 26; Edith Thomas, *La Libération de Paris* (Paris: Mellottée, 1945), 73.

17. Jacques Bardoux, *La Délivrance de Paris: Journal d'un Sénateur, Octobre 1943–Octobre 1944* (Paris: Fayard, 1958), 361; Thomas, *La Libération de Paris*, 73.

18. Capitaine Even, "La 2ième D. B. de son Débarquement en Normandie à la Libération de Paris," *Revue Historique de l'Armée*, March 1952, 121; Ferdinand Dupuy, *La Libération de Paris Vue d'un Commissariat de Police* (Paris: Librairies-Imprimeries Réunis, 1944), 35.

19. Quoted in Olivier Wieviorka, *Normandy: The Landings to the Liberation of Paris* (Cambridge: The Belknap Press of Harvard University Press, 2008), 350–351; Charles Williams, *The Last Great Frenchman: A Life of General de Gaulle* (New York: John Wiley and Sons, 1993), 270.

20. Oral history of General Alain de Boissieu, in Philippe Ragueneau and Eddy Florentin, eds., *Paris Libéré: Ils Étaient Là!* (Paris: France-Empire,

1994), 306; Clara Longworth de Chambrun, *Shadows Lengthen: The Story of My Life* (New York: Scribner's, 1949), 228; *L'Humanité* article, in Philippe Nivet and Yvan Combeau, *Histoire Politique de Paris au XXe Siècle* (Paris: Presses Universitaires de France, 2000), 165.

21. Albert Camus, *Actuelles: Chroniques, 1944–1948* (Paris: Gallimard, 1950), 19–21.

22. Lévi-Valensi, ed., *Camus at* Combat, 17.

23. Holbrook Bradley, *War Correspondent: From D-Day to the Elbe* (New York: iUniverse, 2007), 70; Emlen Etting, "Going in with Leclerc," *Atlantic Monthly* 174, no. 6 (1944): 41–42.

24. Oral history of Raymond Dronne, in Philippe Raguneau and Eddy Florentin, eds., *Paris Libéré: Ils Étaient Là!* (Paris: France-Empire, 1994), 238.

25. William T. Hornaday to Richard Sommers, November 17, 1971, page 2, Papers of William T. Hornaday, Archives Vertical File Building 950, Bay 5, Row 190, Face A, Shelf 7, Box 35, Folder 14, United States Army Heritage and Education Center, Carlisle, Pennsylvania; Blumenson, *Breakout and Pursuit*, 611.

26. Quoted in Jean Lacouture, *De Gaulle: The Rebel, 1890–1940* (New York: W.W. Norton, 1990), 564.

27. Hornaday to Sommers, 2; David Nichols, ed., *Ernie's War: The Best of Ernie Pyle's World War II Dispatches* (New York: Touchstone, 1986), 352.

28. Pierre Bourdan, *Carnet de Retour avec la Division Leclerc* (Paris: Plon, 1965), 150–151.

29. Blumenson, *Breakout and Pursuit*, 613, 614; Martin Blumenson, "The Liberation of Paris," *World War II* 15, no. 3 (2000): 58.

30. Irwin Shaw, "Morts pour la Patrie," in Samuel Hynes et. al., eds., *Reporting World War II*, Part Two, *American Journalism, 1944–1946* (New York: Library of America, 1995), 252.

31. Choltitz, *De Sébastopol à Paris*, 242.

32. Lacouture, *De Gaulle*, 568.

33. Collins and Lapierre, *Is Paris Burning?*, 236; Alain de Boissieu, *Pour Combattre avec de Gaulle, 1940–1946* (Paris: Plon, 1981), 252–253.

Boissieu was captured in 1940 but managed to escape to Russia, which was then an ally of Germany. The Russians imprisoned him until July 1941, when they sent him to London to join de Gaulle. In addition to the Paris campaign, he also fought at Dieppe and in Africa. He married de Gaulle's daughter Elisabeth in 1946 and served as chief of staff of the French Army from 1971 to 1975.

34. Some sources report that Dronne entered through the nearby Porte de Gentilly. Even, "La 2ième D. B.," is one such source. It is possible that Dronne divided his forces. There is also disagreement about exact times that events occurred. These times and entry points come from Dronne himself, in his oral history in Raguneau and Florentin, eds., *Paris Libéré*, 240.

35. Dronne, in Raguneau and Florentin, eds., *Paris Libéré*, 241. Some sources indicate that Leclerc had ordered Dronne to head directly for the prefecture, but Dronne himself did not mention these orders in any of his later recollections. Dronne went on to serve under Leclerc all the way to Hitler's headquarters in Berchtesgaden and then in Indochina. He was later elected to the National Assembly as a Gaullist.

36. Jean Galtier-Boissière, *Mon Journal Pendant l'Occupation* (Paris: Jeune Parque, 1944), 276; Doutard, quoted in Richard D.E. Burton, *Blood in the City: Violence and Revolution in Paris, 1789–1945* (Ithaca, NY: Cornell University Press, 2001), 238; Lebar-Renaud, quoted in Campaux, ed., *La Libération de Paris*, 37.

37. Yvonne Féron, *Délivrance de Paris* (Paris: Librairie Hachette, 1945), 51; Hilary Footitt and John Simmonds, *France 1943–1945* (New York: Holmes and Meier, 1988), 137; Burton, *Blood in the City*, 238–240.

38. Eparvier, *A Paris sous la Botte*, 26–27; Adrien Dansette, *Histoire de la Libération de Paris* (Paris: Fayard, 1946), 357; Dupuy, *La Libération de Paris*, 38; Braibant, *La Guerre à Paris*, 557–558.

39. Even, "La 2ième D. B.," 125; Etting, "Going in with Leclerc," 42.

40. Philippe Barat, *Pavés Sanglants* (Paris: Armand Fleury, 1945), 84; Simone de Beauvoir, *Force of Circumstance* (New York: Putnam's, 1964), 4.

41. Collins and Lapierre, *Is Paris Burning?*, 258–259.

42. Ibid.

Chapter Nine

1. David Nichols, ed., *Ernie's War: The Best of Ernie Pyle's World War II Dispatches* (New York: Touchstone, 1986), 351–352.

2. Pierre Maudru, *Les Six Glorieuses de Paris* (Paris: Société Parisienne d'Édition, 1944), 50.

3. Nichols, ed., *Ernie's War*, 352.

4. Robert Aron, *France Reborn* (New York: Scribner's, 1964), 286.

5. Pascale Moisson, *Anecdotes . . . sous la Botte* (Paris: L'Hamattan, 1998), 125; Adrian Dansette, *Histoire de la Libération de Paris* (Paris: Fayard, 1946), 364; Irwin Shaw, "Morts pour la Patrie," in *Reporting World War II*, Part Two, *American Journalism, 1944–1946* (New York: Library of America, 1995), 261–262.

6. Larry Collins and Dominique Lapierre, *Is Paris Burning?* (New York: Simon and Schuster, 1965), 271–272; Thomas H. Wolf, "My Brush with History: The Liberation of Paris," *American Heritage* 45, no. 5 (1994): 29; Charles Codman, "The Americans Arrive," *Atlantic Monthly* 174, no. 6 (1944): 45 (this article is a letter Codman wrote to his wife on August 27); Jeremy A. Crang, "Document: General de Gaulle Under Sniper Fire in Notre Dame Cathedral, 26 August 1944: Robert Reid's BBC Commentary," *Historical Journal of Film, Radio, and Television* 27, no. 3 (2007), 399.

7. Jacques Bardoux, *La Délivrance de Paris: Journal d'un Sénateur, Octobre 1943–Octobre 1944* (Paris: Fayard, 1958), 366.

8. Collins and Lapierre, *Is Paris Burning?*, 275.

9. Kenneth Crawford, "The Battle for Paris," *Newsweek*, September 11, 1944, 32; Charles C. Wertenbaker, "Paris Is Free," *Time*, September 4, 1944, 35.

10. Codman, "The Americans Arrive," 45; Pierre Bourdan, *Carnet de Retour avec la Division Leclerc* (Paris: Plon, 1965), 150–174.

11. Bourdan, *Carnet de Retour*, 176; Moisson, *Anecdotes*, 124; Gilles Perrault and Pierre Azema, *Paris Under the Occupation* (Paris: Vendôme, 1987).

12. Eric Hazan, *The Invention of Paris: A History in Footsteps* (London: Verso, 2010), 131.

13. Oral history of Jacques Massu, in Philippe Raguneau and Eddy Florentin, eds., *Paris Libéré: Ils Étaient Là!* (Paris: France-Empire, 1994), 288. Massu later led the revolt of French Army officers in Algeria. He was relieved of command in 1960, although he continued a distinguished military career. In 1968, then serving as commander of French forces in Germany, Massu pledged support for de Gaulle against antigovernment demonstrators, but only if de Gaulle gave an amnesty to all French officers punished as a result of their opposition to French policy in Algeria. Shaw, "Morts pour la Patrie," 254, 260.

14. Personal Papers of William Sylvan, US First Army War Diary, United States Army Heritage and Education Center, Carlisle, Pennsylvania, entry for August 25.

15. Shaw, "Morts pour la Patrie," 254.

16. Jean Lacouture, *De Gaulle: The Rebel, 1890–1944* (New York: W. W. Norton, 1990), 568; Henri Michel, *Paris Résistant* (Paris: Albin Michel, 1982), 319; Dansette, *Histoire de la Libération de Paris*, 370–371; Collins and Lapierre, *Is Paris Burning?*, 283.

17. S. Campaux, ed., *La Libération de Paris* (Paris: Payot, 1945), 183.

18. There are many versions of this story, but the most logical and believable is in Dansette, *Histoire de la Libération de Paris*, 377–378.

19. Christine Levisse-Touzé, *Paris Libéré, Paris Retrouvé* (Paris: Découvertes Gallimard, 2004), 68.

20. Dansette, *Histoire de la Libération de Paris*, 381–386; and oral history of Maurice Kriegel-Valrimont, in Philippe Raguneau and Eddy Florentin, eds., *Paris Libéré: Ils Étaient Là!* (Paris: France-Empire, 1994), 100.

21. Bardoux, *La Délivrance de Paris*, 366; Shaw, "Morts pour la Patrie," 252.

22. Oral history of Raymond Dronne, in Philippe Raguneau and Eddy Florentin, eds., *Paris Libéré: Ils Étaient Là!* (Paris: France-Empire, 1994), 246.

23. Alain de Boissieu, *Pour Combattre avec de Gaulle, 1940–1946* (Paris: Plon, 1981), 253.

24. Général [Dietrich] von Choltitz, *De Sébastopol à Paris: Un Soldat Parmi des Soldats* (Paris: Aubanel, 1964), 256. Choltitz died in 1966 in

Baden-Baden, which, ironically enough, was then the headquarters of the French occupation force in Germany.

25. Charles Williams, *The Last Great Frenchman: A Life of General de Gaulle* (New York: John Wiley and Sons, 1993), 273.

26. Oral histories of Alain de Boissieu and Henri Rol-Tanguy, in Philippe Raguneau and Eddy Florentin, eds., *Paris Libéré: Ils Étaient Là!* (Paris: France-Empire, 1994), 59.

27. Oral history of Roger Stéphane, in Philippe Raguneau and Eddy Florentin, eds., *Paris Libéré: Ils Étaient Là!* (Paris: France-Empire, 1994), 112.

28. Lacouture, *De Gaulle*, 573; Charles De Gaulle, *Lettres, Notes, et Carnets,* vol. 5, *Juin 1943 à Mai 1945* (Paris: Plon, 1983), 297–298.

29. Collins and Lapierre, *Is Paris Burning?*, 326.

30. Levisse-Touzé, *Paris Libéré, Paris Retrouvé*, 73; Yvonne Féron, *Délivrance de Paris* (Paris: Librairie Hachette, 1945), 55.

31. Quoted in Levisse-Touzé, *Paris Libéré, Paris Retrouvé*, 95.

32. Quoted in Yvonne Féron, *Délivrance de Paris*, 55.

33. Lacouture, *De Gaulle*, 575; Martin Blumenson, *Breakout and Pursuit*. The US Army in World War II: The European Theater of Operations (Washington, DC: Center of Military History, 1961), 623.

34. *Life*, September 4, 1944, 26.

35. Matthew Cobb, *The Resistance: The French Fight Against the Nazis* (London: Pocket Books, 2009), 269; Perrault and Azema, *Paris Under the Occupation*, 56; James Tobin, *Ernie Pyle's War: America's Witness to World War II* (New York: Free Press, 2006), 21. Nichols, ed., *Ernie's War*, 353, presents a less crass (and less believable) version: "Anybody who does not sleep with a woman tonight is just an exhibitionist."

36. Albert Camus, *Actuelles: Chroniques, 1944–1948* (Paris: Gallimard, 1950), 22; Andrzej Bobkowski, *En Guerre et en Paix: Journal 1940–1944* (Paris: Éditions Noir sur Blanc, 1991), 613–614.

37. Willis Thornton, *The Liberation of Paris* (London: Rupert Hart-Davis, 1963), 211.

38. Lacouture, *De Gaulle*, 576–577; Blumenson, *The US Army in World War II*, 625. The Deuxième Division Blindée did eventually return to the V Corps on September 8.

39. Charles Braibant, *La Guerre à Paris* (Paris: Corrêa, 1945), 559; Williams, *The Last Great Frenchman*, 274.

40. Maurice Kriegel-Valrimont, *Mémoires Rebelles* (Paris: Éditions Odile Jacob, 1999), 69; Cobb, *The Resistance*, 269.

41. Moisson, *Anecdotes*, 128.

42. Féron, *Délivrance de Paris*, 87–88; Crang, "Document," 394. Some of Reid's original audio of the broadcast, complete with sounds of the shooting, can be heard at http://new.fr.music.yahoo.com/robert-reid/tracks/german-snipers-fire-on-de-galle-as-he-enters-notre-dame--60999376. Note the misspelling of de Gaulle in the URL.

43. Helen Kirkpatrick, "Daily News Writer Sees Man Slain at Her Side in Hail of Lead," in *Reporting World War II*, 264; Crang, "Document," 394.

44. Crang, "Document," 395; Kirkpatrick, "Daily News Writer," 265; De Gaulle, *Lettres, Notes, et Carnets*, 298. De Gaulle used the phrase "une vulgaire tartarinade," a reference to an 1872 comic novel entitled "Tartarin de Tarascon" by Alphonse Daudet. The hero, Tartarin, is a braggart who invents his reputation as a great hero and a hunter of wild beasts but cannot in reality shoot straight. My thanks to my friend and Dickinson College professor Dominique Laurent for his help with this reference. Harold C. Lyon, "Operations of 'T Force', 12th Army Group, in the Liberation and Intelligence Exploitation of Paris, France, 25 August–6 September 1944 (Northern France Campaign)," Unit History 02–12 1949, United States Army Heritage and Education Center, Carlisle, Pennsylvania.

45. Ferdinand Dupuy, *La Libération de Paris Vue d'un Commissariat de Police* (Paris: Librairies-Imprimeries Réunis, 1944), 49; Emmanuel Blanc, "Les Six Jours de Feu du Palais de Justice," in S. Campaux, ed., *La Libération de Paris* (Paris: Payot, 1945), 52–53; Féron, *Délivrance de Paris*, 54–55; Moisson, *Anecdotes*, 128. *La Marseillaise* opens with the lines, "Allons enfants de la Patrie / le jour de gloire est arrivé" (Come on children of the fatherland / the day of glory has arrived).

46. Bardoux, *La Délivrance de Paris*, 380.

47. Simone de Beauvoir, *Force of Circumstance* (New York: Putnam's, 1964), 4, 16; Jacqueline Gaussen-Salmon, *Une Prière dans la Nuit: Journal d'une Femme Peintre sous l'Occupation* (Paris: Documents Payot, 1992), 221;

Pleas B. Rogers Papers, Archives Building 950, Bay 5, Row 167, face P, Shelf 6, United States Army Heritage and Education Center, Carlisle, Pennsylvania.

48. A. J. Liebling, "Letter from Paris," *New Yorker*, November 3, 1944, 42.

49. Raymond Massiet, *La Préparation de l'Insurrection et la Bataille de Paris* (Paris: Payot, 1945), 224.

50. Braibant, *La Guerre à Paris*, 562; Dronne, in Raguneau and Florentin, eds., *Paris Libéré*, 251.

Conclusion

1. Simone de Beauvoir, *Force of Circumstance* (New York: Putnam's, 1964), 30.

2. Oral history of Daniel Mayer, in Philippe Ragueneau and Eddy Florentin, eds., *Paris Libéré: Ils Étaient Là!* (Paris: France-Empire, 1994), 172.

3. Maurice Kriegel-Valrimont, *Mémoires Rebelles* (Paris: Éditions Odile Jacob, 1999), 71; Henri Michel, *Paris Résistant* (Paris: Albin Michel, 1982), 335; oral history of Maurice Kriegel-Valrimont, in Philippe Ragueneau and Eddy Florentin, eds., *Paris Libéré: Ils Étaient Là!* (Paris: France-Empire, 1994), 102.

4. There are today 1,061 members of the Ordre de la Libération, honored in a wing of Les Invalides. Members mentioned in this book include Georges Bidault, Alain de Boissieu, Pierre Brossolette, Jacques Chaban-Delmas, Raymond Dronne, Henri Karcher, Philippe Leclerc, Charles Luizet, Jean Moulin, Alexandre Parodi, and the City of Paris.

5. Hilary Footitt and John Simmonds, *France 1943–1945* (New York: Holmes and Meier, 1988), 148–150.

6. Pleas B. Rogers Papers, Archives Building 950, Bay 5, Row 167, face P, Shelf 6, United States Army Heritage and Education Center, Carlisle, Pennsylvania.

7. Charles Braibant, *La Guerre à Paris* (Paris: Corrêa, 1945), 562.

8. The figure of 9,000 comes from Matthew Cobb, *The Resistance: The French Fight Against the Nazis* (London: Pocket Books, 2009), 280, and seems generally accepted, although much higher numbers circulated at the time—a product, undoubtedly, of fear. Also Sisley Huddleston, *France: The*

Tragic Years, 1939–1947, An Eyewitness Account of War, Occupation, and Liberation (New York: Devin-Adair, 1955), 301.

9. Herbert R. Lottman, *The People's Anger: Justice and Revenge in Post-Liberation France* (London: Hutchinson, 1986), 81.

10. Jean Galtier-Boissière, *Mon Journal Pendant l'Occupation* (Paris: Le Jeune Parque, 1944), 284; Lottman, *The People's Anger*, 79.

11. Antony Beevor and Artemis Cooper, *Paris After the Liberation, 1944–1949* (New York: Penguin, 1994), 135; Alan Riding, *And the Show Went On: Cultural Life in Nazi-Occupied Paris* (New York: Alfred A. Knopf, 2010), 334. Arletty (born Arlette-Léonie Bathiat) gave a great double entendre when she said, "In my bedroom, there are no uniforms." She was imprisoned and had her right to act restricted for a brief period then resumed her career, later starring in *The Longest Day*, a 1962 film about the D-Day landing. Chanel lived in such luxury that the Ritz still boasts about it on its web page, although the hotel notes that she was seeking a haven from "the frenzied world of Jazz Age society," not the poverty and misery of occupied Paris. More about her romance with the Nazi spy Hans Günther von Dinklage can be found in Hal Vaughn, *Sleeping with the Enemy: Coco Chanel's Secret War* (New York: Alfred A. Knopf, 2011). The subject of the shavings is treated in greater detail in Fabrice Virgili, *Shorn Women: Gender and Punishment in Liberation France* (Oxford: Berg, 2002).

12. Brenton G. Wallace, *Patton and His Third Army* (Harrisburg, PA: Military Service Publishing Company, 1946), 74–75.

13. Pascale Moisson, *Anecdotes . . . sous la Botte* (Paris: L'Harmattan, 1998), 121.

14. de Beauvoir, *Force of Circumstance*, 11; Louis S. Rehr, *Marauder: Memoir of a B-26 Pilot in Europe in World War II* (Jefferson, NC: McFarland, 2004), 132.

15. Catherine Gavin, *Liberated France* (London: St. Martin's, 1955), 80; Janet Flanner, *Paris Journal, 1944–1965* (New York: Atheneum, 1965), 4; Joseph Evans, "City of Light but No Heat, Paris Lives with Its Clothes On," *Newsweek*, January 29, 1945, 50–52; Beevor and Cooper, *Paris After the Liberation*, 190.

16. Holbrook Bradley, *War Correspondent: From D-Day to the Elbe* (New York: iUniverse, 2007), 81–82; Beauvoir, *Force of Circumstance*, 11, 25, 28, 52.

17. Dominique Veillon, *Vivre et Survivre en France, 1939–1947* (Paris: Payot et Rivages, 1995), 293; Galtier-Boissière, *Mon Journal Pendant l'Occupation*, 289; Martin Blumenson, *Breakout and Pursuit*. The US Army in World War II: The European Theater of Operations (Washington, DC: Center of Military History, 1961), 627.

18. Tom Siler, "Paris: The GI's Silver Foxhole," *Saturday Evening Post* 217, no. 3 (1945): 26–27; "Paris: The City of Light Comes Out of the Darkness Again," *Life*, October 2, 1944, 90; "Paris Delivered," *National Geographic* 87, no. 1 (1945): 83.

19. Beauvoir, *Force of Circumstance*, 15.

20. "Paris: The City of Light," 87; "Life Correspondents See the New Paris," *Life*, September 11, 1944, 38; "Paris Creations," *Life*, October 2, 1944, 32.

21. "Paris Is Free Again," *Life*, September 11, 1944, 36. The Eisenhower quotation comes from the multimedia exhibit at Le Mont Valérien, Suresnes, France. A nineteenth-century fortress in suburban Paris, it is now an impressive museum commemorating the location of Germany's primary execution site during the occupation. Among those shot here were the members of Paris's first organized Resistance cell, formed at the Musée de l'Homme and led by Boris Vildé.

22. Gilbert Joseph, *Une Si Douce Occupation: Simone de Beauvoir, Jean-Paul Sartre, 1940–1944* (Paris: A. Michel, 1991), 357.

23. Victor Hugo, "A l'Arc de Triomphe," in *Les Voix Intérieures, Oeuvres Complètes, Poésie, VI* (Paris: Eugène Renduel, 1837), 50.

INDEX

Abetz, Otto, 126–128, 131
Abwehr, 130
Action (newspaper), 198, 217
Alençon, 98–99, 101
Algeria, 31–32, 41, 133, 235
American Military Government
  (AMGOT), 43–44
Anti-Semitism, 24, 32, 51, 105, 127,
  130
Arc de Triomphe, 30, 223, 227,
  241
Army Group B, 90, 215, 219
Army Group West, 65
Asnières, 115–116, 120
Atlantic Wall, 61
Auschwitz, 23, 75
Avenue des Champs Élysées, 195,
  226–228, 238, 241
Avenue Foch, 22–23, 71, 77, 259

Barat, Philippe, 171–172, 219
Barbie, Klaus, 36

Bardoux, Jacques
  impressions of Germans, 76, 130,
    231
  impressions of the lack of Allied
    aid, 73
  impressions of the mood of Paris,
    1–3, 14–15, 23–24, 71, 165,
    205, 224
Barton, Raymond, 230
Bastille Day, 53, 71–72
BBC, 3–6, 8–9, 101, 108, 122, 135
  role in the Resistance, 5–6
  announcement of the liberation of
    Paris, 204–205
Bender, Emil "Bobby," 159, 185
Bidault, Georges 217, 237, 242
Billotte, Pierre, 215–216, 222,
  228–229
Black Orchestra, 74–75
Blanc, Emmanuel, 138, 198, 244
Bobkowski, Andrzej, 20, 107–108,
  140, 239

Boineburg, Wilhelm von, 62–63, 77, 79

Bois de Boulogne, 10–11, 35, 105, 200–201, 233

Boissieu, Alain de, 207, 215–216, 233

Bourdan, Pierre, 212, 225

Bourget, Pierre, 3

Bradley, Holbrook, 208

Bradley, Omar N.
  thoughts on the liberation of Paris, 55, 58, 70, 155, 182, 189–192, 210–213, 234
  thoughts on the liberation of Rome, 68–69
  and Mortain, 93
  and Falaise, 97

Braibant, Charles
  thoughts on the Normandy campaign, 4, 8–9
  thoughts on the Paris food shortage 18,
  thoughts on the German occupiers, 78, 101–102, 130
  thoughts on the liberation of Paris 135–136, 200, 246

Brasillach, Robert, 252

Bussières, Amédée, 115, 117–118, 138

Café Les Deux Magots, 139, 142

Cagoule, 32

Camus, Albert, 43, 187–188, 199, 207–208, 239

Casablanca Conference, 31, 33

Cathédrale Notre Dame, 141, 144, 146, 148, 243, 258

Cazaux, Yves, 4, 71, 131, 137, 157–158

Chanson d'Automne (Verlaine), 6

Childers, Thomas, 58–59

Choltitz, Dietrich von, 83, 86
  and Pierre Taittinger, 90–91, 109
  and Raoul Nordling, 127–128, 148–152, 159, 185–186
  attitude and strategy toward Paris, 86–91, 96, 119, 125, 128, 148–149, 151, 196, 201–203
  communications with Hitler, 83–87, 192–193, 214
  disillusionment with German strategy, 86–87, 150
  negotiates truce with Paris insurgents, 159–160, 167, 185–186, 193, 204, 214–215
  response to Paris police strike, 118–120, 122, 124, 136, 141, 144, 148–150
  reputation in urban warfare, 85–86
  surrender, 219–220, 228–231, 233–234

Churchill, Winston, 3, 5, 12–13, 57, 71
  relationship with Charles de Gaulle, 31, 39, 41, 204

Clark, Mark, 68–69

Cocteau, Robert (Gallois), 179–184, 188–191, 193, 211, 234

Codman, Charles, 223, 225

Collaborators, 16, 24, 91, 108–109, 126, 188

and the Resistance, 43, 46, 102,
104–106, 128, 131, 134, 175,
188, 199, 208, 249
and Vichy leadership, 16,
104–106, 129, 249
communications, 4, 76–77, 130
épuration, 130–131, 251–252
fear of reprisals, 105–106, 121,
128
life in Paris, 15, 21–22, 30
Parisian attitudes toward, 21–22,
188, 232
within the Paris police, 111, 115,
118
Combat (newspaper), 43, 109, 153,
187–188, 199, 208, 239
Combined Bomber Offensive, 11
Comité Parisien de la Libération
(CPL), 7, 53, 59, 247
Communist Party, 4, 158, 163, 236,
250–251
and the Gaullists, 37–38, 40–43,
104, 142–143, 156, 207, 236,
238, 247, 249
and the general strike, 71, 73
and the Paris police, 24, 73,
112–114, 117, 142–143
and the Resistance, 7, 28, 34,
36–37, 40, 44, 47, 53, 107,
174
fears of, 7, 14, 22, 41, 48, 100,
104–105, 113, 207, 210, 250
support of Soviets, 40, 52–53, 59
thoughts about truce, 153, 168,
174, 211
Confédération Générale du Travail
(CGT), 44, 72

Conseil National de la Résistance
(CNR), 35, 37
Cunningham, Sir Andrew, 13

Darlan, Jean, 32
de Beauvoir, Simone, 106, 171, 219,
245, 247, 255–256
de Gaulle, Charles, 7, 28–31, 37,
217, 244
and the communists, 37–38,
40–43, 52, 104, 207, 238, 247,
249, 251
and Chaban, 47–49, 103,-104,
124, 168–169, 230
attitude toward épuration, 252
and Luizet, 133, 140
and Parodi, 48, 143
and Vichy, 128–129
as head of the provisional
government, 41–42, 44, 48, 60,
177, 185, 204–206, 249
BBC addresses, 8–9, 29
leadership of Free France, 7, 30,
33, 41–42
liberation strategies, 156, 206,
222, 228, 231, 233
Normandy campaign, 57
Paris police, 24, 115, 133, 138,
140, 236, 238, 242
relationship with the Allies,
31–32, 39–41, 43–44, 59–60,
160, 182, 211, 247, 258
Resistance, 25, 27–30, 33–35, 40,
44, 47–49, 103–104, 238, 242,
250
return to Paris, 233–244
de Gaulle, Philippe, 231

Delmas, Jacques (Chaban)
  and the communists, 53
  and de Gaulle, 47, 103–104, 108,
    230
  and the FFI, 48–49, 103, 124,
    168
  and the Paris police strike, 116,
    134, 146, 157
Deuxième Division Blindée (Second
    Armored Division), 42, 97–101,
    108, 155–156, 234, 258
  entry into Paris, 182, 192–193,
    202, 205, 209, 212–215,
    225–226, 231, 239
  victory parade, 241–242
Dio, Louis, 222
Doisneau, Robert, 157
Drancy, 23, 114, 137, 147, 252
Dronne, Raymond, 108, 192, 209,
    215–218, 232–233, 246
Duras, Marguerite, 3, 37, 78
Dutourd, Jean, 217

Eden, Anthony, 12
Eisenhower, Dwight D.
  and Giraud, 32
  and de Gaulle, 39, 41, 160, 182,
    211
  and Falaise pocket, 94
  and the Normandy campaign, 5,
    9, 13, 56–58, 98
  bombing of Paris, 11–13
  Paris liberation strategy, 42–43,
    59, 155, 182–183, 189, 191,
    233, 240–241, 258
  thoughts of strategic importance
    of Paris, 55, 65–70, 80–81,
    132, 160–161, 182, 245, 258

Élysée Palace, 235
Épuration, 175, 251–255
Etting, Emlen, 208–209, 218–219

Falaise-Argentan pocket, 93–100,
    102, 124–125, 127, 130, 132
Fascism, 24, 38, 108, 113, 126, 139
Flanner, Janet, 19, 255
Food shortage, 177, 225
  after Allied bombings, 17–23
  and the Allies, 67, 71, 106, 154,
    239–240, 245, 256–257
  for average Parisians, 52, 71, 73,
    197, 205, 255–256
  for Germans, 78, 101, 106–107
Forces Françaises de l'Intérieur
    (FFI), 25, 45–46, 51, 102–103,
    245–250, 258–259
  and the Allies, 44, 58–59,
    189–191, 258
  and Chaban, 48, 124
  and Choltitz, 90–91, 119, 122,
    128, 148–152, 160–161, 167,
    185, 201, 229
  and the Gaullists, 47, 115, 134,
    140–141, 143, 158, 176–177,
    203, 217, 234, 236, 238,
    240–242, 247–250
  and the Normandy campaign, 6,
    10, 46, 49
  and the Paris police, 102,
    116–118, 122, 134, 136–137,
    140
  barricades, 170–175, 179
  épuration, 130–131, 254
  fears of, 47–49, 90, 104–106,
    121, 128, 176, 207, 238, 240
  German surrender, 230–231

lack of weapons, 41, 46, 49, 92, 94, 100, 122–123, 175

leadership and membership, 45–46, 200

mission to contact the Allies, 179–181

uprising of, 102–103, 107, 109, 117, 124, 134, 145–147, 154, 156–162, 175–178, 185, 192, 198–202, 204, 217, 219, 226–227, 232

thoughts on liberating Paris, 46, 165, 198–199

truce, 152–153, 167–169, 189

Franco-Prussian War, 206

Francs-Tireurs et Partisans (FTP), 45. *See also* FFI

French Army, 28–30, 45, 48, 217, 25, 248–249

French Expeditionary Corps, 42, 68

French Parliament, 232, 249

French Revolution, 25, 49, 53, 105, 252

French Senate, 1–2, 15, 73, 108, 205, 226

French Fourth Republic, 39, 235

French Third Republic, 38, 235

Fresnes, 10, 23, 73, 126–127, 137, 147, 252

Front National de la Police, 112–113, 116–117

Galtier-Boissière, Jean, 3, 104, 121–122

Gare de l'Est, 131, 175, 200

Gare Montparnasse, 231, 233–234, 258

Gaussen-Salmon, Jacqueline, 3, 23

Gavin, Catherine, 255

German Army, 34, 175, 247

and the Allies, 4, 42, 65, 68–70, 74

and Choltitz, 83–85, 87–91, 97, 124, 150, 215, 253

and the Paris police, 114, 120

and the Soviets, 38, 51, 59, 74

actions during the Paris barricades, 175–177

during the Normandy campaign, 4, 62–64, 80, 130

morale of, 78, 88, 167, 175–176

Mortain and Falaise operations, 92–95, 124–125

strategy for Paris, 62–65, 96–97, 125, 149–150, 165–167

German Supreme Command West, 6

Gerow, Leonard, 99–100, 156–157, 182, 209–213, 241, 245

Gestapo, 11, 36, 64, 85, 88, 131

and the assassination attempt on Hitler, 75–78

and Choltitz, 85, 167–203

and the Resistance, 23, 45, 112–115, 120, 159

Giraud, Henri, 31–35

Goebbels, Joseph, 51

Grand Palais, 195–197, 238

Hamon, Léo, 109, 144, 153–154, 158

Hampton, Wade, 99

Haussmann, Baron, 169

Heller, Gerhard, 76, 87–88, 100

Hemingway, Ernest, 202

Henriot, Philippe, 51
Herriot, Edouard, 128–129
Hesse, Kurt, 63–64, 97, 161,
    202–203
Hitler, Adolf
  and Choltitz, 83–87, 89,
      192–193, 202, 214
  attempts to assassinate, 65, 73–77
  attitude toward truce, 65
  Mortain counteroffensive, 92–93
  strategies for holding Paris, 84,
      89, 97, 125, 141, 162, 192–193
Hodges, Courtney, 156–157, 161
Hold, Kurt, 63
Honneur de la Police, 112, 116–117
Hornaday, William, 156
Hôtel de Ville, 137, 158, 162,
    216–219, 236–237, 240
Hôtel Meurice, 90, 157, 159–160,
    214–214, 226, 229–230
Huddleston, Sisley, 15–17,
    251–252
Hugo, Victor, 111, 169–170, 259
Humbert, Agnès, 30

Île de la Cité, 123, 138–139,
    143–145, 172, 222, 243
Institut Allemand, 76
International Brigades, 44, 139
Italy, 38–39, 42–43, 58, 61, 68–69,
    107

Jade Amicol (Claude Ollivier), 70,
    186
Jeunesse Patriotique, 24
Jewish population
  German and Vichy propaganda
      about, 4–5, 15

imprisonment of, 23, 85, 111,
    114, 121, 147, 252
Jodl, Alfred, 96–97
Joliot-Curie, Frédéric, 138, 144
Jouhandeau, Marcel, 105–106
Juin, Alphonse, 42, 68, 242
Jünger, Ernst, 4, 50, 77, 100

Karcher, Henri, 229–230
Kirkpatrick, Helen, 243–244
Kluge, Guenther von, 65, 75–76,
    78–80, 96–97, 118–119, 124
Koenig, Marie-Pierre, 6, 10, 47–49,
    204, 242–243, 245
Kriegel-Valrimont, Maurice, 71, 92,
    121, 153, 230–231, 248

L'Humanité (newspaper), 47, 71,
    114, 187, 252
La Défense de la France
    (newspaper), 52
La Marseillaise, 137–138, 187, 232,
    241, 244, 250
Langlade, Paul Girot de, 213,
    222–224, 227–228
Laval, Pierre, 5, 32, 128–130, 138,
    150, 176–177
Le Figaro, 243
Le Franciste (newspaper), 4
Le Franc-Tireur (newspaper)37–38,
    236, 238
Léautaud, Paul, 105
Leclerc, Philippe, 42, 98, 108
  and the Second Armored Division,
      42, 98, 108, 241
  entry into Paris, 191–193,
      205–206, 209–211, 213, 215,
      222

relationship with the Americans, 98–100, 156–157, 161, 182, 184, 190–191, 210–211, 213, 241

role in the German surrender, 230–231, 233–234, 242

thoughts on liberating Paris, 99, 155

Lepoutre, Robert, 138

Little Gray Mice, 101

Longworth de Chambrun, Clara, 105, 176, 207–208

Luftwaffe, 90, 204, 226

Luizet, Charles, 132–134, 139–140, 148, 205, 228, 231

Lyon, Harold, 183, 244

Maginot Line, 28, 67

Mandel, Georges, 51

Maquis, 5, 24–25, 58

Marshall Plan, 256

Marshall, George, 81, 182

Marshall, S. L. A., 223

Massiet, Raymond, 25

Massu, Jacques, 227

Massu, Suzanne, 239

Maudru, Pierre, 145–146, 165

Mayer, Daniel, 247–248

McNair, Lesley J., 80

Métro, 255
    German use of, 1, 153
    Parisians' limited use of, 20–21, 101, 106
    Resistance use of, 145–146, 159, 174, 233
    workers' strike, 123–124

Milice, 51, 73, 113–115, 120, 131, 227, 244

Mitterrand, François (Morland), 78

Moats, Alice, 14–16, 19–20, 22, 25–26, 53

Model, Walter, 124–125, 142, 152, 186

Moisson, Pascale, 223, 225, 243–244, 254

Monod, Robert, 178–181

Monte Cassino, 69–70

Montgomery, Bernard, 56, 58, 94

Morandat, Yvon, 176–177, 217

Mortain, 92–95, 101

Moulin, Jean, 27–28, 34–36, 47–48, 258

Munich Conference, 126

Nazi Party, 24, 27–28, 63, 167, 195, 252, 255
    and Otto Abetz, 126–127
    and Choltitz, 85–86
    and the attempted assassination of Hitler, 74–78
    attitudes toward Paris, 88, 95

Nazi-Soviet Pact of 1939, 40

Nordling, Raoul, 125
    attempts to negotiate peace, 126–128, 147–149, 151–152, 154, 228
    mission to meet with de Gaulle, 185–187
    and the Paris police strike, 120–121, 140–141, 147, 151–152
    relationship with Choltitz, 86, 128, 148–152, 159–160, 167, 185–186

Nordling, Rolf, 187, 191, 211

Normandy Campaign, 2–15, 17–18,
    52, 56–65, 130
  and the food crisis in Paris, 21
  and de Gaulle, 57, 60
  and the Second Armored
    Division, 97–98
  German reaction to, 24, 50, 56,
    78–80, 88, 219
  Resistance reaction to, 25, 46–47,
    49–50, 53
North Africa, 32–33, 42, 44, 129,
    133, 256

Office of Strategic Services, 5
Operation Anvil/Dragoon, 58,
    95–96
Operation Bagration, 51–52
Operation Cobra, 79–80, 83
Operation Overlord, 56–58, 69. *See
    also* Normandy campaign.
Oradur massacre, 24–25, 78, 101,
    107, 198

Palais du Luxembourg, 90, 97, 176,
    186, 192, 226, 232–233
Paris Commune, 40, 206–207,
    238
Paris Police, 111–112, 140, 165,
    176, 236, 258–259
  and the Gaullists, 133–134, 140,
    177, 217, 231, 236, 249
  and the Resistance, 24, 73, 102,
    112–116, 121–123, 238
  before the police strike, 23–24,
    64, 72, 90, 92, 101
  general strike of, 102, 111–123,
    136–138
  seizure of the Préfecture de Police,

138–140, 142–148, 151–152,
    173–174, 183, 206, 222
Parodi, Alexandre, 48, 109
  arrest of, 159–160
  Paris police strike, 134, 146,
    159
  relationship with the Resistance,
    49, 53, 103–104, 124,
    142–143, 176
  role as de Gaulle's representative,
    48, 159–160, 177, 217
Perrault, Gilles
  thoughts on liberation, 225–226,
    239
  thoughts on life in occupied Paris,
    2, 10, 121, 171
  thoughts on German occupiers,
    10, 88, 131
Pétain, Henri-Philippe, 5, 16, 29–30,
    32, 104–105, 129–130
Petit Parisien (newspaper), 91
Place de l'Étoile, 223
Place de la Concorde, 90, 226–227,
    232, 242–244, 246
Place de la Nation, 200
Place de la République, 90, 175,
    200, 226, 232
Police et Patrie, 112, 117
Polish Home Army, 107, 158
Pré, Roland, 116
Préfecture de Police, 123, 236, 246,
    258
  and the liberation of Paris,
    204–206, 218, 222, 228
  and the German surrender, 230
  seizure by the Paris police,
    137–149, 150–154, 158, 162,
    173–175

Provisional Government of the
    French Republic, 7, 40–42,
    138, 177, 238, 241
Pyle, Ernie, 166, 212, 221–222,
    239

Radio Paris, 51, 76, 130
Radio Rome, 4, 8
Rastenburg, 73–75, 83–84, 86–87,
    92
Rehr, Louis, 255
Reid, Robert, 223–224, 243–244
Resistance, 21, 25–53, 92, 132,
    187–192, 231
  and the Allies, 22, 25, 37, 40, 58,
    60, 104, 129, 155–156,
    178–184, 198, 258
  and Choltitz, 90–91, 128, 148,
    150–152, 159–160, 167
  and collaborators, 22, 43, 208,
    251
  and the communists, 7, 28, 34,
    36–37, 40, 44, 47, 53, 107, 174
  and de Gaulle, 25, 27–30, 33–35,
    40, 44, 47–49, 103–104, 238,
    242, 250
  and the Gaullists, 133, 140, 143,
    207
  and the Germans, 56, 60, 64,
    77–78, 127–128, 136, 146,
    151, 162
  and the Gestapo, 23, 45, 112–115,
    120, 159
  and the Paris police, 24, 73, 102,
    112–118, 121–123
  and the seizure of the prefecture,
    138–142
  barricades, 169–173

disagreement within, 102, 116,
    143, 153–154, 168–169, 203
German arrests of, 10, 23, 75
lack of weapons, 14, 64, 178,
    198–199
liberation of Paris, 198–204, 212,
    216–219, 226–227, 232, 258
membership, 34, 37, 199, 249
Parisian attitudes toward, 34, 49,
    106, 108, 207
truce, 167–169
uprising, 89, 124, 137, 140–142,
    147, 158–159, 165, 174–178
Rogers, Pleas, 245, 250
Rommel, Erwin, 65
Roosevelt, Franklin D., 13, 31–32,
    39–41, 44, 60
Roy, Claude, 140, 197
Rue des Saussaies, 23, 77, 131, 162
Rundstedt, Gerd von, 65, 75

Sartre, Jean-Paul, 106, 199, 258
Shaw, Irwin, 213, 223, 227–228,
    231–232
Sibert, Edward, 190
Siegfried Line, 67
Soustelle, Jacques, 43–44
Soviet Union, 25, 38, 52, 74, 250
  French Communist Party support
    of, 40, 52–53, 59–60
  German and Vichy propaganda
    about, 4–5, 16
  Operation Bagration, 51–52
  Red Army, 74, 76, 83, 136
  Warsaw Uprising, 107–108
Special Operations Executive (SOE),
    5
Speidel, Hans, 220

St. Denis, 71, 115–116, 120

St. Lô, 80, 83

Stauffenberg, Claus von, 73–75

Stéphane, Roger, 234

Stülpnagel, Karl-Heinrich von, 74–78

Sylvan, William, 161

T Force, 155–156, 183, 244

Taittinger, Pierre, 24, 90–91, 97,
    109, 149, 158, 252

Tanguy, Henri (Rol), 44–45,
    248–249
  attempts to obtain weapons, 46,
    92, 123, 178–179, 200
  barricades, 163, 173–176
  Paris police strike, 102, 116–117,
    121–123, 134, 136–140,
    142–143
  Préfecture truce, 153, 158, 168
  role as FFI commander, 45–49,
    102–103, 124, 134, 143, 147,
    158–159, 201, 236, 242, 248
  role in American entry to Paris,
    179
  role in German surrender,
    230–231, 233–234
  thoughts on strikes, 53, 71–72,
    92, 115

Thomas, Edith, 205

Thorez, Maurice, 40, 251

Tollet, André, 7, 14, 73, 142, 153

Trappes, 11–12

Truscott, Lucian, 68

Tulle, 25, 78, 101, 107

United States of America, 69, 245,
    256–258

and Choltitz, 185–187, 203

and de Gaulle, 31–33, 37–44, 60,
    103, 124, 182, 233–236,
    240–241, 250, 257–258

and French military leadership,
    210–212, 245

and the German surrender, 232,
    234

and the Resistance, 40, 178–184,
    258

and Vichy leadership, 128–129

attitudes toward liberation of
    Paris, 55–56, 60, 65–66, 70, 81,
    98–100, 132, 154–155,
    160–161, 167, 182–183,
    189–191, 212, 245

bombing of Paris railway network
    (Transportation Plan), 1, 11–17,
    70

enemy view of, 5, 65, 166, 202

entry into Paris, 155–156,
    212–213, 215, 223, 227

fear of communists, 40, 52, 207,
    249

Normandy campaign, 5, 57,
    61–62, 98

Operation Cobra, 79–81

Parisians' view of, 22, 25, 92,
    162, 198

Sherman tanks, 215–216

thoughts on the postwar status of
    France, 43, 59–60, 250

V-1 rockets (also V-2, V-3), 50, 56

V-E Day, 247–248

Vélodrome d'Hiver (Vel d'Hiv), 114,
    252

Vercors, 24–25, 58, 107
Vichy, 16, 53, 130, 227
  and the Americans, 31, 39, 42,
    44, 129
  and the communists, 43, 168
  and de Gaulle, 30–31, 129–130,
    236
  and the Germans, 10, 24, 36, 64,
    91, 150
  and Giraud, 32
  and the Paris police, 111–115,
    117, 120
  and the Resistance, 10–11, 27,
    35–36, 38, 43, 118, 129–130,
    208, 249
  attitudes toward, 2, 16, 34, 37,
    71, 104–105, 112, 192
  leadership of, 5, 128–129
  propaganda, 5, 9, 13, 15–16, 51,
    195
Villon, Pierre, 168–169

Walborn, Claire, 176–177
Warsaw Rising, 107–109, 124, 158,
    168, 189, 196
Wolf, Thomas, 166, 223